WOMEN *of* WISDOM

About the Author

Paula Marvelly was born in 1967 and educated at The City of London Freemen's School, Ashtead Park, Surrey. She read English at Royal Holloway College, University of London, and European Studies at Selwyn College, University of Cambridge. Her first book, *The Teachers of One: Conversations on the Nature of Non-Duality* is a collection of interviews with some of the world's foremost teachers of *advaita* Vedanta. She currently lives in the south of France.

WOMEN *of* WISDOM

A journey of enlightenment by
women of vision through the ages

PAULA MARVELLY

WATKINS PUBLISHING
LONDON

This edition published in the UK 2005 by

Watkins Publishing, Sixth Floor, Castle House, 75-76 Wells Street,
London W1T 3QH
Distributed in USA and Canada by Publishers Group West

1 3 5 7 9 10 8 6 4 2

Designed and typeset by Ed Pickford

Printed and bound in Great Britain

Library of Congress Cataloging in Publication data available

ISBN 1 84293 162 8

www.watkinspublishing.com

Acknowledgements

I have inadvertently plagiarized everything I have read and am therefore indebted to all the authors I have consulted. Nevertheless, it is vital that I acknowledge my unreserved gratitude to the following texts, which have formed the philosophical, literary and mythological foundations of this book:

History of Mysticism: The Unchanging Testament, S Abhayananda
An Anthology of Sacred Texts by and about Women, Serinity Young
Myth of the Goddess: Evolution of an Image, Anne Baring &
    Jules Cashford

My sincerest gratitude also goes to the following who have given me immeasurable love, support and guidance: my family – Jean, Bert and Colin Marvelly; Michael Mann; Alan Jacobs; Anne Irwin, Will Rasmussen; Anne Corkhill; Stella Konsta; Claire Fuller; Robert Genower; and my English students at Hurtwood House. I would also like to express my thanks to all the publishers who have given permission to use quotations from their publications.

With regard to the text itself, I have decided to refrain from footnoting within the main body of the text, however, endnotes for all quotations can be found at the back of the book. A comprehensive bibliography is also included should the reader wish to investigate a topic further. I have also left out all diacritical marks on all foreign words, including proper names, to enable a smoother read.

For
Mum, Dad and Colin,
Elizabeth and Tommy

Contents

I, WOMAN, am that wonder-breathing rose
That blossoms in the garden of the King.
In all the world there is no lovelier thing,
And the learned stars no secret can disclose
Deeper than mine – that almost no one knows.
The perfume of my petals in the spring
Is inspiration to all the birds that sing
Of love, the spirit's lyric unrepose.

Under my veil is hid the mystery
Of unaccomplished eons, and my breath
The Master-Lover's life replenisheth.
The mortal garment that is worn by me
The loom of Time renews continually;
And when I die – the universe knows death.

'The Mystic Rose'
Elsa Barker

Prologue

> Let us then begin at the beginning, and remind ourselves of a few
> of the trite and primary facts which all practical persons agree to
> ignore. That beginning, for human thought, is, of course, the I, the
> Ego, the self-conscious subject which is writing this book, or the
> other self-conscious subject which is reading it; and which declares,
> in the teeth of all argument, I AM. Here is a point as to which we
> all feel quite sure. No metaphysician has yet shaken the ordinary
> individual's belief in his own existence. The uncertainties only
> begin for most of us when we ask what else *is*.[1]

Evelyn Underhill's words, in her classic text, *Mysticism*, immediately
cut to the chase – the only fact of which there can be absolutely no
doubt is I AM. And as she also points towards, very few people truly
know that I AM, owing to the veil of ignorance and illusion that separates humankind from his or her essential inner being.

There are, however, a number of people throughout the course of
history who have tasted the joy of their immortal selves, the freedom
of the immanent Source, the infinite bliss of I AM. And some of those
have sought to explain this ineffable state. But because the indefinable defies definition, that is when the uncertainties begin ...

All religions and faiths contain an esoteric heart, a mystical belief
that I AM is in fact synonymous with God. However, cultural differences have meant that the presentation of this fact is as diverse as
there are waves on the sea. There is, however, a consensus of interpretation: that the unmanifest, the Absolute, the primal Source from

which the universe came and will ultimately return, is perceived as masculine; and that the manifest, the created world, the dance and drama of daily life, is perceived as feminine. Needless to say, these are all concepts. But useful concepts to work with, until there is a complete understanding that God is in fact everything, the masculine and the feminine, and yet, at the same time, ultimately beyond both.

Through the millennia of time, attention has shifted its focus from the veneration of the immanent, feminine principle in the form of a Mother Goddess to the transcendent, masculine principle in the form of a Father God; from nature and her bounty to a sterile voice in the void. Moreover, qualities generally associated with the feminine – intuition and emotion, passivity and chaos – have been subsumed by those generally associated with the masculine – reason and logic, activity and structure. Unfortunately this has resulted in the dominance of the masculine principle over the feminine and, inevitably, men over women. In practice, this has produced numerous misogynistic atrocities and the annihilation of women's human rights the world over.

In order for there to be any real sense of I AM, the eternal subject within all of us, free from dogma and prejudice, there has to be an abandonment of all analytical reasoning and objective knowledge. Only through the realm of direct experience and intuitive sensibility can there ever be a taste of the true Self. Many male mystics have pointed to this nondualist vision through their writings and example. Nevertheless, there have been many female mystics who have also alluded to that ineffable place. Indeed, the emotional and psychological disposition of women makes them aptly suited to lose themselves in the agonies and ecstasies of the mystical relationship between the individual soul and the divine Beloved – merging through their mutual love into One. And it is their story that we are now going to follow in their exploration of the sacred feminine.

chapter one

Enheduanna

From the first native tribesman to Palaeolithic and Neolithic man – all experienced life and the very universe itself as a personification of the Great Primordial Mother Goddess. Everything was seen as her manifestation: birds and beasts, mountains and meadows, rivers and seas. The changing seasons, experienced as both the abundance of the late-summer harvest and the devastation of winter storms, were aspects of her infinite expression. Artefacts discovered from prehistoric times, including statues of fertile goddesses and painted female images in caves and on vases and pots, confirm that the vision of the cosmos was seen as a revelation of the sacred feminine, a celebration of the manifested aspect of the One.

The changing faces of the moon also began to be associated with the life cycles of the Mother. Birth, transformation and death as well as the woman's menstrual cycle were synonymous with the moon's recurring phases – waxing (the maiden), full (the pregnant mother) and waning (the old wise woman) – which in turn represented the changing aspects of the phenomenal world. Moreover, the moon's final phase of three days' darkness, where its features are subsumed in shadow, symbolized the underlying constancy of consciousness, the omnipresent totality of the universe in which everything else was contained.

For centuries, the divine feminine as the Mother of the Universe was perceived and worshipped in such a way; indeed, the universal recurrence of goddess and lunar iconography can be charted between the great cultures from Old Europe to the Indus Valley. But the advent of the Bronze Age (3500 BCE to 1250 BCE) saw momentous changes that profoundly altered this view. The discovery of bronze, an alloy of copper and tin, was to provide not only more powerful and flexible tools for farming but also weapons of killing and defence, used to protect and win land to accommodate the ever growing, hierarchical population.

Mesopotamia, the land between the Euphrates and Tigris rivers incorporating Sumeria, Akkadia, Assyria and Babylonia and where our journey begins, was principally an agricultural community living in accord with nature. Worshipping a universal mother goddess, the Mesopotamians lived a relatively peaceful existence up until this time, guided by an intuitive feminine wisdom. However, this was soon to be violated. Invading migratory warriors – Aryan tribes from the steppe lands between the Dnieper and Volga rivers, north of the Black and Caspian Seas, as well as Semitic tribes from the Syro-Arabian desert – started to impose their own patriarchal customs.

Thus, the perpetual fear of violence and subordination to invaders subsequently brought about a profound shift in the consciousness of mankind. A self-interested awareness thus began to place survival and the quest for individual power as the primary focus of life, and the notion of the 'hero', passing tests of strength and courage, started to emerge – a superhuman male role model for the rest of the tribe to worship, and above all, emulate.

Most importantly, death is no longer seen as the end of a recurring phase in the rhythm of the world. It is the end, a complete finality, with no hope of rejuvenation or rebirth. With this limiting and consequentially fearful world view comes about, inevitably, a split in mankind's relationship with the whole. And thus, the immanent Mother Goddess is gradually replaced by the emergence of a transcendent and separate Father God. Where there was harmony, sustenance and peace, now there is discord, degeneration and war. A pantheon of sky gods starts to emerge to validate these masculine forces, which are separate and above creation – lightning and thunder, storm and fire. Moreover, with the decline of the sacred feminine, the position of women in society also starts to deteriorate to such a point that they become subordinate to, and even possessions of, men.

Creation myths, therefore, reflected this change. According to Mesopotamian mythology, long before the beginning of space and time, there existed only the primordial sea, Nammu – a limitless, undifferentiated ocean of the Mother Goddess. Nammu then gave birth to a cosmic mountain, within which were the beginnings of the differentiated world: An, the god of the heavens, and Ki, the goddess of the earth. Together, An and Ki conceived a son, Enlil, Air or Breath, who would eventually carry off his mother, Ki, to be his wife. In other words, the omnipotent position of the mother, the feminine principle, is usurped by the son, the masculine principle, through an act of separation and violence.

But one idol, worshipped by the Mesopotamians, reconciled the ruptured components of the masculine and feminine, moulding them back into a unified equalitarian whole. Inanna, the Sumerian goddess of the moon (known as Ishtar in neighbouring Babylonia) embodied the waxing and waning world within her very arms. Believed to be the great-great-granddaughter of Nammu, she reminded her devotees through the myths told about her that life is a process, filled with many trials and triumphs, leading to a state of transformation and renewal, all the while cherished in the One.

Inanna was one of the three great goddesses of the Bronze Age. She is represented both astrologically by the stars Sirius and Venus and pictorially as a woman with wings, flanked either side by two owls – the Sumerian word, '*ninna*' in fact means 'owl' and one of her many epithets is 'Divine Lady Owl'.

Many stories feature Inanna, including the famous legend of 'Inanna's Descent into the Nether World'. In it, Inanna goes down to the land of the dead, where her sister, Queen Ereshkigal, reigns supreme. She sacrifices Inanna by hanging her up like a carcass for three days. During this time all fertility on the earth completely ceases. The god, Ea, manages to win Inanna's release and she is resurrected back to earth where life's vitality is restored. Nevertheless, Inanna is forced to appoint a sacrifice in her place and she chooses her husband, Dumuzi. In a story that echoes the later Greek myth in which Persephone, daughter of Demeter, is carried off by Hades to the underworld, Inanna's is a tale rich in metaphor and the relationship between living and dying in an eternal recurring dance of darkness and light.

In a time which saw the invention of the art of writing through hieroglyphs and cuneiform script, stories like these were finally given a recorded voice. Temple hymns to Inanna from the period establish once again that everything returns to the sacred feminine:

Begetting Mother am I, within the Spirit I abide and none see me.
In the word of An I abide, and none see me
In the word of Enhil I abide, and none see me
In the word of the holy temple I abide, and none see me.[1]

Moreover, she is the controller of destinies, the omnipresent Divine:

To thee I cry, O lady of the gods,
Lady of ladies, goddess without peer,
Ishtar who shapes the lives of all mankind,
Thou stately world queen, sovereign of the sky,
And lady ruler of the host of heaven –
Illustrious is thy name … O light divine,
Gleaming in lofty splendour o'er the earth –
Heroic daughter of the moon, oh! hear …[2]

Around this time, a priestess was also recording her own reflections on the nature of her beloved Inanna and her name was Enheduanna. The first recorded poetry to be identified by an individual of either gender, it was discovered in 1922 when the ancient city of Ur in Sumer (now southern Iraq) was excavated by archaeologists. Composed in cuneiform and inscribed on clay tablets,

Enheduanna's temple hymns resonate passionately with her veneration of the sacred feminine:

> *Lady of all powers,*
> *In whom light appears,*
> *Radiant one*
> *Beloved of Heaven and Earth,*
> *Tiara-crowned*
> *Priestess of the Highest God,*
> *My Lady, you are the guardian*
> *Of all greatness.*
> *Your hand holds the seven powers:*
> *You lift the powers of being,*
> *You have hung them over your fingers,*
> *You have gathered the many powers,*
> *You have clasped them now*
> *Like necklaces onto your breast.*[3]

The daughter of King Sargon of Akkad, Enheduanna was appointed in around 2300 BCE to the position of High Priestess of Nanna, the moon god, at the temple of Ur. Indeed, her portrait on a small alabaster disc, also unearthed along with her poems, shows her presiding over a libation ritual. Very soon, however, Enheduanna redirected her devotion to Nanna's daughter, Inanna, elevating her above the moon god. In nearly fifty temple hymns, including a series of three long poems dedicated specifically to Inanna, her poetry is in no doubt that Inanna is the Queen of Heaven and Earth. Through the voice of the goddess, she proclaims:

> *I the Lady*
> *circling the sky*
> *circling the earth*
>
> *I Inanna*
> *circling the sky*
> *circling the earth*[4]

What sets Enheduanna's work apart from other script of the period is her sense of individuality, her self assuredness in a time of increasing male dominance. Growing up in a time of profound change, she too witnessed the shift from the belief in the immanence of the feminine Spirit, imbuing all of manifested nature, to the new 'civilized' idea of a masculine God, separate from all his creation. Enheduanna's poetry is therefore suffused with the confidence and self-awareness of a powerful, all-knowing woman, reasserting her precious position in the cosmos:

> *I*
> *I am Enheduanna*
> *High Priestess of Nanna*
>
> *I*
> *Enheduanna   Jewel of An*
> *Let me say a prayer to you*[5]

Despite having been composed over four millennia ago, the unshakeable sense of self belief is palpable. Her female voice can be heard resounding through the centuries. Wisdom and strong emotion resonate from the very heart of her verse and in particular through her three long poems addressed to Inanna: 'Inanna and Ebih', 'Lady of Largest Heart', and 'The Exaltation to Inanna'. Using her position at the temple as upholder of the Mesopotamian concept of Me, meaning wisdom, Enheduanna was able to reddress the balance between the masculine and feminine principles and present a unified, nondualist vision of the universe.

'Inanna and Ebih', relates the story of a battle between Inanna and a defiant mountain called Ebih – a place of paradise, a Garden of Eden, devoid of conflict and struggle. Inanna, by contrast, represents the natural world; a similar environment of beauty and yet seething with the rhythmical dualities of life. The poem is reminiscent of the biblical story of Genesis, which describes the soul's passage from a secluded place of innocence to a rugged landscape of experience; the psyche's journey from the naivety of a child to the wisdom of an adult:

> *my hands like falcon claws*
> *slash heads*
> *like the FIRST SNAKE*
> *I come out of the mountains*[6]

A familiar symbol of the sacred wisdom in the natural world, the snakelike Inanna has come to bring knowledge and self conscious- ness to the universe. (Interestingly, the snake is used in later patriarchal religions as a symbol of evil and deception.) Similar in style to Kali, the Hindu goddess of destruction and death, Inanna represents the antithetical forces of nature, not as a Fallen, patriar- chal world, but one which is the differentiated expression of the radiance of the Divine:

> *Inanna*
> *child of the Moon God*
> *a soft bud swelling*
> *her queen's robe cloaks the slender stem*
> *on her smooth brow she paints*
> *fire beams and fearsome glint*
>
> *fastens carnelian*
> *blood-red and glowing*
> *round her throat*
>
> *and then her hand clasps*
> *the seven-headed mace*
> *she stands as in youth's prime*
> *her right hand grasps the mace*
>
> *steps, yes she steps her narrow foot*
> *on the furred back*
> *of a wild lapis lazuli bull*

and she goes out
white-sparked, radiant
in the dark vault of evening's sky
star-steps in the street
through the Gate of Wonder[7]

Enheduanna continues her mystical wisdom in her next poem, 'Lady of Largest Heart'. With vivid imagery, she writes a series of intense and emotional epithets in praise of Inanna's enigmatic character: her beauty and charisma, her mercy and compassion, her wisdom and wrath:

YOU mistress of the powers of heaven
YOU unequalled in the earth around you
YOU exalted all on your own
   heaven and earth cannot gird your fame[8]

Just like living in the world with all its mysteries of life and death, love and loss, so too is everything contained within the vastness of Inanna's heart:

she wears
the carved-out ground plan
of heaven and earth[9]

Inanna's divine heart encompasses the entire fabric of the universe, a place where servant and mistress are united, where lover and Beloved become One:

to have a husband   to have a wife
to thrive in the goodness of love
are yours Inanna[10]

Indeed, the sacred practice of performing sexual intercourse in the temples devoted to Inanna and Ishtar were important rituals in

Mesopotamia. As the 'Hierodule of Heaven', meaning 'servant of the holy', making love within the precincts of a goddess was believed to pour divine energy back into life, thus helping increase the land's fertility.

The third poem, 'The Exaltation of Inanna' tells of an actual event whereby Enheduanna is literally usurped from her temple by a male priest and banished into the wilderness. It is the powerful and gruesome story of a woman's displacement by the brute force of a man. Enheduanna appeals to Inanna for help:

> *speak to An*
> *he will free me*
> *tell him 'Now'*
> *he will release me*[11]

Not only does Enheduanna want freedom from her male usurper but she also wants release from the bondage of the patriarchal culture she lives in. She yearns for a return to complementary principles, the harmonization of female and male and it is Inanna who hears her prayer:

> *child of yours   I am a captive*
> *bride of yours   I am a captive*
> *it is for my sake your anger fumes*
> *your heart finds no relief*[12]

The poem reinforces the intensity and interdependence of the relationship between Inanna and Enheduanna – they are goddess and devotee, they are lover and Beloved, they are mother and child. In praise and awe, the High Priestess of Inanna, Enheduanna, sings of her goddess's greatness and the glory of her celestial name:

> *mistress of the scheme of order*
> *great Queen of queens*

babe of a holy womb
greater than the mother who bore you
You all knowing
You wise vision
Lady of all lands
life-giver for the many
faithful Goddess
worthy of powers
to sing your praise is exalted

You of the bountiful heart
You of the radiant heart
I will sing of your cosmic powers

truly for your gain
you drew me toward
my holy quarters
I
The High Priestess
I
Enheduanna[13]

Babylonia and Assyria retained the image of the great Mother Goddess, in the form of Ninhursag, for centuries after Enheduanna's day. Nevertheless, the advent of the Iron Age (beginning 1250 BCE) saw Mesopotamian law consolidated into the *Code of Hammurabi*, in which the status of women was explicitly spelt out. Although they were allowed certain legal and economic rights, the code categorically stated that authority within the home belonged to men – women were merely the disposable property of their husbands. Furthermore, the Babylonian creation myth, the *Enuma Elish*, from the same period, recounts the story of the conquest and murder of the original Mother Goddess, Tiamat, by the god, Marduk, her great-great-great-grandson.

It is not surprising, therefore, that long after she had died,

Enheduanna's poetry was copied and sung in the temples devoted to Inanna and Ishtar – a powerful female voice trying to re-establish harmony in the cosmos and the rightful place of the sacred feminine.

chapter two

Hatchepsut

In the neighbouring lands of ancient Egypt, the immanent life force was also revered and honoured. The Egyptians understood that underlying the apparent duality of daily life was an all-pervading unity, known as *Neter*, within which manifested the phenomenal world, *neteru*, of goddesses and gods as well as all the birds and beasts and human beings of mortal life.

Dating back as far as 3100 BCE and lasting up until the birth of Christ, the ancient Egyptian civilization was one of the most sophisticated cultures in the known world. As society expanded and thus became more structured and patriarchal, creation mythology describing the birth of the universe inevitably started to evolve. Similar to Mesopotamia, we again hear of a watery chaos: in one story, the 'great flood' is called Nu, a primordial male energy, which gives birth to a High Hill, the god Atum (or Aten), the 'Complete One'. Atum then masturbates the celestial pantheon into life – the god, Shu (Air or Light), and the goddess, Tefnut (Moisture or Order), who in turn together conceive Nut, the goddess of the sky, and Geb, the god of the earth.

An older tradition, however, relates that the heavenly sea is feminine, from which the Primordial Mother manifests in the form of Hathor, a great cow nourishing and sustaining the world through her ever flowing rain-milk. As she swims in the ocean of her divine being, she carries the sun god, Ro, in between her horns

Hathor could also be personified as a woman, either as the counterpart or the daughter of Re. But whatever her outward form, she was praised as the 'Golden One' and many temple poems were written in her praise:

> *All hail, jubilation to you, O Golden One ...*
> *Sole ruler, Uraeus [Egyptian cobra] of the Supreme Lord himself!*
> *Mysterious One, who gives birth to the divine entities,*
> *Forms the animals, models them as she pleases, fashions men ...*
> *O Mother! ... Luminous One who thrusts back the darkness,*
> *Who illuminates every human creature with her rays,*
> *Hail Great One of many names ...*[1]

The Golden One is hailed by many other names but none so ubiquitously as Isis, Queen of Heaven, Earth and the Netherworld. The only female deity to be worshipped long before the fourth millennia BCE right up until the second century CE, Isis surpassed all other goddesses in Egypt and even found expression in the ancient world of Greece. Pictorially, she is represented as a beautiful woman with soaring wings, as well as being the star of Sirius and the immortal Tree of Life, the sycamore. She was intimately connected with royalty and the protection of Pharaohs owing to her associated powers of life, death and wisdom. Born of Nut and Geb, Isis was also perceived as the Primordial Mother Goddess of the entire universe.

Many myths feature her story but the most important links her with her brother, the god Osiris. Gestating together in the same womb, the siblings form an inseparable bond leading to their eventual marriage. But their other brother, Seth, murders Osiris in a fit of jealousy, and dismembers his body, scattering it throughout the land. Devastated, Isis gathers it up and with the final part, Osiris's penis, she impregnates herself, subsequently giving birth to their son, Horus. Raising him secretly in a swamp, Horus is unfortunately killed by a scorpion's sting. Lamenting once again, Isis is able to restore Horus to life through the aid of her sister, Nephthys, and the god of wisdom, Thoth.

What this legend represents is the recurring cycle of birth, death and regeneration. Just like the tale of Inanna and her descent into the underworld, hymns to Isis immortalize her sacred beauty and her power to restore eternal life:

> *I play the sistra before your beautiful face,*
> *Isis, Giver of Life, residing in the Sacred Mound,*
> *Eye of Re who has no equal in heaven and on earth.*
> *Great of love, mistress of women,*
> *Who fills heaven and earth with her beauty ...*[2]

Interestingly, it is Osiris who dominates Egyptian mythology and is immortalized in *The Egyptian Book of the Dead*, the 3,500-year-old manuscript written by an anonymous poet; describing the passage of the soul after death, it becomes identified with Osiris and is guided through a series of psychological realms (similar to the bardo states of the *Tibetan Book of the Dead*) until it finds union with the universe. Nevertheless, Isis's role in the regeneration of Osiris is given due acknowledgement, as temple texts make claim:

> Thy mother has come to thee, that thou mayst not perish away; the great modeller she is come, that thou mayst not perish away. She sets thy head in place for thee, she puts together thy limbs for thee; what she brings to thee is thy heart, is thy body. So dost thou become he who presides over his forerunners, thou givest command to thy ancestors and also thou makest thy house to prosper after thee, thou dost defend thy children from affliction.[3]

Yet another name for the Golden One was Maat. In Egypt, Maat was the embodiment of the universal principles of harmony and truth. As the figure of a goddess, Maat wears an ostrich feather on her head, symbolizing the counterbalance measuring the hearts of men and women at their death upon the scales of justice. A concept known also in Mesopotamia as Me, Maat is the underlying order of the cosmos, the feminine aspect of consciousness:

I have come to you, I am Thoth, my two hands united to carry Maat.
… Maat is in every place that is yours … You rise with Maat,
You live with Maat, you join your limbs to Maat, you make Maat
Rest on your head in order that she may take her seat on your forehead.
You become young again in the sight of your daughter Maat,
You live from the perfume of her dew.
Maat is worn like an amulet at your throat, she rests on your chest,
The divine entities reward you with Maat, for they know her wisdom …

Your right eye is Maat, your left eye is Maat …
Your flesh, your members are Maat …
Your food is Maat, your drink is Maat …
The breaths of your nose are Maat …
You exist because Maat exists,
And vice versa.[4]

Maat could never be taken for granted – it had to be upheld and honoured. And part of that responsibility fell on the Pharaohs' shoulders. As gods incarnate on earth, Egyptian kings would pledge to rule justly and wisely in exchange for the harmonious flow of the seasons, the annual inundation cycle of the Nile and the eternal rising and setting of the moon and sun. However, a handful of female 'kings' were appointed to rule, and one woman in particular was responsible for one of the longest periods of peace and prosperity Egypt has ever seen.

One of only six women believed to have governed in her own right, Hatchepsut, eldest daughter of King Tuthmosis I and his consort, Queen Ahmose, ruled roughly between 1503–1482 BCE during the eighteenth Dynasty. Married at twelve to her half-brother, King Tuthmosis II, she initially shared the throne acting at his queen consort, 'God's Wife and Great Royal Wife' and bore him two daughters, Neferure and Meritre-Hatchepsut. Owing to the fact that there was no legitimate male heir, the premature death her husband inspired Hatchepsut to proclaim herself as king and assume the office of Pharaoh. Like the male kings before her, hieroglyphs in the Temple of Amen (also known as Amun or Amon and king of all the gods) leave autobiographical details of her reign:

I have done this with a loving heart for my father, Amen;
Initiated in his secret of the beginning,
Acquainted with his beneficent might,
I did not forget whatever he had ordained.
My majesty knows his divinity,
I acted under his command;
It was he who led me,
I did not plan a work without his doing.[5]

This obelisk inscription at Karnak, commissioned by Hatchepsut herself, asserts her spiritual right to rule for, as she explicitly states, it was not her will but the will of the gods.

In order to legitimize her godlike authority further, a series of cartoons at her mortuary temple, Djeser-Djeseru, at Deir el-Bahri in Thebes, depict her divine birth. Amen is shown as visiting Queen Ahmose in her bedchamber where he fills her nostrils with the breath of life. Hatchepsut's subsequent birth is heralded by all the gods and she is presented as a future king of Egypt. As the Karnak obelisk makes clear:

Amen, Lord of Thrones-of-the-Two-Lands;
He made me rule Black Land and the Red Land as reward,
No one rebels against me in all lands.
All foreign lands are my subjects,
He placed my border at the limits of heaven,
What Atum encircles labours for me.
He gave it to him who came from him,
Knowing I would rule it for him.
I am his daughter in very truth,
Who serves him, who knows what he ordains.
My reward from my father is life-stability-rule,
On the Horus throne of all the living, eternally like Re[6]

Other images of Hatchepsut painted on temple walls depict her suckling milk at the udders of the cow goddess, Hathor, symbolizing again her immortal status on earth.

Surviving statues of Hatchepsut in her youth show a beautiful woman, with an oval face and high forehead, almond-shaped eyes and pointed chin, with a rather prominent nose – but as she unashamedly says of herself:

> To look upon her was more beautiful than anything; her splendour
> and her form were divine; she was a maiden, beautiful, blooming.[7]

Daughter of a deity, she was the preserver of Maat – universal harmony in a world perpetually threatened by instability and chaos. Excavations of a small tomb on the West Bank at Thebes revealed pottery jars and amphorae, stamped with seals confirming her rank: 'The Good Wife Hatchepsut' and 'The Good Goddess Maatkare', literally meaning 'Maat is the Ka of Re' or 'Truth is the Soul of the sun god Re'.

As part of their complex creation mythology, the Egyptians also believed that the universe had a soul called *Ka*, a concept not dissimilar to that of *Neter*. *Ka* was depicted as a large bird, often a blue phoenix, from which all of creation was made. Moreover, each individual had a separate soul called *Ba*, which upon death, would assume the form of a bird and fly up and embrace its bird mother – *Ba* would thus merge back into *Ka*, duality dissolving in the One. As 'The Good Goddess Maatkare', Hatchepsut was therefore seen as the personification of Maat, the feminine equilibrial source of the universe, from which the masculine gods, like Re, were given form.

Although women in Egypt enjoyed, on the whole, a liberal status in society, its structure was predominantly patriarchal, with official and religious offices controlled mainly by men. Despite Hatchepsut's immortal roots, such a setup must have provoked the need within her to be taken more seriously because, somewhat bizarrely, she begins to be perceived as male, presumably in an attempt to validate her rule. Thus, unlike the promoted sensuality of later, more illustrious Egyptian queens such as Cleopatra and Nefertiti, Hatchepsut is portrayed as a handsome man, dressed in male clothing, sporting the traditional Pharaoh's false beard. The obelisk inscription also verifies her adopted male gender:

I swear, as I am loved of Re,
As Amen, my father, favours me,
As my nostrils are refreshed with life and dominion,
As I wear the white crown,
As I appear with red crown,
As the Two Lords have joined their portions for me,
As I rule this land like the son of Isis,
As I am mighty like the son of Nut,
As Re rests in the evening bark,
As he prevails in the morning bark,
As he joins his two mothers in the god's ship,
As sky endures, as his creation lasts,
As I shall be eternal like an undying star,
As I shall rest in life like Atum –
So as regards these two great obelisks,
Wrought with electrum by my majesty for my father Amen,
In order that my name may endure in this temple,
For eternity and everlastingness ...[8]

A female voice given expression through a male ... perhaps Hatchepsut is Egypt's equivalent of modern Western woman – assertive, powerful, competing in a world predominantly controlled by man. But by blurring the boundaries of her gender, she manages to transcend the confines of her mortal sex; by identifying with the deities, she lives for all eternity, her influence leaving a blazing trail through the stars.

Hatchepsut reigned for over twenty years. Legend has it that she was romantically involved with one of her advisors, Senenmut, who succeeded in charming and seducing her. Held under his spell for years, she rewarded him with financial gain and personal power.

Tragically, however, he betrayed Hatchepsut's trust by inscribing his own name on the inner doors of her mortuary temple, Djeser-Djeseru, in a bid for his own immortality. Instantaneously, Senenmut was stripped of all his privileges and then, mysteriously, disappeared. But by destroying Senenmut, Hatchepsut effectively destroyed herself. Bereft of his guidance and unable to govern alone, she soon lost all ability to reign. Within two years, her control over Egypt had crumbled and she was usurped by her stepson, Tuthmosis III, who assumed the position of Pharaoh.

Now an 'old' woman of between thirty-five and fifty-five, she died of natural causes in early February 1482 BCE though her body has never been identified. Interestingly, after her death, serious attempts were made to delete her memory from the history of Egypt – her temples and monuments were desecrated; her portraits and cartouches were vandalized; and details of her rule were omitted from the official list of kings. It took the intervention of the priest and historian, Manetho, living in approximately 300 BCE, to preserve her memory under the pseudonym, Amensis, until modern history was able to reveal her true identity.

One of Hatchepsut's earliest chosen tomb sites was situated high up on the west face of a cliff in Wadi Sikkat Taka ez-Zeida, over-looking the Nile Valley. Excavated by the famous Egyptologist Howard Carter at the end of the nineteenth century, he had discovered one of three magnificent sarcophagi commissioned by the 'king' herself. Although the tomb was later abandoned by Hatchepsut as a burial chamber, the lid of the excavated sarcophagus is inscribed with a prayer to the goddess, Nut:

The King's Daughter, God's Wife, King's Great Wife, Lady of the Two Lands, Hatchepsut, says, 'O my mother, Nut, stretch thyself over me, that thou mayest place me among the imperishable stars which are in thee, and that I may not die.'[9]

And die you never shall.

chapter three

Vach

As well as the great empires of Mesopotamia and Egypt in the West, another great civilization was emerging in the north-west Indian subcontinent in the East, situated in the Indus Valley. The recently unearthed cities of Harappa and Mohenjo-daro show evidence that a race of people, known as the Dravidians, date as far back as 2500 BCE. Like the Mesopotamians, they too had their own primitive mythology which understood the nature of creation – an omnipresent absolute Being in which manifested the phenomenal universe.

Around 1500 BCE the Aryans invaded. Originating from the steppe lands between the Dnieper and Volga rivers north of the Caspian and Black Seas, they brought with them their unique philosophical belief system, which was intrinsically the same in its mystical basis. Moreover, they already had their own orally transmitted collection of devotional songs in praise of the Divine, collectively known as the *Vedas* (meaning 'knowledge').

Over time, both interpretations of the one universal truth would merge and develop into the complex religious system we now know as the Hindu faith ('Hindu' being a corruption of the name 'Sindhu', a major river in northern India). Nevertheless, for many centuries, the two cultures developed independently: for the Dravidian population, the undifferentiated consciousness was known as Siva, or the male principle, and the creative spirit of the world, Shakti, or the female principle; for the Aryans, undifferentiated consciousness was called

Brahman, or the Absolute, and the creative spirit, maya, or illusion. (Interestingly, a further classification would be made centuries later by the sage Kapila, who lived around 800 BCE; in his philosophical system of *Samkhya*, also meaning 'knowledge', he makes his own distinction; undifferentiated consciousness was called Purusha, and the creative spirit was called Prakriti.)

By the time the oral tradition was transcribed into written Sanskrit, it would combine the diversity of all the names and labels given to the unmanifest and manifest aspects of the universe from both cultures. Thus, during the period between 2000 BCE and 1000 BCE, various priests and legalists, sages and poets started to compile four distinct texts, namely the *Rig Veda* (composed of hymns), the *Yajur Veda* (sacrificial formulae), the *Sama Veda* (melodies) and the *Atharva Veda* (magical spells). It is the *Rig Veda*, consisting of 1,071 hymns divided into ten books or mandalas, which comprises the mystical wisdom of oneness and the *advaita* doctrine of Vedanta (the philosophy contained at the end of the *Vedas*).

It is book ten, the final mandala, of the *Rig Veda*, which describes the beginning of creation:

Then, neither the non-Real nor the Real existed.
There was no sky then, nor the heavens beyond it.
What was contained by what, and where, and who sheltered it?
What unfathomable depths, what cosmic ocean, existed then?

Then, neither death nor deathlessness existed;
Between day and night there was as yet no distinction.
That ONE by its own power breathlessly breathed.

In the beginning, darkness lay wrapped in darkness;
All was one undifferentiated sea.
Then, within that one undifferentiated existence,
Something arose by the heat of concentrated energy.

What arose in That in the beginning was Desire,
Which is the primal seed of mind.

The wise, having searched deep within their own hearts,
Have perceived the bond between the Real and the unreal.

They [the wise] have stretched the cord of their vision,
And they have perceived what is higher and lower:
The mighty powers are made fertile
By that ONE who is their Source ... [1]

Out of the undifferentiated Self, the manifested world is born into its myriad components – lightness and dark, mankind and beast, land and sea. Moreover, the complementary aspects of masculine and feminine also inaugurate themselves in a distinct pantheon of mythological creatures, goddesses and gods. And as with Mesopotamia and Egypt, the first forms of reverence focused on the sacred feminine. Indeed, terracotta figurines found in the Indus Valley show a highly developed Mother Goddess worship cult, which is reflected in the Vedic texts.

In the *Rig Veda*, she is the goddess Aditi, the 'Deva Mata', Mother of the Universe:

Aditi, Mighty Mother, true to Law, [was] brought forth ...
Ye who have gathered up your gifts, celestial and terrestrial food,
Let your rain come to us fraught with the mist of heaven. [2]

She is also Saraswati, a powerful river (usually associated with the Ganges), originating in heaven and flowing down to earth, flooding the world with her celestial grace:

I sing a lofty song, for she is mightiest, most divine of Streams.
Saraswati will I exalt with hymns and lauds, and, Vasistha, Heaven
*   and Earth.*
When in the fullness of their strength the Purus dwell, Beauteous One,
*   on thy two grassy banks,*
Favour us ... [3]

And in the *Atharva Veda*, she is Prithivi, Mother Earth·

Truth, greatness, universal order, strength, consecration, creative fervour, spiritual exaltation, the sacrifice, support the earth. May this earth, the mistress of that which was and shall be, prepare for us a broad domain.[4]

Many seers or rishis who composed their perennial philosophy in the *Rig Veda* were men but a number of poems are believed to have been written by women. In a time when women were of equal standing as their husbands and purdah and sati (or suttee) were not, as yet, common practice, they were eligible for study and initiation into the supreme knowledge. Out of ten identified, one woman in particular who conveys her mystical wisdom more profoundly than any other of her female contemporaries is the poetess, Vach.

Coincidentally sharing the same name as Vach, the goddess of learning (meaning 'word' and sometimes synonymous with Saraswati), little is known of her life except that she was the daughter of the sage, Ambhrina. Her beautiful description of absorption in the Source also occurs in the tenth mandala of the *Rig Veda*. Such is its power and emotional intensity that it is still chanted today and has come to be known as the *Devi Sukta*, a devotional song in praise of Devi, the generic Hindu name of the goddess:

I walk with the Rudras and the Vasus,
I, with the Adityas and all the gods;
I bear up the two, Mitra and Varuna,
I, Indra and Agni, I, the two Ashwins.

I sustain the pressed-out soma,
I, Twashtri, Pushan and Bhaga;
I give wealth to him that brings oblation,
To the worshipper devout, and him that presses soma.

I am the queen, the bestower of riches,
I was the first to know among the holy ones;
Me, the gods put in many places,
Making me enter and dwell abundantly.

By me, whoever eats food, and whoever sees,
Whoever breathes, and whoever hears what is said,
They dwell in me, though they know it not;
Listen, O wise, to thee I say what is true.[5]

In whatever form she manifests, Vach proclaims that the universal 'I'
pervades the entire universe. And this is the implicit message of the *Rig
Veda* – duality in unity, phenomenon in noumenon, many in the One:

Verily I myself speak all this,
What is welcome to the gods and men;
Whoever I love I make strong,
I make him a Brahma, a sage and a seer.

I spread out the bow of Rudra for him
To slay the unbeliever with his arrow;
I make strife among the people;
I pervade all the earth and heaven.

I give birth to the father on the head of all this;
My source is in the midst of waters in the sea;
Thence I spread through all the worlds;
And touch this heaven with my eminence.

It is I who blow as the winds blow,
Taking hold of all the worlds;
Past heaven and past this earth
I have by greatness become such.[6]

Again, like the poems of Enheduanna and hymns to Hatchepsut,
Vach has created the image of a female power dancing amidst heaven
and earth, wielding her bow of truth. She is the creatrix, the Shakti,
the feminine aspect of the Divine. Other women who are also known
to have been involved in the composition of the hymns of the *Rig
Veda* include Lopmudra, Apala, Vishwavara, Sikata, Nivavari, Godha

and Ghosha. Together, they sing of the sacrificial love of the Absolute and the passion of praising God's myriad name.

As time moved on, the core nondualist teaching would be crystallized even further and find expression in the Upanishads, the philosophical appendages to each Veda. Literally meaning 'sitting beneath', the Upanishads are the crest jewel of mystical knowledge. Of the 108 Upanishads believed to exist and composed during the first millennium BCE, their common motif is the merging of the individual self (atman) with the universal Source (Brahman), through active contemplation, purity of heart and the simple grace of God. It is the dissolution into the all-pervading consciousness, says the *Isa Upanishad*, that freedom from the bondage of suffering and the bliss of everlasting peace can be found:

> *When a man or woman*
> *Understands and knows*
> *That the Self or Consciousness*
> *Reality, Love,*
> *Has become all that exists,*
> *What possible trouble or sorrow*
> *Can affect*
> *He or she who has seen*
> *That seamless Unity?*[7]

Although the authorship of the Upanishads is unknown, many speak of feminine wisdom and none so beautifully as the *Devi Upanishad*:

> *'Great goddess, who art thou?'*
> *She replies: 'I am essentially Brahman.*
> *From me has proceeded the world comprising Prakriti and Purusha, the*
>   *void and Plenum.*
> *I am all forms of bliss and non bliss.*
> *Knowledge and ignorance are Myself …*
> *I am the entire world.*

I am the Veda as well as what is different from it.
I am unknown. Below and above and around am I.'[8]

It is the *Brihadaranyaka Upanishad*, however, that speaks of the wisdom of two actual women: Gargi, daughter of the sage Vachaknu, and Maitreyi, wife of the sage Yajnavalkya. Like Vach, nothing more is known of their lives except that which is mentioned in the Upanishad. Both come to the understanding of the universal Brahman through their perseverance in the discovery of the ultimate understanding: Gargi, through her repeated questioning of the sage, Yajnavalkya, at a philosophical tournament held by King Janaka; and Maitreyi, wife of the same sage Yajnavalkya, upon his departure to the forest and the settlement of his worldly affairs. It is only Maitreyi, out of both his wives, who asks about the nature of immortality:

'Maitreyi!' said Yajnavalkya, 'Lo, verily, I am about to go forth from this state. Behold! Let me make a final settlement for you and that Katyayani [his second wife].'

Then said Maitreyi: 'If now, sir, this whole earth filled with wealth were mine, would I be immortal thereby?'

'No,' said Yajnavalkya. 'As the life of the rich, even so your life would be. Of immortality, however, there is no hope through wealth.'

Then Maitreyi said: 'What should I do with that through which I may not be immortal? What you know, sir – that, indeed, tell me!'

Then said Yajnavalkya: 'Ah! Lo, dear as you are to us, dear is what you say! Come, sit down. I will explain to you. But while I am expounding, do you seek to ponder thereon.'

Then said he: 'Lo, verily, not for love of the husband is a husband dear, but for love of the Soul [atman] a husband is dear.

'Lo, verily, not for love of the wife is a wife dear, but for love of the Soul a wife is dear.

'Lo, verily, not for love of the sons are sons dear, but for love of the Soul sons are dear.

'Lo, verily, not for love of the wealth is wealth dear, but for love of the Soul wealth is dear.

'Lo, verily, not for love of Brahmanhood is Brahmanhood dear, but for love of the Soul Brahmanhood is dear.

'Lo, verily, not for love of Kshatriyahood [warrior caste] is Kshatriyahood dear, but for love of the Soul Kshatriyahood is dear.

'Lo, verily, not for love of the worlds are the worlds dear, but for love of the Soul the worlds are dear.

'Lo, verily, not for love of the gods are the gods dear, but for love of the Soul the gods are dear.

'Lo, verily, not for love of the beings are beings dear, but for love of the Soul beings are dear.

'Lo, verily, not for love of all is all dear, but for love of the Soul all is dear.

'Lo, verily, it is the Soul that should be seen, that should be hearkened to, that should be thought on, that should be pondered on, O Maitreyi. Lo, verily, with the seeing of, with the hearkening to, with the thinking of, and with the understanding of the Soul, this world-all is known.'[9]

Never before, or possibly since, has the mystical message been recorded in such a precise and profound way. And by honouring the feminine principle, harmony is kept in balance in a universe full of complements. In our contemporary times where the sexes vie for dominance, Vach and her sisters point to the underlying purpose that should be hearkened to, pondered upon – the understanding of the atman in which everything is ultimately known.

India was one of the first great cultures to recognize the equality, and even supremacy, of the voice and form of the feminine. Indeed the Vedic period was a time when women had, on the whole, equal rights. However, as society expanded and became more and more sophisticated during the Upanishadic era, women's position in society came increasingly under the governance of men. Texts like the *Manu Smriti* ('The Laws of Manu'), a collection of instructions on how to order one's life and compiled in approximately the third century BCE, did indeed advocate the sacredness of the female form:

Women must be honoured and adorned by their fathers, brothers, husbands and brothers-in-law, who desire [their own] welfare.

Where women are honoured, there the gods are pleased; but where they are not honoured, no sacred rite yields rewards.[10]

Nevertheless, Manu subsequently goes on to say that if a wife is barren, dishonourable or merely displeases her husband, she may be superseded at any time – a rule that does not appear to apply to the man. Unfortunately, these types of misogynistic attitudes towards women were starting to emerge in many other continents across the globe. Paradoxically, however, Indian society would continue to revere the concept of the feminine principle right up until modern times, which would act as a model that the rest of the developed world would eventually come to emulate.

chapter four

Makeda, Queen of Sheba

Around the beginning of the second millennium BCE, a small group of people, led by Terah and his son, Abraham, set out from the city of Ur, Enheduanna's birthplace, and travelled northward across the Euphrates River to Haran, in modern-day Iraq. Here it is said that Abraham heard God speaking directly to him. If His followers obeyed His commandments and settled in 'The Promised Land' of Canaan in the south, God said to Abraham, they would become His 'chosen people'. Abraham and his people, also known as Hebrews, immediately agreed to this 'covenant' and the Judaic religion, the earliest monotheist faith, was born.

For several hundred years, the descendants of Abraham lived as nomads in Canaan, worshipping their God, whom they called Yahweh (or Elohim, which translates as 'I am'). Joseph, a descendent of Abraham, then led a number of the Hebrew tribe into Egypt, where they were forced into slavery. The remaining Canaanites, however, over the next four hundred or so years, developed their own religious culture, which evolved from their Judaic and Babylonian inheritance. Embracing both the newly emerging separate Father God of the Hebrews with the more traditional all-encompassing Mother Goddess, a dual interpretation of the Truth started to flourish. The transcendent male aspect of the Divine they called El (the 'First' and the root of 'Elohim') or Ba'al ('the Lord'); the immanent female aspect, they called Elat (the feminine form of El) or Ba'ala (the feminine form of Ba'al).

Indeed, Elat had evolved from the Canaanite mother goddess, Asherah, who in turn was a variant of Inanna and Ishtar. As wife of El, the father god of the Canaan pantheon, Elat was called 'Lady of the Sea' and 'Mother of the Gods', linking her to Nammu, Isis and Aditi. Archaeological evidence from the period suggests that Asherah was even worshipped as the wife of Yahweh. Pictorially, Asherah is seen nourishing creation with the offering of her breasts; she is also depicted on carvings and statues as either a lion or a sycamore tree.

Anath, daughter of Asherah, and included alongside the Canaanite goddesses, was also revered for her female power. Known as 'Lady of Heaven' and 'Lady of the Mountain', she is the sister-wife of Baal, who too must descend into the underworld to rescue her husband from his evil brother, Mot. Echoing once again the stories of Inanna and Ishtar, Anath is symbolic of the recurring seasons of life, death and regeneration in the temporal world.

One goddess, however, whose fame was far greater than any of her female counterparts was Astarte (or Ashtoreth in Hebrew), meaning 'that which issues from the womb'. It is unclear as to whether Astarte is a goddess in her own right or she is a synthesis of Asherah and/or Anath. Whatever her heritage, the cult of Astarte, the Mother Goddess, was widespread throughout Canaan. Again, she is referred to as 'Lady of Heaven' and 'Virgin of the Sea' and is typically shown standing on a lion, holding a lotus flower in one hand and serpents in the other, and, in some cases, wearing a horned headdress, reminiscent to Hathor. She is also represented by the moon as well as the morning and evening stars.

In the twelfth century BCE, the Hebrews who had originally left Canaan under Joseph were now to return under a new leader, Moses, bringing with them their monotheist Judaic faith, together with a code of social conduct in the form of the Ten Commandments. Despite their common theological roots, conflict arose between the two peoples, each side claiming the supremacy of their own philosophical idea over the other. Sadly, this resulted in the systematic slaughter of the Canaanites by the Hebrews. Although some Hebrews accommodated the cult of Astarte within their belief system, perceiving her as the wife of Yahweh, the sacred feminine was no longer revered in the tangible form of a goddess. Furthermore, Yahweh's instruction to worship no graven images gave legitimacy to the deconsecration of Astarte; moreover, the belief in the immanence of the sacred feminine in nature was replaced with the idea that Reality only lived *behind*, and not within, the world of appearance.

The Hebrew Bible, essentially known as the Old Testament, charts the history of God's 'chosen people' and the veneration of Yahweh. In particular, the Judaic creation myth reinforces the transcendent aspect of the Father God not as a bountiful evolutionary power but as a sterile voice coming out of the void, creating the universe in a series of delineated steps over the course of seven days.

Moreover, the story of Adam and Eve reinforces the arising dominance of the masculine over the feminine. Interestingly, two creation myths were originally composed: the first, written in approximately 400 BCE and known as the Priestly myth, recounts a tale in which Adam and Eve are created simultaneously as equals. But it is an earlier myth, written in roughly 850 BCE, which has formed the Judaic, Christian and Islamic inheritance, and it states:

And the Lord God formed man of the dust of the ground, and breathed into his nostrils the breath of life; and man became a living soul.[1]

Furthermore:

And the Lord God caused a deep sleep to fall upon Adam, and he slept: and he took one of his ribs, and closed up the flesh instead thereof;

And the rib, which the Lord God had taken from man, made he a woman, and brought her unto the man.

And Adam said, 'This is now bone of my bones, and flesh of my flesh: she shall be called Woman, because she was taken out of Man.'[2]

Not only does this subvert the original concept of the feminine principle as being the life-generating force but woman is now miraculously born of man – a biological impossibility!

Moreover, the serpent and the Tree of Knowledge, traditional symbols of the sacred feminine, now become sources of evil. And even sexuality itself, the very epiphany of male and female union, is little more than an act of lust, with the woman herself reduced to a demonic temptress. Indeed, many later Christian mystics would engage in self flagellation and bodily abasement, owing to the idea that anything to do with the flesh was essentially wicked. It is no coincidence that Mary, the mother of Christ, was perceived to be a virgin and therefore divorced from any association with sexual intercourse.

Thus, by dishonouring the feminine and in turn defaming the cult of Astarte by introducing their own patriarchal mythology, the Hebrews effectively accelerated the 'holy war' of masculine *against* feminine and, in turn, man against woman. Moreover, under the emerging Judaic code, laid down in the *Torah* (the first five books of the Hebrew Bible), women were excluded from most forms of religious ceremonies in the synagogues as well as study of their Judaic faith.

Against all the odds, the suppressed spirit of the sacred feminine managed to retain a voice in a collection of fifteen texts written in Greek, known as the *Apocrypha*, meaning 'hidden books', owing to the fact that they were all excluded from the orthodox canon of Jewish literature. Here, Astarte resurfaces under a new guise, in the form of Hokhmah, meaning 'wisdom'. Similar in concept to Me in Mesopotamia, Maat in Egypt and Sophia in Ancient Greece, Hokhmah forms the very heart of the *Apocrypha*. One book in particular, entitled *Ecclesiasticus* and written by Jesus Ben Sirach, a Jew living in Egypt and writing in approximately 180 BCE, speaks of the immanent creative force of the universe:

> *The sand of the sea, the drops of rain,*
> *and the days of eternity – who can count them?*
> *The height of heaven, the breadth of the earth,*
> *the abyss, and wisdom – who can search them out?*

Wisdom was created before all other things,
and prudent understanding from eternity
the root of wisdom – to whom has it been revealed?
Her subtleties – who knows them?[3]

Moreover, Hokhmah is a personification of the Mother Goddess and is rightfully honoured once again:

She will come to meet him like a mother,
and like a young bride she will welcome him.
She will feed him with the bread of learning,
and give him the water of wisdom to drink.[4]

Sadly, Jesus Ben Sirach did not have the courage of his convictions and he goes on to support the split in gender relations by stating: 'Of the woman came the beginning of sin, and through her we all die.'[5] He forgot, sadly, that through her we are all, in fact, given the gift of life.

Another interesting character emerges from history who also challenged the religious status quo. Solomon, King of Israel – a unified kingdom between Assyria and Egypt – lived in approximately 1000 BCE and has been accredited with writing over 3,000 proverbs and 1,005 psalms (recorded in the fourth century BCE) as well as one of the books of *Apocrypha*, entitled the *Wisdom of Solomon*. Meaning 'sun' or 'peace', Solomon was born to King David and Bathsheba and famed for his great wealth and for having hundreds of wives. Although his life was devoted to the service of Yahweh, he also paid reverence to the sacred feminine. As it states in 1 Kings 11:5: 'Solomon became a follower of Astarte, the goddess of the Sidonians.' He built many pagan temples in honour of the goddess and in Jerusalem, the image of Astarte was used to adorn Solomon's Temple.

In the *Wisdom of Solomon*, the King eulogizes the feminine form of knowledge:

Wisdom is radiant and unfading,
and she is easily discerned by those who love her,

and is found by those who seek her.
She hastens to make herself known to those who desire her.
One who rises early to seek her will have no difficulty,
for she will be found sitting at the gate.
To fix one's thought on her is perfect understanding,
and one who is vigilant on her account will soon be free from care,
because she goes about seeking those worthy of her,
and she graciously appears to them in their paths,
and meets them in every thought.[6]

Moreover, her presence becomes an intoxicating vision of the Beloved:

I loved her and sought her from my youth;
I desired to take her for my bride,
and became enamoured of her beauty.
She glorifies her noble birth by living with God,
and the Lord of all loves her.
For she is an initiate in the knowledge of God,
and an associate in his works.
If riches are a desirable possession in life,
what is richer than wisdom, the active cause of all things?[7]

Moreover, the Book of Proverbs, also attributed to Solomon and included in the Old Testament, praises the omniscient feminine:

The Lord possessed me in the beginning of his way, before his works of old.

I was set up from everlasting, from the beginning, or ever the earth was.

When there were no depths, I was brought forth; when there were no fountains abounding with water.

Before the mountains were settled, before the hills was I brought forth.

While as yet he had not made the earth, nor the fields, nor the highest part of the dust of the world.

When he prepared the heavens, I was there: when he set a compass upon the face of the depth.

When he established the clouds above: when he strengthened
the fountains of the deep:

When he gave to the sea his decree, that the waters should not pass
his commandment: when he appointed the foundations of the earth:

Then I was by him, as one brought up with him: and was daily
his delight, rejoicing always before him;

Rejoicing in the habitable part of his earth; and my delights were
with the sons of men.[8]

A great lover of women, it is no surprise, therefore, that when
Solomon encountered a queen of outstanding beauty and wisdom, he
immediately fell in love with her, wanting to possess her as his own.
Numerous legends abound about the life of this female figure
throughout Arabia, Persia, Ethiopia and Israel, but of her title there
is little doubt – she was Makeda, the Queen of Sheba.

Fanciful tales of Islamic, Arabian and Jewish origin involve magic
carpets, talking birds and even teleportation. More realistic portraits,
however, appear in the Old Testament, in 1 Kings and 2 Corinthians,
the Quran as well as the Ethiopian Bible, the *Kebra Nagast* or 'The
Glory of Kings'. Born of royalty in 1020 BCE in the kingdom of
Sheba or Saba, modern-day Yemen, she succeeded her father to the
throne upon his death, at the age of fifteen. It is said that she
possessed both a fierce intelligence and an exquisite beauty, despite a
number of accounts testifying to the fact that she had a deformed foot
in the shape of a hoof. The Jewish historian, Josephus, living in the
first century CE, said of her: 'She was inquisitive into philosophy and
on that and on other accounts also was to be admired.'[9]

The kingdom of Saba, which some historians believe also incor-
porated the territories of Ethiopia and Egypt, was a wealthy country,
famous for its precious stones and exotic spices. Links had long been
established between Saba and its neighbours, trading frankincense
and myrrh up the 'Incense Road' along the Rea Sea into the land of
Israel. Like all great nations, the Sabaeans had their own pantheon of
goddesses and gods, which also included worshipping the universal
Mother Goddess as Astarte.

Known as Bilqis by the Arabians, possibly meaning 'concubine' and Makeda by the Ethiopians, meaning 'greatness' or 'Great One', the Queen of Sheba upon hearing of Solomon's wise reputation desired to see him for herself. Speaking to her subjects, she is recorded as saying in the *Kebra Nagast*:

> *Wisdom is*
> *sweeter than honey,*
> *brings more joy*
> *than wine,*
> *illumines*
> *more than the sun,*
> *is more precious*
> *than jewels.*
> *She causes*
> *the ears to hear*
> *and the heart to comprehend.*
>
> *I love her*
> *like a mother,*
> *and she embraces me*
> *as her own child.*
> *I will follow*
> *her footprints*
> *and she will not cast me away.*[10]

With 797 camels, laden with precious gifts, Makeda set out for Jerusalem. Solomon was overjoyed at her arrival in his court and immediately gave her a luxurious apartment and showed her around his palace. However, Makeda had not come to stand in awe of his wealth; she had come to hear his wise counsel and she started to ask him philosophical questions as well as to test him with riddles. Over the following six months she conversed daily with Solomon on all manner of profound matters. Overcome by his insight, Makeda addressed him thus:

'I look upon thee and I see that thy wisdom is immeasurable and thine understanding inexhaustible, and it is like unto a lamp in the darkness.'[11]

But Solomon replies:

'Wisdom and understanding spring from thee thyself.'[12]

Eventually, Makeda knew it was time to return to her own country but Solomon could not bear to let her go and begged her to remain with him as his principal wife. He ponders his predicament:

'A woman of such splendid beauty hath come to me from the ends of the earth! What do I know? Will God give me seed in her?'[13]

Makeda was, however, a virgin and she refused his sexual advances so Solomon decided to seduce her instead. He ordered a lavish feast, full of spicy foods, after which he asked Makeda to rest in his bedchamber. Makeda agreed on the condition that he must not attempt to have her by force, to which Solomon agreed, on his own condition that she too must not take anything from the palace without permission. In the middle of the night, with a raging thirst, Makeda got up to drink some water. Solomon, who had only been pretending to sleep, grabbed her by the arm and asked if she were not breaking her vow – what, after all, is more precious than water? She acquiesced and demanded to be released from her vow. This meant that Solomon was also released from his and he subsequently satisfied his carnal passion with her. Accounts of this tale suggest that Makeda enjoyed the physical union with Solomon, from which a child was later conceived by the name of Menelek.

One of the most beautiful love poems dating from this period is the *Song of Songs*, although it wasn't actually written down until 100 BCE. Traditionally, this sacred marriage text is attributed to Solomon and the object of his affection is believed to be Makeda, though there is no firm evidence to confirm this. Interestingly, despite its intoxicating blend of sexual ecstasy and mysticism, the *Song of Songs* finds a place in the Old Testament.

In poetry more akin to earlier Mesopotamian verse, the mystical marriage between lover and Beloved is explored in exquisite style:

> *Let him kiss me with the kisses of his mouth –*
> *For thy love is better than wine.*
> *Thine ointments have a goodly fragrance,*
> *Thy name is as ointment poured forth;*
> *Therefore do the maidens love thee.*
> *Draw me, we will run after thee.*
> *The king hath brought me into his bedchambers;*
> *We will be glad and rejoice in thee,*
> *We will find thy love more fragrant than wine.*
> *Sincerely do they love thee.*[14]

And of Makeda's physical form, he writes through her voice:

> *I am dark, but comely,*
> *O ye daughters of Jerusalem,*
> *As the tents of Kedar,*
> *As the curtains of Solomon.*[15]

In their sexual union, Sheba and Solomon merge into the bliss of their mutual love:

> *I am a rose of Sharon,*
> *A lily of the valleys.*
>
> *As a lily among thorns,*
> *So is my love among the daughters.*
>
> *As an apple tree among the trees of the wood,*
> *So is my beloved among the youths.*
> *I delight to sit in his shadow*

And his fruit is sweet to my taste.
He brought me to the banqueting house,
And his banner of love was over me.

Stay me with flagons, comfort me with apples;
For I am lovesick.
His left hand is under my head,
And his right hand doth embrace me.[16]

And like the universal Mother Goddess, they are nourished in the bosom of the sacred feminine:

O that thou wert as my brother,
That sucked the breasts of my mother!
When I should find thee without, I would kiss thee;
Yea, and none would despise me.

I would lead thee, and bring thee
Into my mother's house,
That thou mightest instruct me:
I would cause thee to drink of spiced wine
Of the juice of my pomegranate.

His left hand should be under my head,
And his right hand should embrace me.[17]

When he had grown into a young man, Menelek also travelled to Jerusalem, to meet his father for the first time. Solomon was so impressed by his valiant and noble son that he tried to persuade him to stay but Menelek longed to return the land of his mother. Sadly, Solomon had to let him go, however, he was accompanied home by an entourage of Solomon's own family, thus further establishing his royal lineage within Ethiopia.

Makeda is attributed with praising the name of wisdom upon her son's return:

I fell
because of wisdom,
but was not destroyed:
through her I dived
into the great sea,
and in those depths
I seized
a wealth-bestowing pearl.

I descended
like the great iron anchor
men use to steady their ships
in the night on rough seas,
and holding up the bright lamp
that I there received,
I climbed the rope
to the boat of understanding.

While in the dark sea,
I slept,
and not overwhelmed there,
dreamt: a star
blazed in my womb.

I marvelled
at that light,
and grasped it,
and brought it up to the sun.
I laid hold upon it,
and will not let it go.[18]

Makeda's poetry is powerful and prophetic. Like her female predecessors, Makeda's love of Hokhmah has been tested but the journey into the unknown yields even greater knowledge than before. It is said that Makeda relinquished goddess worship of Astarte in favour of Yahweh, unifying her country in one monotheist religion – whether this was in honour of her love for Solomon we can only speculate. However, like Inanna, Ishtar and Anath, a voyage into the 'other' world brought about the process of rebirth, redemption and renewal.

Interestingly, in the manner of his own father, Menelek was also involved in an act of trickery. Leaving Jerusalem, he stole away with him the Ark of the Covenant, containing the tablets of the law as given to Moses by Yahweh, taking it back to Ethiopia, where he would later become king.

It is said that after Makeda left Jerusalem, coupled with the later departure of Menelek and the Ark, Solomon's state of mind deteriorated and, in turn, so too did the state of Israel. Many historians also state that he became obsessed with his own glory and his love of extravagance, fuelled by increased taxes, which contributed to an ever-increasing corrupt society, torn asunder by civil war.

Like Enheduanna and Hatchepsut, Makeda remains essentially an enigmatic character and her biography is sketchy at best. Recent scholarship even suggests that she was an Egyptian queen, synonymous with Maakhah Tamar II. Whatever her identity, her charismatic memory is a reminder of the female voice empowered with the wisdom of Hokhmah.

Unfortunately, however, the feminine principle continued to be suppressed in the Judaic faith for the following two and a half millennia. Eve, and her predecessor Lilith, (who according to Judaic legend was created by Yahweh and fought unsuccessfully with Adam for her equality and independence) form the overwhelming misogynistic flavour of the Hebrew Scriptures. Moreover, strict laws regarding women's behaviour, as recorded in the *Mishnah* particularly surrounding menstruation, miscarriage and childbirth, continued to exist until modern times.

The voice of the goddess surfaces again in other cultures and religious traditions but it is not until the Middle Ages in Europe within the Kabbalistic tradition that she emerges once more in the Jewish faith in the form of Shekhinah, the sacred feminine.

chapter five

Sappho

One particular civilization where the nondualist teaching came into its own and whose philosophical legacy formed the basis of Western thought was Ancient Greece. Many Greek thinkers during the first millennium BCE, influenced through cultural links with Egypt, Mesopotamia and the Indus Valley, were conversant with an immanent mystical power.

The legacy of one illumined individual, whose perennial philosophy became the cornerstone of Greece's Golden Age during the sixth century BCE, was the martyred sage, Socrates. Born in 469 BCE in Athens, he championed what became known as the Socratic Method – deconstructing philosophical argument in order to arrive at one unchanging Truth, which he called the 'Good'. Although he never wrote a word, Socrates' Method was immortalized by his devoted disciple, Plato.

In Book VII of *The Republic*, Plato describes Socrates' 'Analogy of the Cave', which illustrates the difference between the world of shadows, or maya, and the one everlasting Reality. After Socrates' death in 399 BCE through drinking hemlock, his mystical vision was also apperceived by, amongst others, the Roman Emperor Marcus Aurelius (121–180 CE) as well as the great philosopher, Plotinus (205–270 CE), both of whom spoke of a universal, all-pervading Being. In another of Plato's famous works, *Symposium*, the nature of love, discussed over dinner, is presented through

Diotima, a Mantinean priestess and Socrates' teacher. Expounding the nature of beauty, she demonstrates how falling in love with its pursuit can lead to a love of the Divine:

> 'The correct way,' she said, 'for someone to approach this business [the pursuit of love] is to begin when he's young by being drawn towards beautiful bodies. At first, if his guide leads him correctly, he should love just one body and in that relationship produce beautiful discourses. Next he should realize that the beauty of any one body is closely related to that of another, and that, if he is to pursue beauty of form, it's very foolish not to regard the beauty of all bodies as one and the same. Once he's seen this, he'll become a lover of all beautiful bodies ... After this, he should regard the beauty of minds as more valuable than that of the body, so that, if someone has goodness of mind even if he has little of the bloom of beauty, he will be content with him, and will love and care for him, and give birth to the kinds of discourse that help young men to become better ... After practices, the guide must lead him towards forms of knowledge, so that he sees their beauty too ... he will be turned towards the great sea of beauty and gazing on it he'll give birth, through a boundless love of knowledge, to many beautiful and magnificent discourse and ideas ...
>
> He will suddenly catch sight of something amazingly beautiful in its nature; this, Socrates, is the ultimate objective of all the previous efforts ... this beauty always *is*, and doesn't come into being or cease; it doesn't increase or diminish ... It will appear as in itself and by itself, always single in form; all other beautiful things share its character, but do so in such a way that, when other things come to be or cease, it is not increased or decreased in any way nor does it undergo any change.[1]

Greek mythology abounds with references to immortal beauty and in particular towards the feminine form. Legend states that in the beginning, the universe was formed out of nothingness into a pantheon of immortal beings, called *protogonoi*, meaning 'first born', who formed the fabric of the cosmos. Consisting both male and female elements, each *protogonos* is the embodiment of a specific quality or substance. The female *protogonoi* comprise Ananke (Destiny), Hemera (Day), Chaos (Air), Nyx (Night), Tethys (Fresh Water), Thalassa (Sea Water) and Thesis (Creation). But it is Gaia who is the most illustrious for she is Mother of the Earth and all the gods. Often depicted as a buxom woman half emerging from the earth, there are many poems written in her praise, one of the most beautiful being the 'Homeric Hymn to Gaia':

O universal mother, who dost keep
From everlasting thy foundations deep,
Eldest of things, Great Earth, I sing of thee;
All shapes that have their dwelling in the sea,
All things that fly, or on the ground divine
Live, move, and there are nourished – these are thine;
These from thy wealth thou dost sustain; from thee
Fair babes are born, and fruits on every tree
Hang ripe and large, revered Divinity!

The life of mortal men beneath thy sway
Is held; thy power both gives and takes away!
Happy are they whom thy mild favours nourish,
All things unstinted round them grown and flourish.
For them, endures the life-sustaining field
Its load of harvest, and their cattle yield
Large increase, and their house with wealth is filled.

Such honoured dwell in cities fair and free,
The homes of lovely women, prosperously;
Their sons exult in youth's new budding gladness,
And their fresh daughters free from care or sadness,
With bloom-inwoven dance and happy song,
On the soft flowers the meadow-grass among,
Leap round them sporting – such delights by thee
Are given, rich Power, revered Divinity.

Mother of gods, thou wife of starry Heaven,
Farewell! Be thou propitious, and be given
A happy life for this brief melody,
Nor thou nor other songs shall unremembered be.[2]

Gaia is the immanent creative force, sustaining and nourishing all of creation. Indeed, priestesses at Delphi, known for their oracular powers, made their invocations to Gaia long before any of the Greek gods were paid due homage.

The rising dominance of the masculine principle was, nonetheless, perpetuated in a number of other creation myths, the principal tale being preserved in Hesiod's *Theogony* (c. 700 BCE). In this tale Gaia, who is born of Chaos, unites with her first born, Uranus, ruler of Heaven, and gives birth to three violent giants. Uranus, sick of the sight of them, imprisons them all in a secret place, whereupon one of them, Chronos, carries out a plot to castrate Uranus. Defeating him thus, Chronos then becomes ruler of the universe. The pattern is subsequently repeated by the next generation whereby Chronos eats his first five children born of his sister-queen, Rhea, but is outwitted by the remaining child, Zeus, who in turn also becomes Father God of the universe. Zeus then swallows his first wife, Metis, while she is pregnant. Thus, the final and complete control of female fertility is represented by the birth of Athena, goddess of wisdom, from Zeus's head.

Despite the arising of the powerful male principle, Greek wisdom is personified in the form of the goddess, Athena. Symbolically represented by the olive tree and pictorially either with helmet and girdle or, in an older image, wreathed in serpents, she lends her name to the capital of Greece. Known also as 'Pallas', meaning 'shaker' or 'brandisher' (of a weapon or even the ignorant minds of humankind), her temple is the famous Parthenon, meaning 'maiden', in Athens. As the guardian of reason and intermediary between mortal man and the gods, she appears most famously in Homer's *Odyssey* – the tale of Odysseus' epic journey home from the Trojan Wars. Through her *'metis'*, meaning 'counsel' and taken from her mother of the same name, Athena guides her male protégé, Odysseus, through a series of tests in his voyage of self discovery and mastery. The opening of the Homeric 'Hymn to Athena' reiterates her beauty and wisdom:

> *Pallas Athena*
> *I shall sing,*
> *the glorious goddess*
> *whose eyes gleam,*
> *brilliantly inventive,*
> *her heart relentless,*
> *formidable maiden,*
> *guardian of cities* ...[3]

Another female Greek deity who is the goddess of the hunt as well as the soul of the wilderness is Artemis. Also known as the Moon Goddess, she is often shown as a winged woman accompanied by lions, deer and other creatures of the forest. Unlike the cool logic of Athena, Artemis embodies the wild and passionate forces of creation. And together with Hecate, the three-headed goddess of sorcery and witch-craft, they together represent life, death and regeneration, like their counterparts Inanna and Ishtar in Mesopotamia and Kali in India. The Homeric 'Hymn to Artemis' pays reverence to her warrior-like form:

> *Artemis I sing*
> *with her golden arrows*
> *and her hunting cry*
> *the sacred maiden*
> *deer-huntress*
> *showering arrows*
> *sister of Apollo* ...[4]

There is one goddess, however, who triumphs over all others. Born of the sea and immortalized in Botticelli's *Birth of Venus*, her fame and beauty are world renowned, for she is Aphrodite, 'the Golden One'. The tale of the 'Judgement of Paris' relates how Paris chooses Aphrodite over Hera and Athena, believing her to be the fairest of them all. (His reward is Helen of Troy but it comes at the price of precipitating the Trojan Wars.)

Sensuality personified, Aphrodite is attended by the Five Graces – *Euphrosyne* (Joyous), *Aglea* (Brilliance), *Thalia* (Flowering), *Himeros* (Desire) and *Eros* (Love). According to Hesiod, when Chronos castrated his father, he threw his genitals into the sea. Foam formed around Uranus's penis whereupon it was tossed along the waves to Cyprus. Reaching the shore, Aphrodite (also called Cypris) emerges from the spume – '*aphros*' in fact means 'foam'. The Homeric 'Hymn to Aphrodite' heralds the beauty of this electrifying goddess:

> *Golden crowned, beautiful*
> *awesome Aphrodite*
> *is who I shall sing,*
> *she who possesses the heights*
> *of all*
> *sea-wet Cyprus*
> *where Zephyros swept her*
> *with his moist breath*
> *over the waves*
> *of the roaring sea*
> *in soft foam.*
>
> *In their circles of gold*
> *the Hours joyously*
> *received her*
> *and wrapped*
> *the ambrosial garments around her.*
> *On her immortal head*
> *they laid a crown of gold*
> *that was wonderfully made*
> *and in*
> *the pierced lobes of her ears*
> *they hung*
> *flowers of copper*

from the mountains
and precious gold ...[5]

Aphrodite epitomizes the interconnectedness of all creation and the perpetual cycle of rebirth, sustained through the nourishing power of love. Worshipped at her temple in Paphos, Aphrodite is often accompanied by dolphins, swans, geese and doves in artistic form as well as being associated with the evening star, Venus. She is the lover of Adonis who is slain by a boar, with the condition of his resurrection being that he must split his time between Persephone in Hades and Aphrodite on earth.

When we consider the extent to which goddesses were revered and honoured in ancient Greece, it is difficult to reconcile it with the manner in which ordinary women were treated in daily life. Women were excluded from participating in civic democracy and were generally perceived as being irrational and lacking intelligence. Hesiod's *Theogony* perpetuates this misogyny through his story of Pandora, who in the manner of Eve, is blamed for being responsible for transforming man's peaceful existence on earth into one of conflict and death. The first woman on earth, she is given a sealed box by the gods and told never to open it. Pandora's curiosity finally overwhelms her, however, and she opens the box, from which innumerable plagues and sorrows escape into the world.

Perhaps, therefore, Athena, Artemis and Aphrodite represent feminine ideals, removed from flesh and blood reality, thus leaving the masculine psyche inspired and yet relatively unchallenged. But when faced with the real-life embodiment of beauty and wisdom, attitudes radically shift. This may also account for the bizarre way in which society treated the woman poet, Sappho, who in many ways embodied the ideals of Aphrodite, her patron goddess.

Born on the island of Lesbos, off the coast of modern Turkey, Sappho was a writer and priestess living in approximately 600 BCE. We only know a small amount of her work for most of it, up to nine papyrus rolls, was destroyed by fire in two separate incidents – the first, at the great library at Alexandria in 272 CE, which was started by the Roman Emperor Lucius Aurelianus, and then a second fire at the Temple of Serapis in 391 CE, started by the Roman Emperor Theodosius, both in an attempt to obliterate pagan and non-Christian manuscripts contained within them. The only remaining evidence of her poetry, therefore, comes to us either through quotations in various books passed from era to era, or on surviving pieces of broken pottery and papyrus leavings, discovered only in the last years of the nineteenth century in the town of Oxyrhynchus in Egypt.

There are many complex interpretations of Sappho's verse. Some commentators have focused on stories surrounding her tragic love for a ferryman, Phaon, and her apparent suicide; others have concentrated on her sexuality and the perceived female homoerotic elements in her work. Whether or not she endorses lesbianism we can never know but of one thing we can be in no doubt – her poetry is the celebration of sexual love. Moreover, her literary genius, often sidelined in modern times, was given due reverence in its day – Plato called Sappho the Tenth Muse. (It must be remembered, however, that Plato believed that any man who had not lived a virtuous life would be reincarnated as a woman.) The later Roman poet Ovid (43 BCE – 17 CE) was not so favourable and wrote salacious comments about her. This is somewhat surprising since he too went on to compose his own series of love poetry, the *Amores*, as well as a set of handbooks on the art of lovemaking, the *Ars Amatoria*, inspired, he claimed, by the goddess Venus herself.

Of Sappho's life, we know very little – an entry in the *Suda*, an historical and literary encyclopaedia written in the tenth century CE, states that she had a family, including a husband and daughter, but this cannot be proven. Whatever her situation, she was subject to the prevailing ancient-world attitudes towards women, who were seen only as property of their menfolk with their role firmly within the precincts of the home. The only public activity they were privy to was to supervise cults of the deities such as the god Dionysus and the goddess Aphrodite.

Translating from the Greek, Sappho's verse is in the genre of the lyric – short, personal monodies or poems sung by a single voice. Infused with intense erotic desire, she implores the immortal goddess of love to help her in her quest for her beloved:

Shimmering,
              iridescent,
                             deathless Aphrodite,
child of Zeus, weaver of wiles,
                                         I beg you,
do not crush my spirit with anguish, Lady,
but come to me now, if ever before
you heard my voice in the distance
and leaving your father's golden house
drove your chariot pulled by sparrows
swift and beautiful
over the black earth, their wings a blur
as they streaked down from heaven
                                         across the bright sky –

and then you were with me, a smile
playing about your immortal lips
as you asked,
                        what is it this time?
                                         why are you calling again?
And asked what my heart in its lovesick raving
most wanted to happen:
                                         'Whom now
should I persuade to love you?
Who is wronging, Sappho?
She may run now, but she'll be chasing soon.
She may spurn gifts, but soon she'll be giving.
She may not love now, but soon she will,
                                         willing or not.'

Come to me again now, release me
from my agony, fulfil all
that my heart desires, and fight for me,
                                         fight at my side, Goddess.[6]

During a period in history when the segregation of the sexes in public life was rife, it is little wonder that Sappho alludes predominantly to the society of women and the figure of the goddess – her comfort, her inspiration, her guide:

>   *down from the mountain top*
>
> *and out of Crete,*
>   *come to me here*
> *in your sacred precinct, to your grove*
> *of apple trees,*
>   *and your altars*
>   *smoking with incense,*
>
> *where cold water flows babbling*
> *through the branches,*
>   *the whole place*
>   *shadowed with roses,*
>   *sleep adrift down*
> *from silvery leaves*
>   *an enchantment*
>
> *horses grazing in a meadow*
>   *abloom with spring flowers*
> *and where the breezes blow sweetly,*
>
>   *here, Cypris,*
> *delicately in golden cups*
>   *pour nectar*
> *mixed for our festivities.*[7]

Throughout her work, Sappho employs all the imagery and symbolism recurrent with the divine goddess and the fertility of her bountiful nature – roses, apples, trees, the moon:

from Sardis
often turning your mind here

we thought you were like a goddess
      everyone looked at you
she loved the way you moved in the dance

now among the women of Lydia

as at sunset the rose-fingered moon
      outshines all stars, spreading her light
over the salt sea, the flowering fields,

and the glimmering dew falls, roses
      bloom amid delicate starflowers
chervil and sweet clover

she walks back and forth, remembering
      her beloved Atthis,
the tender soul consumed with grief

to go there   *this*
minute   *much*
talks   *in the middle*

It is not easy for us to equal
goddesses in beauty

      Aphrodite
    poured nectar from
a golden

      Persuasion

    the Geraesteum
      dear ones

    nothing[9]

Ecstasy and agony – Sappho understands the alchemy of love. Sometimes unrequited, sometimes our heart's fulfilment:

Lucky bridegroom,
the marriage you have prayed for has come to pass
and the bride you dreamed of is yours ...

Beautiful bride,
to look at you gives joy; your eyes are like honey,
love flows over your gentle face ...

Aphrodite
has honoured you above all other[9]

For Sappho, Aphrodite was her patron muse. However, other goddesses, along with Athena and Artemis, were also revered in ancient Greece. Demeter, the Corn Mother, and her daughter Persephone, the Corn Maiden, were also worshipped, particularly at the annual festival of Thesmophoria at the temple of Eleusis in Attica. The great-great-granddaughter of Gaia, Persephone, was seized by Hades whilst out gathering flowers and carried off to the underworld. As Demeter wandered in search of her lost daughter, the Earth grew desolate and all vegetation withered away. Since Persephone had eaten six seeds of the pomegranate, the food of the dead, she was compelled to return to the underworld for six months of each year. Like Inanna and Isis, Persephone represents the cycle of birth, death and renewal.

Moreover, in the neighbouring Roman Empire (lasting roughly between the third century BCE and the third century CE), Hellenistic culture was adapted and synthesized into another distinct mythology. Indeed, many Greek deities had their specific Roman counterpart, for example Aphrodite was Venus, Artemis was Diana and Athena was Minerva. Another Roman goddess of Anatolian lineage, Cybele, was also popular; known as the Magna Mater, she was 'Mother of the Gods' and goddess of fertility and rejuvenation, typically depicted with lions and snakes, roses and pomegranates.

Similarly, Isis, the Egyptian Queen of Heaven, Earth and the Netherworld, found her place in Roman life and became immortalized in Apuleius' *The Golden Ass* – the tale of a young man, Lucius, who after being turned into an ass for a whole year in order to learn about the banality and misery of mortal life, is saved through his devotion to Isis.

Despite the fracture in society's perception of the feminine – as a goddess, an object of reverence; as a woman, a second-class citizen – the female voice still manages to triumph. In the words of Sappho herself:

The Muses have made me happy
in my lifetime

and when I die
I shall never be forgotten[10]

chapter six

Therigatha Nuns

From this state of limited consciousness, I appear once again to be a separate form within samsara; but from the state of expanded awareness, all of samsara is a manifestation of myself. I am a single, undifferentiated Mind, yet I shine forth, like the radiant beams of the Sun, as a universe of countless living beings, all made of my light. All beings are united in me, for I am their consciousness, their form, their very being. Never are there any separate selves; that is only an illusion produced by the limiting of consciousness. All are but players in the outflowing radiance of the one Being. These transient forms live but for a moment, but I, One, live forever. Though I appear as many, I am forever One, forever serene.[1]

Thus spake the Buddha under a peepul tree in Bodh-Gaya upon the moment of his enlightenment. After a long and arduous path of striving and effort, the 'Enlightened One' realized the ineffable Truth of all existence – that he was, ultimately, beyond the world of name and form, birth and decay, the ocean of samsara.

In Kapilavatthu (in modern-day Nepal), Siddhartha Gautama of the Sakya clan was born to a king, Suddhodana, and his wife, Maya, in around 586 BCE. Unfortunately, his mother died seven days after the delivery and thus her sister, Pajapati Gotami, also married to Suddhodana, raised Siddhartha as his own. At the time of Siddhartha's birth, a holy man predicted that the boy would either end up ruling the world or renouncing it. To ensure that his son would grow up as a great king, Suddhodana surrounded him with great luxury and splendour. At sixteen, Siddhartha married the princess, Yashodara, and together they had a son, Rahula. All went well until he reached the age of twenty-nine. Travelling one day outside the palace gates, Siddhartha encountered four aspects of human existence that he had never seen before – a sick person, an old man, a corpse and a wandering ascetic.

Profoundly shocked by the experience, he decided right then and there to renounce his family and all his wealth and find the meaning of suffering and liberation from it. After six years of extreme austerities and intense study, Siddhartha Gautama realized the path to peace was in fact the 'Middle Way', the moderate life that encompasses meditation and the ability to discriminate between a life that is bound by samsara, the world of illusion and suffering, and nirvana, the underlying, all-pervading consciousness.

During the centuries approaching the turn of the new millennium, the mystical tradition of the Vedas and Upanishads was being subverted by the priestly class into a ritualistic religion steeped in superstition and dogma, supervised by an unenlightened Brahmin hierarchy. What the Buddha set out to do was brush away the multifarious descriptions of the one Self, such as Siva, and Shakti, Brahman and atman, as well as god and goddess mythology, all of which sought to objectify the formless state. Instead, he put greater emphasis on the actual *experience* of the Self, a place beyond name and form, and yet knowable to those who had tasted it. Thus by calling Reality 'nirvana', meaning 'extinction' or 'non-being', he hoped to put an end to the increasingly diverse interpretations of the One. Indeed, the Buddha would often be asked to comment on a number of metaphysical arguments about the nature and origin of the universe, upon all of which he would remain silent. What is the point, he would argue, when knowledge of oneself is not even known?

Choosing to share this simple and yet profound insight into Truth, Siddhartha travelled to a large deer park in Benares to give what has now come to be known as the 'Sermon of the Turning of the Wheel of Law', which was only recorded 300 years after his death. In his discourse, he expounds the 'Four Noble Truths': that there is suffering; that there is a cause of suffering (owing to the false belief in the illusory ego); that there is a remedy to suffering (enlightenment); and that there is the cessation of suffering (through the destruction of ignorance by the practice of the 'Noble Eightfold Path' – right understanding, right intention, right speech, right action, right livelihood, right effort, right mindfulness, right concentration). The Buddha, also known as the Tathagata, the 'attainer of Truth', subsequently established a sangha or order of monks called *bhikkus* where the Dharma (also known as *Dhamma*), the Buddhist doctrine on the nature of Reality, was taught.

Regarding the ordination of women into the sangha, however, the Buddha was adamant that they were not to be allowed in. Believing that the female nature was prone to waywardness and possessed by the power of seduction, he feared that the monks would be adversely affected by their presence. However, owing to the fact that many men during this time had either died in battles between warring clans or had decided to become monks, many women were left on their own, feeling displaced and lacking moral guidance. Pajapati, Siddhartha's foster mother, thus became a source of support and strength for many women in the district. Moreover, inspired by the transformation in her foster son, she too was overcome by the desire to be initiated into the supreme knowledge. But she was repeatedly rebuffed by the Buddha and it took the intervention of a monk, the Venerable Ananda, to resolve the crisis:

> Now at one time the Buddha was staying among the Sakyans at Kapilavatthu in the Banyan Monastery. Mahapajapati Gotami went to the place where the Buddha was, approached and greeted him, and, standing at a respectful distance, spoke to him: 'It would be good, Lord, if women could be allowed to renounce their homes and enter into the homeless state under the Dharma and discipline of the Tathagata.'
>
> 'Enough, Gotami. Don't set your heart on women being allowed to do this.' [A second and a third time Pajapati made the same

request in the same words and received the same reply.] And thinking that the Blessed One would not allow women to enter into the homelessness, she bowed to him, and keeping her right side towards him, departed in tears.

Then the Blessed One set out for Vesali. Pajapati cut off her hair, put on saffron-coloured robes, and headed for Vesali with a number of Sakyan women. She arrived at Kutagara Hall in the Great Grove with swollen feet and covered with dust. Weeping, she stood there outside the Hall.

Seeing her standing there, the Venerable Ananda asked, 'Why are you crying?'

'Because, Ananda, the Blessed One does not permit women to renounce their homes and enter into the homeless state under the Dharma and discipline proclaimed by the Tathagata.'

Then the Venerable Ananda went to the Buddha, bowed before him, and took his seat to one side. He said, 'Pajapati is standing outside under the entrance porch with swollen feet, covered with dust, and crying because you do not permit women to renounce their homes and enter into the homeless state. It would be good, Lord, if women were to have permission to do this.'

'Enough, Ananda. Don't set your heart on women being allowed to do this.' [A second and a third time Ananda made the same request in the same words and received the same reply.]

Then Ananda thought: The Blessed One does not give his permission. Let me try asking on other grounds.

'Are women able, Lord, when they have entered into homelessness, to realize the fruits of stream-entry, once-returning, non-returning and *arhatship* [one who is free from cravings]?'

'Yes, Ananda, they are able.'

'If women then are able to realize perfection and since Pajapati was of great service to you – she was your aunt, nurse, foster mother; when your mother died, she even suckled you at her own breast – it would be good if women could be allowed to enter into homelessness.'

'If then, Ananda, Pajapati accepts the Eight Special Rules, let that be reckoned as her ordination.'[2]

The Buddha had acquiesced but there were conditions. The Eight Special Rules, not to be confused with the Noble Eightfold Path, were additional precepts to be adhered to by nuns only. These included the first rule, which stated that a nun, a *bhikkhuni*, even of a hundred years' standing, should bow down before a monk ordained even for just one day; and the final rule, which expressed that admonition of monks by nuns was expressly forbidden, whereas admonition of nuns by monks was not. Pajapati and her fellow women reluctantly accepted these stipulations and went on to establish a community of Buddhist sisters. But the issue of women's rights was not to go away and Pajapati was to raise the subject again:

'I would ask one thing of the Blessed One, Ananda. It would be good if the Blessed One would allow making salutations, standing up in the presence of another, paying reverence, and the proper performance of duties, to take place equally between both *bhikkhus* and *bhikkhunis* according to seniority.'

And the Venerable Ananda went to the Blessed One [and repeated her words to him].

'This is impossible, Ananda, and I cannot allow it. Even those teachers of false Dharma don't permit such conduct in relation to women; how much less can the Tathagata allow it?'[3]

It is difficult for us to appreciate the cultural context of Buddha's refusal and whether Pajapati was successful or not, we do not know. Despite her frustration, however, this did not stop her veneration for the Buddha for revealing to her the Dharma. Indeed, such was Pajapati's gratitude that she joined her Buddhist sisters in composing poetry and songs in praise of the Buddha and his teaching. Grouped together, their exquisite lyrics are collectively known as the *Therigatha*: *Theri* means 'women elders', or 'women who have grown old in knowledge'; *gatha* means 'verse', 'stanza' or 'song'.

Such creative outpourings of women formerly from all strata of society – widows, wives, single women and prostitutes – thus became a living testament that enlightenment was exclusively for all, not just men or the upper echelons of the caste system. Initially handed down orally through the generations, the seventy-three poems of the *Therigatha* were finally recorded in the first century BCE in the literary language of Pali. Indeed, the profound simplicity of the nuns' individual experience, written in stanzas of four verses, each of eight syllables, is utterly compelling. Every poem was later prefixed by a narrative story, including a short biographical sketch of the particular authoress, by Dhammapala in the fifth century CE as part of his larger work, the *Paramattha Dipani*, or 'The Elucidation of the Ultimate Meaning'.

Pajapati, meaning 'leader of a great assembly', and also known as Mahapajapati ('Maha' meaning 'great') was the Great Mother of the Buddhist tradition. It was prophesized at her birth that she, along with her sister Maya, would be the mother of a great religious leader. Her sublime poetry reveals her powerful wisdom and the attainment of *arhatship*, the state of perfection and the end of rebirth:

Homage to you Buddha,
best of all creatures,
who set me and many others
free from pain.

All pain is understood,
the cause, the craving is dried up,
the Noble Eightfold Way unfolds,
I have reached the state where everything stops.

I have been
mother,
son,
father,
brother,
grandmother;
knowing nothing of the truth
I journeyed on.

But I have seen the Blessed One;
this is my last body,
and I will not go
from birth to birth
again.

Look at the disciples all together,
their energy,
their sincere effort.
This is homage to the buddhas.

Maya gave birth to Gautama
for the sake of us all.
She has driven back the pain
of the sick and dying.[4]

Pajapati lived to be 120 years old. Upon her death, it is said that miracles occurred around her. Having been in such an eminent position in the order, she had many disciples whom she helped realize the ultimate Truth – some say as many as 500 nuns were under her care.

Another illustrious nun was Patacara. Renowned for her charisma and brilliance in teaching, she too oversaw the spiritual welfare of up to thirty women. According to legend, she was born into a banker's family in the town of Savatthi, where her parents arranged for her to marry a local suitor. Sadly, she was already in love with one of her father's servants. Defying their wishes, therefore, she eloped with her lover and subsequently had two children. After many years, Patacara wished to see her parents again so, accompanied by her family, they set off for Savatthi. Unfortunately, as they walked through the forest, her husband was bitten by a poisonous snake and instantaneously died. Furthermore, resting under a tree stricken at her loss, a hawk swooped down and stole her younger child. And then later, crossing a swollen river, the elder boy was swept away by a strong current. Paralyzed with grief, she finally arrived at the home of her parents only to discover that the roof of their house had collapsed the night before and that they too had died under the falling debris.

It just so happened that the Buddha was staying in Savatthi at the time and, beside herself with torment, Patacara sought his help. Full of compassion for the broken woman, he told her that no one could help her because suffering was part of everyday life. It is said that he then described to her the path of the Middle Way and, addressing her directly, said: 'Sister, recover your presence of mind!' Immediately, her turmoil ended and she was initiated into the sangha.

Patacara's poem recounts her later experience of total enlightenment. Its vivid immediacy emphasizes the importance of this profound moment. Entering the cell, we almost hold our breath in anticipation of her ultimate breakthrough:

> *When they plough their fields*
> *and sow seeds in the earth,*
> *when they care for their wives and children,*
> *young brahmins find riches.*
>
> *But I've done everything right*
> *and followed the rule of my teacher.*
> *I'm not lazy or proud.*
> *Why haven't I found peace?*
>
> *Bathing my feet*
> *I watched the bathwater*
> *spill down the slope.*
> *I concentrated my mind*
> *the way you train a good horse.*
>
> *Then I took a lamp*
> *and went into my cell,*
> *checked the bed,*
> *and sat down on it.*
> *I took a needle*
> *and pushed the wick down.*

When the lamp went out
my mind was freed.[5]

Unlike the impassioned cries of Enheduanna, Vach and Sappho, the Therigatha nuns coolly recount their mystical wisdom. In keeping with the Buddhist tradition, their point of view is precise, mindful, detached. In fact, the sensoriness of worldly experience is positively shunned as is physical beauty, a trait highly regarded by the Mesopotamians, Indians and Greeks. And the poetry of Khema illustrates this point.

Born into a wealthy family in Sagala, Khema was the chief consort of King Bimbisara. Such was her beauty it was said that her complexion was like molten gold. The Buddha would often preach in the royal household but Khema was uninterested in listening to discourses on the transitoriness of beauty and pleasure, being vain and conceited by nature. Nevertheless, hearing about the loveliness of the Buddha's own hermitage grove, she was intrigued to see it for herself. Upon her arrival, the Buddha made the image of a goddess whose beauty far surpassed even her own appear before her. Then the image changed to a woman of middle age and then of old age, with grey hair, wrinkled skin and decaying teeth. The message of the image was obvious – Khema understood immediately the nature of impermanence.

The Buddha then continued to explain to her that those who were devoted to physical beauty were bound to the world, whilst those who renounced it were free. It is said that Khema was instantly enlightened and her poem recalls the subsequent loathing she had for the body and its sensual delights. Tempted by Mara, the embodiment of evil and death, she transcends the physical world and knows satisfaction only through honouring the teaching:

[Mara:]
Come on, Khema!
Both of us are young
and you are beautiful.
Let's enjoy each other!
It will be like the music of a symphony.

[Khema:]
I'm disgusted by this body.
It's foul and diseased.
It torments me.
Your desire for sex
means nothing to me.

Pleasures of the sense are
swords and stakes.
The elements of mind and body
are a chopping block for them.
What you call
delight
is not delight for me.

Everywhere the love of pleasure
is destroyed,
the great dark
is torn apart,
and Death,
you too are destroyed.
Fools,
who don't know things
as they really are,
revere the mansions of the moon
and tend the fire in the wood
thinking this is purity.

But for myself,
I honour the Enlightened One
the best of all
and, practising his teaching,
am completely free from suffering.[6]

Immediately afterwards, Khema left King Bimbisara and became a nun.
Another Buddhist sister mentioned in the *Therigatha* is Kisa Gotami

('Kisa' meaning 'thin'). She too came from Savatthi, albeit a poor family, which is probably the reason for her name. But she had illustrious connections – her mother's brother was Suddhodana, the father of the Buddha, thus making Siddhartha Gautama her cousin. Kisa Gotami married and had a son but, unfortunately, he died while still a toddler. The effect was so devastating that she lost her mind. In her inconsolable state, she picked up her dead child and wandered from house to house in the hope of finding the medicine that would bring her son back to life. On her travels, an old man redirected her to the Buddha, whom, taking pity on her, told her to bring to him a white mustard seed from the house where nobody had ever passed away. Innocently, she set off to accomplish the task but inevitably, she could not find one single household that had never tasted death. The truth thus dawned upon her – no one is exempt from dying. After collecting up her dead child and leaving him in the forest, Kisa Gotami then asked for the Buddha's ordination.

Her subsequent poetry details the wisdom of a woman formerly burdened with the misery of human life:

[I]
The Sage looked at the world
and said –
with good friends
even a fool can be wise.

Keep good company,
and wisdom grows.
Those who keep good company
can be freed from suffering.

We have to understand suffering
the cause of suffering,
its end,
and the Eightfold Way –
these are the Four Noble Truths.

[II]
The Guide of a restless,
passionate humanity has said –
to be a woman is to suffer.
To live with co-wives is suffering.
Women can give birth
and, becoming depressed,
cut their throats.
Beautiful young women eat poison,
but both will suffer in hell
when the mother-murdering foetus
comes not to life.

[IV]
I have practised the Great
Eightfold Way
straight to the undying.
I have come to the great peace
I have looked into the mirror
of the Dharma.

The arrow is out.
I have put my burden down.
What had to be done has been done.

Sister Kisa Gotami
with a free mind
has said this.[7]

Kisa Gotami knew exactly what it meant to be a woman – the hardships, the sorrow, the torment. Her words are as true today as they
ever were. She also understood, as did all her Buddhist sisters, that
the teaching not only set her free from her own suffering but from
the prejudices of a misogynistic society.

Paradoxically, the Buddha, the supreme Enlightened One,

continued to have doubts about admitting women into the sangha right up until his death at the age of eighty. Confiding in Ananda, he supposedly stated:

> If ... women had not received permission to renounce their homes and enter into homelessness under the Dharma and discipline proclaimed by the Tathagata, then would the pure religion ... have lasted long, the good law would have stood for a thousand years. But since ... women have now received that permission, the pure religion ... will not last so long, the good law will now stand fast for only five hundred years. Just ... as houses in which there are many women but few men are easily violated by robber burglars; just so ... under whatever Dharma and discipline women are allowed to renounce their home and enter into homelessness, that religion will not last long. And just ... as when the disease called mildew falls upon a field of rice in fine condition, that rice does not continue long; just so ... under whatever Dharma and discipline women are allowed to renounce their homes and enter into homelessness, that religion will not last long ... And just ... as a man in anticipation builds an embankment to a great reservoir, beyond which the water should not overpass, just even so ... have I laid down these Eight Chief Rules for the *bhikkhunis*, not to be disregarded throughout their whole life.[8]

It is hard to imagine why a wise teacher, advocating a philosophy so free from dogma, retained such a prejudiced position. Interestingly, his prophesy in one sense was to come true – by the fifth century CE, the sangha of Buddhist nuns had, to all intents and purposes, died out and it would take the pioneering work of Ayya Khema (1923–) in the twentieth century to establish Parappuduva Nuns' Island, just off the coast of Sri Lanka, and re-establish the individual rights of women Buddhists.

Moreover, as the centuries passed after the Buddha's death, the pure Buddhist teaching became diluted into multifarious interpretations and essentially split into two 'vehicles': the lesser vehicle of Theravada Buddhism in southern India, which believes in a personal and final enlightenment; and the greater vehicle of Mahayana Buddhism, in northern India, which believes that enlightenment should be postponed in order for the individual to reincarnate and help all other sentient beings.

Inevitably, a complex Buddhist mythology would also emerge, including the deification of the sacred feminine. This is precisely not what the Buddha had wanted but perhaps it does serve to neutralize the negative perception of women and reaffirm their equal ability to realize the Self.

chapter seven

Mary Magdalene

By the time Christianity became a fully-fledged monotheist religion in the West, the image of the goddess was, to all intents and purposes, subsumed beneath a swathe of patriarchal dogma. However, the figure of Mary, mother of Jesus Christ, continues the lineage of the archetypal sacred feminine and her ubiquitous form over the centuries is testament to her position both in the cosmic order and the human psyche.

Like her female counterparts Inanna and Ishtar, Hathor and Demeter, Mary gave birth to a child who descended into the underworld and was later resurrected. Moreover, her more traditional name of 'Maria' takes its etymological root from the Latin, '*mare*', meaning 'sea'. Again, like her deistic sisters Nammu, Isis and Nut who all emerged from a watery birth, Mary is the immanent embodiment of the Divine. Often depicted wearing an elaborate sea-blue robe, she is still hailed today as the Great Mother, Queen of Heaven, a living conduit of the God:

> *Hail Mary,*
> *full of Grace,*
> *the Lord is with thee.*
> *Blessed art thou among women,*
> *and blessed is the fruit*
> *of thy womb, Jesus.*

Holy Mary,
Mother of God,
pray for us sinners now,
and at the hour of death.[1]

Indeed, within the Eastern Orthodox Church, Mary was given due prominence and even called the *Theotokos*, the 'Godbearer' or 'Mother of God'. Moreover, women in general were esteemed in religious activities and could assume liturgical positions within the Church's structure. Constantinople, the centre of Eastern Orthodoxy, is in fact known by the title, 'City of the Theotokos' in honour of Mary.

However, the Catholic Church was not so accommodating – Mary was no longer perceived as a mother goddess, symbolic of the life-giving Source. She was now reduced to a mortal woman, untainted by sexual desire, and used to right the wrong created by her forebear, Eve, whose 'sin' was to know herself and enjoy the carnal pleasures of the flesh. Only by being a virgin, impregnated by the Holy Spirit, can Mary assume a respectable position within the Christian faith. (As we shall see, the wisdom tradition of gnosis perceives the Holy Spirit to be feminine, thus making the whole concept of the Immaculate Conception even more bizarre.)

Patriarchal interpretations of the Christian message were further reinforced by St Paul in the sixth decade CE in his correspondence to the Church at Corinth. First, he outlines his views on women in general:

> Wives, submit yourselves unto your own husbands, as unto the Lord.
>
> For the husband is the head of the wife, even as Christ is the head of the Church: and he is the saviour of the body.
>
> Therefore as the Church is subject unto Christ, so let the wives be to their own husbands in everything.[2]

And in terms of her ability to honour the Divine, Paul was in absolutely no doubt:

Let your woman keep silence in the churches: for it is not permitted unto them to speak; but they are commanded to be under obedience, as also saith the law.

And if they will learn anything, let them ask their husbands at home: for it is a shame for women to speak in the church.[3]

Moreover, Paul goes on to explain that:

I will, therefore, that men pray everywhere, lifting up holy hands, without wrath and doubting.

In like manner also, that women adorn themselves in modest apparel, with shamefacedness and sobriety; not with braided hair, or gold, or pearls, or costly array.

But (which becometh women professing godliness) with good works.

Let the woman learn in silence with all subjection.

But I suffer not a woman to teach, not to usurp authority over the man but to be in silence. For Adam was first formed, then Eve.

And Adam was not deceived, but the woman being deceived was in the transgression.

Notwithstanding, she shall be saved in childbearing, if they continue in faith and charity and holiness with sobriety.[4]

Here we have the root of Christian misogyny, branded onto the female gender, aided and abetted by the earlier Church Fathers of the second century CE, Tertullian and Irenaeus. St Augustine of the fifth century CE had also taken up the anti-female stance, in spite of attributing his conversion to Christianity to his mother, Monica, by declaring that Eve was more to blame for the Fall than Adam – unlike he, she was not made in the image of God. (All this from a man who never married and lived in 'sin' with an unmarried concubine.)

As with any organization that grows around a teacher who never wrote a word, the sayings of Jesus himself became distorted and twisted for individual purpose. Indeed, when we actually consider his words through the mouths of his apostles, we discover that not only is there no mention of original sin, but that he also makes his companions of women and prostitutes. Moreover, humanity's interpretation of Jesus being the only begotten Son of God, through whom salvation can exclusively be gained, is not borne out through his message. In the New Testament Gospel of St Luke, Christ affirms, 'The kingdom of God is within you,'[5] pointing not to a transcendent heaven removed from everyday life but an immanent place of salvation, inherent within each and every living being.

As a realized sage, Jesus was pointing to the state where opposites have been reconciled and where one's heart and mind have become one with God. Thus, the story of the resurrection is not so much fact but a myth in its truest sense – it is a metaphorical interpretation of the soul's journey from a state of ignorance to self discovery and subsequent transformation.

Moreover, in the Gospel of St John, Jesus says:

'I am the way, the truth, and the life: no man cometh unto the Father, but by me …

Believest thou not that I am in the Father and the Father in me? The words that I speak unto you I speak not of myself but the Father that dwelleth in me, he doeth the works …

I will not leave you comfortless: I will come to you.

Yet a little while, and the world seeth me no more; but ye see me: because I live, ye shall live also.

At that day ye shall know that I am in my Father and ye in me and I in you.'[6]

This is exactly the same nondualist message of the mystics and echoes the words of Moses, who also proclaimed 'I am Who I am',[7] knowing that the phenomenal word is permeated by God. As the Gospel of St John makes clear:

In the beginning was the Word [Logos], and the Word was with God, and the Word was God.

The same was in the beginning with God.

All things were made by him; and without him was not anything made that was made.

In him was life; and the life was the light of men.[8]

Logos is synonymous with Prakriti, Shakti and maya – the manifestory aspect of consciousness, duality in the One. Thus, whilst the Catholic Church was to interpret Logos solely as the incarnation of Jesus Christ giving it final authority at the Council of Chalcedon in 451 CE, a number of religious sects were to flourish around the Mediterranean espousing the esoteric teaching of mysticism and the fact that the Logos is within all of humankind.

Referred to as Gnostics (taken from the Greek word, '*gnostikoi*', an adjective meaning 'insightful' or 'intuitive'), they drew their wisdom from the mystical traditions of India, Persia, Egypt and ancient Greece. Many cults grew under the blanket term of Gnosticism, including the Manichaeans, Hermetics, Valentinians, Stoics and a whole host of others, producing a vast array of literature of varying insight into the Truth. One particular exponent was Simon Magus, a first-century CE disciple of John the Baptist and founder of the Simonian sect of Gnostics, who codified a nondual structure of the universe, incorporating both the masculine and feminine principles, and which was to be preserved by the Church Father, Hippolytus:

There are two aspects of the One. The first of these is the Higher, the Divine Mind of the universe, which governs all things, and is masculine. The other is the lower, the Thought [*epinoia*] which produces all things and is feminine. As a pair united, they comprise all that exists …

Since He, Himself, brought forward Himself, by means of Himself, manifesting to himself His own Thought, it is not correct to attribute creation to the Thought alone. For She [the Thought] conceals the Father within Herself; the Divine Mind and the Thought are intertwined. Thus, though [they appear] to be a pair, one opposite the other, the Divine Mind is in no way different from the Thought, inasmuch as they are one …

> [Thus], … there is one Divine Reality, [conceptually] divided as Higher and lower; generating Itself, nourishing Itself, seeking Itself, finding Itself, being mother of Itself, father of Itself, sister of Itself, spouse of Itself, daughter of Itself, son of Itself. It is both Mother and Father, a Unity, being the Root of the entire circle of existence.[9]

It is said that Simon Magus was always accompanied by a woman, Helen, who was a converted prostitute from Tyre and whom he believed to be the reincarnation of Helen of Troy. Deriving from the Hebrew word, 'Selene', meaning 'moon', Simon says of Helen:

In the beginning the Father intended to bring forth the angels and
   the archangels.
His thought leaped forth from him, this thought,
Who knew Her father's intention.
Thus she descended to the lower realms.
She bore angels and powers, who then created the world.
But after she thus bore them, she was held captive by them.
She suffered every indignity from them.
And she could not return to the Father,
In a human body she came to be confined,
And thus from age to age she passed from body to body,
Into one female body after the other …
Thus she became the lost sheep.[10]

Here we hear the familiar lament not only of the decline of the appreciation of the sacred feminine but also the universal journey of the soul, bewildered by the world, searching tirelessly for its lost home.

Further spiritual tracts were produced during this period; however, it was not until the middle of the twentieth century that two important discoveries were made that have fundamentally altered our perception of the religious beliefs that were prevalent during the early decades of the first millennium. In 1947 the *Dead Sea Scrolls*, a collection of Hebrew and Aramaic manuscripts, were discovered in a series of caves in Jordan, at the north-western end of the Dead Sea in the area of Khirbet Qumran. The 600 or so manuscripts, originally written on leather or papyrus, have been attributed to members of a previously unknown Jewish brotherhood, similar in nature to the Essenes. The scrolls include manuals of discipline, hymn books, biblical commentaries and apocalyptic writings.

Of much greater importance was the discovery by a peasant of the name Mohammad Ali, two years earlier in 1945 near the town of Nag Hammadi in Upper Egypt, of a clay jar in which there were thirteen papyrus leather-bound books containing fifty-two texts. Written in Coptic (the last stage of the Egyptian language) about 1,500 years ago, they are translations from earlier texts written in Greek. Collectively known as the *Gnostic Gospels*, they bring to light the extent to which the mystical teachings existed during this period. Focusing on a diverse range of subject matter, the *Gnostic Gospels* include creation mythology, discussions on the nature of reality and the soul, hagiography of the apostles, issues pertaining to Sophia, the divine feminine, and the teachings of Jesus Christ.

It is believed that these texts were widely known in their day but the Roman Emperor Constantine (known for boiling his wife alive as well as murdering his own son) had other ideas about their future. In 325 CE, he convened the Council of Nicaea where the official texts of the Bible were decided: those texts that were deemed acceptable we now know as the New Testament; those texts that supported the Gnostic position were burned. And those who disagreed with the Emperor's decision were instantaneously exiled.

Of the Gnostic texts, the nondualist vision is none so beautifully and perceptively stated as it is in the *Gospel of Thomas*, the very same Thomas who took Christianity to India. At the very beginning of his tract, he announces the immortal phrase, 'Whoever finds the explanation of these words will not taste death.'[11] His words could be used as a preface to the entire canon of Gnostic scripture, with their emphasis on the annihilation of the ego into the All:

Jesus said: I am the Light that is above
them all, I am the All,
the All came forth from Me and the All
attained to Me. Cleave a [piece of] wood, I
am there; lift up the stone and you will
find Me there.[12]

Moreover, Jesus is very specific that self knowledge is an active process:

Jesus said: Whoever knows the All
but fails [to know] himself lacks everything.[13]

Furthermore, issues pertaining to gender are irrelevant when it comes to discovering the Truth:

They said to Him: Shall we then, being children,
enter the Kingdom? Jesus said to them;
when you make the two one, and
when you make the inner as the outer
and the outer as the inner and the above
as the below, and when
you make the male and the female into a single one,
so that the male will not be male and
the female [not] be female, when you make
eyes in the place of an eye, and a hand
in the place of a hand, and a foot in the place
of a foot, and an image in the place of an image,
then shall you enter [the Kingdom].[14]

Again, Christ proclaims the New Testament message that the Kingdom of Heaven is within. Interestingly, the merging of the 'male and the female into a single one' echoes Jungian psychology centuries later; by reconciling our respective anima and animus, a process of individuation and personal transformation can become complete. Such ideas also find expression through Renaissance thinkers specializing in alchemy and mystical practices, like Leonardo da Vinci, who was particularly fascinated with the image of the hermaphrodite (reflected in the immortal *Mona Lisa*).

Like Simon and Helen, Jesus also had his own special female companion in the figure of Mary Magdalene. A great deal of myth and legend surround her. For a start, it is unclear as to whether Mary of Bethany (Lazarus's sister), the 'sinner' who anointed Jesus' feet with oils, and Mary Magdalene are one and the same. Moreover, portraits of the identified Mary Magdalene in the Canonical Gospels are predominantly pejorative – she is traditionally perceived as a prostitute, possessed of 'seven demons' and full of 'evil spirits and infirmities'.[15]

Nevertheless, the discovery of the *Gospel of Mary Magdalene* has done much to reassert her rightful position in terms of the inheritance of the sacred feminine. In 1896, a fifth-century papyrus, written in Coptic, was bought in Cairo, which contained the text of the *Gospel of Mary Magdalene*, along with a handful of other Gnostic texts. Although it was not in the Nag Hammadi discovery, it is included in the library canon and known as the Berlin Codex. Whether Mary actually composed the original document herself, we can only speculate.

Mary (sometimes called Miriam) is believed to have come from Magdala (also known as Migdal) on the west shore of the Sea of Galilee. (Some commentators have even suggested that Mary was a black pagan priestess from a town of the same name in Ethiopia.) Whatever her inheritance, Mary was the first human being to witness the resurrected Christ. More specifically, Jesus initiated her into the mystical teachings – the knowledge that everything in the universe ultimately returns to its 'roots', the eternal Source of all, the primordial One:

> 'What is matter?
> Will it last forever?'
> The Teacher answered:
> 'All that is born, all that is created,

all the elements of nature
are interwoven and united with each other.
All that is composed shall be decomposed;
everything returns to its roots;
matter returns to the origins of matter.
Those who have ears, let them hear.'[16]

The opening sequence of Mary's Gospel sounds more akin to a passage from an Upanishad than a Christian text. The Teacher then goes on to speak of the true nature of life, the ultimate reality of the universe. By detaching oneself from the physical world, he tells her, inner tranquillity can be found:

Attachment to matter
gives rise to passion against nature.
Thus trouble arises in the whole body;
this is why I tell you:
'Be in harmony ...'
If you are out of balance,
take inspiration from manifestations
of your true nature.[17]

Salvation comes from being free of all our identifications and desires. This is the truth that shall set us all free. The Teacher instructs Mary that heaven is not a place located in a future, distant land; it is present in the here and now, it is in fact within:

Be vigilant, and allow no one to mislead you
by saying:
'Here it is!' or
'There it is!'
For it is within you
that the Son of Man dwells.
Go to him,
for those who seek him, find him [18]

Mary asks the Teacher how it is possible to achieve this, to find the inner Son of Man:

> 'Lord, when someone meets you
> in a Moment of vision,
> is it through the soul [psyche] that they see,
> or is it through the Spirit [Pneuma]?'
> The Teacher answered:
> 'It is neither through the soul or the spirit,
> But the nous between the two
> Which sees the vision ...'[19]

'Nous' is the intuitive faculty of mind (from noumenon); it is the 'third eye' that discerns truth from untruth, the discriminating intelligence of the individual that unites soul and Spirit into One. In the same manner as the teachings of Plato, that which is immutable and eternal can only be known through reason and by transcending all sensory attachment. As the Teacher says:

> 'There where is the nous, lies the treasure.'[20]

Indeed, in the light of the Gnostic interpretation of Jesus' words, the Christian teaching takes on a whole new meaning. Knowing, therefore, that the creation is rooted in the One, the concept of original sin becomes redundant. The Teacher declares:

> 'There is no sin.
> It is you who make sin exist,
> when you act according to the habits
> of your corrupted nature;
> this is where sin lies.'[21]

In other words, there is nothing inherently bad with human nature; it is the indulgence of one's habits and desires that is the problem, and constitutes the only 'sin'. ('Interestingly, the original word, hamartia, generally mistranslated as 'sin' actually means 'missing the mark'; similarly, *metanoia* is not 'repentance' but 'turning about of the mind'.)

The Teacher then continues:

'This is why the Good has come into your midst.
It acts together with the elements of your nature
so as to reunite it with its roots.'[22]

The Good, personified in this instance as the Christ the Saviour, has therefore come to remove the veil of ignorance, in order to reunite mankind with its roots.

The *Gospel of Mary Magdalene* is one of the most radical and yet timeless expositions of the Truth. And yet these profound words are uttered by a woman! Indeed, Peter challenges Mary on this very point:

'How is it possible that the Teacher talked
in this manner with a woman
about secrets of which we ourselves are ignorant?
Must we change our customs,
and listen to this woman?
Did he really choose her, and prefer her to us?'[23]

But Levi (Matthew) leaps to her defence:

'Surely the Teacher knew her very well,
for he loved her more than us.'[24]

Mary's reputation is further validated in another Gnostic gospel, the *Gospel of Philip*. In startling frankness, Jesus' special relationship with Mary is made quite explicit:

The Lord loved Mary more than all the disciples, and often used to kiss her on the mouth. When the others saw how he loved Mary, they said, 'Why do you love her more than you love us?' The

Saviour answered them in this way: 'How can it be that I do not love you as much as I love her?'[25]

And as Christ affirms in the *Gospel of Thomas*:

'Whoever drinks from My mouth
shall become as I am and I myself will become
he, and the hidden things shall be revealed to him.'[26]

As the only disciple to be at both Jesus' crucifixion and resurrection, it is little wonder that Mary Magdalene is known as the 'apostle of apostles'. Similarly, the Gnostic text, *Dialogue of the Saviour*, also found in Nag Hammadi, says she is the 'woman who knew the All'.[27] (It is interesting to note that orthodox thinking attests that it was Peter, not Mary, who was instrumental in proselytizing the words of Christ, being the 'rock' upon which the Catholic Church built its faith.)

As the Teacher says of Mary in the *Gospel of Thomas*:

'See, I have been guiding her
so as to make her into a human [anthropos].
She, too, will become
a living breath, like you.
Any woman who becomes a human
will enter the Kingdom of God.'[28]

Christ makes the specific point of saying than any woman can enter the Kingdom of Heaven through a process of individuation, by becoming human through making 'the male and the female into a single one'. Again, this reflects the Jungian position where masculinity and femininity are reconciled. (Some commentators have also mistranslated '*anthropos*' as 'man', possibly in an attempt to champion the superiority of the male gender; the word '*andros*' would have been used had Christ wanted this interpretation.)

Christ's highest teaching, the knowledge that the Truth is within, applies to everyone who sincerely desires it, as Mary's Gospel makes clear:

> 'Therefore let us atone,
> And become fully human,
> So that the Teacher can take root in us.'[29]

Only then can the journey's end be discovered, can the sound of the Source be heard. The Teacher then concludes:

> 'Henceforth I travel toward Repose,
> where time rests in the Eternity of Time;
> I go now into Silence.'
> Having said all this, Mary became silent,
> for it was in silence that the Teacher spoke to her.[30]

As well as a profound knowledge of the immanent Self, the *Gnostic Gospels* also show an acute understanding of the difference between the Creator and its creative powers, with a number of gospels referring directly to the sacred feminine. The tantalizingly entitled *Thunder, Perfect Mind*, speaks through a female voice of the power of the Infinite:

> For I am the first and the last.
> I am the honoured one and the scorned one.
> I am the whore and the holy one.
> I am the wife and the virgin.
> I am the mother and the daughter.
> I am the members of my mother.
> I am the barren one, and many are her sons ...
> I am the bride and the bridegroom ...
> I am the mother of my father and the sister of my husband,
>   and he is my offspring ...
> I am the silence that is incomprehensible and the idea whose
>   remembrance is frequent.

I am the voice whose sound is manifold and the word whose
   appearance is multiple.
I am the utterance of my name.[31]

And in the Gnostic text, *Trimorphic Protennoia*, the same female voice speaks of her immanent presence:

I am the Invisible One within the All. It is I who counsel those who are hidden, since I know the All that exists in it. I am numberless beyond everyone. I am immeasurable, ineffable, yet whenever I [wish, I shall] reveal myself of my own accord. I [am the head of] the All. I exist before the [All, and] I am the All, since I [exist in] everyone.

I am a Voice [speaking softly]. I exist [from the first. I dwell] within the Silence [that surrounds every one] of them. And [it is] the [hidden Voice] that [dwells within] me, [within the] incomprehensible, immeasurable [Thought, within the] immeasurable Silence.[32]

In a further text from the *Nag Hammadi Library*, *The Sophia of Jesus Christ*, a text describing how twelve men and seven women are gathered to hear the Saviour speak after the resurrection, Mary asks Jesus to clarify further the role of the sacred feminine:

Mary said to him, 'Holy Lord, where did your disciples come from and where are they going and [what] should they do here?' The perfect Saviour said to them: 'I want you to know that Sophia, the Mother of the Universe and the consort, desired by herself to bring these to existence without her male [consort]. But by the will of the Father of the Universe, that his unimaginable goodness might be revealed ...'

   The perfect Saviour said: 'Son of Man consented with Sophia, his consort, and revealed a great androgynous light. His male name is designated, "Saviour, Begetter of All Things". His female name is designated, "All-Begettress Sophia". Some call her "Pistis".'[33]

One other Gnostic text that surfaced long before the Nag Hammadi discovery was the *Pistis Sophia* or 'Faith Wisdom' in Luxor, Egypt in the third century CE. Known as the Askew Codex and bought by the British Museum in 1785, the text describes how Jesus appears twelve years after his ascension and gathers around his closest disciples, including Mary Magdalene, in order to discuss the nature of Sophia. In her repeated questioning of Jesus, it is clear that he favours Mary Magdalene high above her male contemporaries:

> 'Maria [Mary], thou blessed one, whom I will complete in all the mysteries of the height, speak openly, thou art she whose heart is more directed to the Kingdom of Heaven than all thy brothers …
>
>   'Thou are blessed beyond all women on earth, because thou shalt be the *Pleroma* [fullness] of all *Pleromas* and the completions of all completions.'[34]

And most scintillatingly of all, in *On the Origin of the World*, another Nag Hammadi text, not only is the feminine principle honoured in the form of Sophia but Eve herself is given status *above* Adam – in fact, it is *she* who gives Adam his first breath:

> After the day of rest, Sophia sent Zoe, her daughter, being called Eve, as an instructor in order that she might make Adam, who had no soul, arise so that those whom he should engender might become containers of light. When Eve saw her male counterpart prostrate she had pity upon him, and she said, 'Adam! Become alive! Arise upon the earth!' Immediately her word became accomplished fact. For Adam, having arisen, suddenly opened his eyes. When he saw her, he said, 'You shall be called "Mother of the Living". For it is you who have given me life.'[35]

Here, the gnostic interpretation of the story of Genesis is completely overturned as the story of Adam and Eve can now be seen a psychological process of the soul's journey towards self knowledge. Rather than being condemned to a life tainted by original sin, the primordial couple in fact gain immortality through eating the fruit from the Tree of Knowledge. Moreover, in the Gnostic text, *The Reality of the Rulers*, it is the feminine principle, personified as the snake, who urges Adam and Eve to discover wisdom for themselves:

> Then the female spiritual principle came [in] the snake, the instructor, and it taught [them] saying, 'What did he [say to] you? Was it, "From every tree in the garden shall you eat; yet – from [the tree] of recognizing evil and good do not eat?"'
>
> The carnal woman said, 'Not only did he say, "Do not eat," but even, "Do not touch it; for the day you eat from it, with death you are going to die."'
>
> And the snake, the instructor, said, 'With death you shall not die; for it was out of jealousy that he said this to you. Rather your eyes shall open and you shall come to be like god, recognizing evil and good.' And the female instructing principle was taken away from the snake, and she left it behind merely a thing of the earth.[36]

How ironic! Instead of being responsible for the Fall and thus the damnation of the entire human race, Eve is in fact a source of spiritual awakening.

Emperor Constantine did irreparable damage in his suppression of the Gnostic texts. Women the world over have had to suffer unimaginable prejudice as a consequence. But the voice of Truth always rises up eventually – indeed, the Nag Hammadi discovery epitomizes the sheer will and determination of the female spiritual principle to emerge and triumph once again as the guiding light for the human spirit.

chapter eight

Chinese Nuns

By the time the Buddhist teaching started to flourish along the Silk Roads into the Asian continent, the inevitable fragmentation of the Buddha's message, as he had predicted, took effect. Thus, Buddhism adopted many of the creation myths from the Hindu tradition in order to explain the nature of Reality. In the *Visuddhi-Magga*, written by the fifth-century CE Ceylonese philosopher, Buddhaghosa, the beginning of the world is seen as part of a recurring cycle whereby existence manifests itself out of a watery void, destroys itself and then arises once again:

> Now after the lapse of another long period, a great cloud arises. And first it rains with a very fine rain ... After the water has thus been massed together by the wind, it dwindles away, and by degrees descends to a lower level ... This water is sweet, and as it wastes away, the earth which arises out of it is full of sap, and has a beautiful colour, and a fine taste and smell, like the skimmings on the top of thick rice-gruel.
>
> Then beings, who have been living in the Heaven of the Radiant Gods, leave their existence ... and are reborn here on earth.[1]

As Buddhism became more widespread, it split into the two main strands of Mahayana and Theravada. Mahayana established itself in northern India and then travelled east to Tibet, China, Korea and

Japan. An early Mahayanan text, the *Vimalakirti Sutra*, composed in Sanskrit roughly between the first century BCE and the second century CE, focuses on the illusory nature of all created beings. During a conversation between two bodhisattvas, a goddess appears who materializes a rain of flowers. The disciple, Sariputra, also present, then starts to challenge the goddess on issues pertaining to liberation:

> *Sariputra*: 'Pray, what have you attained, what have you realized, that you have such eloquence?'
> *Goddess*: 'I have attained nothing, reverend Sariputra. I have no realization. Therefore I have such eloquence. Whoever thinks, "I have attained! I have realized!" is overly proud in the discipline of the well-taught Dharma.'[2]

Moreover, upon asking her about the issue of gender, the goddess changes herself into a male form and similarly changes Sariputra into a woman, in order to show to him the nature of impermanence and the fact that liberation is not precluded to the female gender:

> 'All women appear in the form of women ... While they are not women in reality, they appear in the form of women. With this in mind, the Buddha said, "In all things, there is neither male nor female."'[3]

(It is a shame that the Buddha didn't have quite the same attitude towards his mother and the other nuns in his sangha.)

Another important Buddhist text in its Chinese translation, the *Lotus Sutra*, composed in India between the first and third centuries CE, also alludes to the sacred feminine in the form of the female celestial bodhisattva, Kuan Yin, meaning 'all hearing'. (The original Sanskrit version speaks of a male deity, Bodhisattva Avalokitesvara, meaning 'all seeing'.) It is believed that rather then being a mistranslation, Kuan Yin became a hybrid of existing Chinese mythology – the primitive images of the Chinese Holy Mother, Sheng Mu, and the goddess of the sea, Matsu.

Also known as 'She Who Listens to the World's Sounds', Kuan Yin is ever attentive to the cries and laments of her devotees and hence is represented with a thousand heads, eyes and arms in order to be well equipped to deal with all the miraculous deeds expected of her. Indeed, in the *Lotus Sutra*, an unnamed female deity extols the virtues and deeds of Kuan Yin, imploring all to worship her name:

> Inexhaustible Knowledge, the bodhisattva Mahasattva Kuan Yin's magnificent spiritual powers are like this. If living beings are intensely passionate and yet they always revere the bodhisattva Kuan Yin, they will be able to give up their desire. If they are intensely hateful yet they always revere the bodhisattva Kuan Yin, they will give up their hatred. If they are greatly disillusioned yet they always revere the bodhisattva Kuan Yin, they will give up their disillusionment.[4]

Like her goddess counterparts from around the world, Kuan Yin also descends to the underworld in order to comfort the dead. Reciting the Buddhist scriptures, the netherworld is transformed into a paradise, all the instruments of torture are turned into lotus blossoms and all its inhabitants are blessed with everlasting happiness.

Worshipped principally by women as the bringer of children, Kuan Yin is often depicted wearing a long white robe, sitting on a lotus flower and cradling a child in her lap. A bird is often shown bringing her a rosary. Sometimes she is holding either a vase full of magical water bringing vitality and wakefulness, a pearl, symbolizing steadfast purity, a peach, representing longevity, or a willow branch, which is the symbol of life itself (the willow is the first tree to come to blossom in the spring and the last to shed its leaves in the autumn). Like Inanna, Isis and Mary, Kuan Yin is the goddess of Heaven and Earth:

> *A mind perfected in the four virtues,*
> *A gold body filled with wisdom,*
> *Fringes of dangling pearls and jade,*
> *Scented bracelets set with lustrous treasures,*

Dark hair piled smoothly in a coiled-dragon bun,
And elegant sashes lightly fluttering as phoenix quills,
Her green jade buttons
And white silk robe
Bathed in holy light;
Her velvet skirt
And golden cords
Wrapped by hallowed air,
With brows of new moon shape
And eyes like two bright stars,
Her jade-like face beams natural joy,
And her ruddy lips seem a flash of red.

Her immaculate vase overflows with nectar from year to year,
Holding sprigs of weeping willow green from age to age.
She disperses the eight woes;
She redeems the multitude;
She has great compassion;
Thus she rules on the T'ai Mountain,
And lives at the South Sea.
She saves the poor, searching for their voices,
Ever heedful and solicitous,
Ever wise and efficacious.
Her orchid heart delights in green bamboos;
Her chaste nature loves the wisteria.
She is the merciful ruler of Potalaka Mountain,
The living Kuan Yin from the Cave of Tidal Sound.[5]

And yet despite being honoured in an abstract form, we see in society yet again a similar situation to that of ancient Greece: the bizarre anomaly of revering the feminine spiritual principle and yet practising an essentially misogynistic stance in daily life. Indeed, in the first century BCE, the scholar Liu Hsiang composed the influential but sexist tract, the *Lieh Nü* or 'Biographies of Women', in which he outlined the subordinated lives of specific female role models, particularly mothers. Its impact was such that it became a standard work for the deportment and behaviour of all Chinese women. Through the voice of Meng Mu, Liu Hsiang writes:

> Now the proper conduct of a woman is found in her skill in preparing the five foods, fermenting wine, caring for her husband's parents, and making clothes and that is all. A woman's duty is to care for the household and she should have no desire to go abroad. The *Book of Changes* says, 'She provides sustenance and avoids going out.' The *Book of Songs* says: 'For her no decoration, no emblems; her only care the wine and food.' This means that it does not belong to the woman to determine anything herself but she has the three obediences. Therefore when young, she has to obey her parents; when married, she has to obey her husband; when her husband is dead, she obeys her son. This is proper etiquette.[6]

Is it any wonder, therefore, that many women sought sanctuary from the burdens of family life. Coupled with the political and sociological upheavals of third-century CE China and the collapse of the ruling Han Dynasty, many women took Buddhist vows, like the Therigatha of India, in order to escape their 'obediences' and the vicissitudes of their daily existence.

One specific document meticulously details the lives of Chinese nuns from this period. The *Pi-ch'iu-ni chuan* or 'Lives of the Nuns', compiled by Shih Pao-ch'ang in approximately 516 CE, contains the short and distilled biographies of sixty-five women arranged in chronological order, starting from the Eastern Chin dynasty (357–361 CE) ending with the Liang dynasty (502–519 CE). Entering the monastery from anything from the age of five up until seventy, the nuns' commitment to the Buddhist Dharma is both exemplary and powerful. As Shih Pao-ch'ang says himself in his preface:

> These nuns then, whom I hereby offer as models, are women of excellent reputation, paragons of ardent morals, whose virtues are a stream of fragrance that flows without end.[7]

Moreover, his mission in collating the stories of the nuns' lives is to offer the world a testament to dedicating one's existence to the pursuit of Truth:

> The first Buddhist nun in the world was Mahaprajapati, [the Buddha's own stepmother]. [From the time of Mahaprajapati] nuns throughout the succeeding generations have ascended the stages of the Buddhist path and realized the fruits of spiritual practice. These illustrious examples of the religious life are like the sun passing through the sky, shedding light and warmth on all.[8]

The whole issue, raised in the Buddha's time by Mahaprajapati herself, concerning women's rights in relation to the sangha is addressed in the 'Lives'. In the biography of Chu Ching-Chien, the nun asks:

> 'Because the scripture speaks of the two terms, monk and nun, can it be that the rules for each group are different?'
>   Fa-shih said, 'Foreign Buddhists say that nuns have five hundred rules to follow as compared to fewer for monks, and that must be the difference. I asked the instructor about this, and he said that the rules for nuns are highly similar and only slightly different from the monks' regulations, but, if I cannot get the complete texts of these rules, then I certainly cannot bestow on women the obligation to observe them. A woman aspiring eventually to become a nun may, however, receive the ten fundamental precepts from the Assembly of Monks only, but, without a [female] monastic instructor to train her on the practice of all the rules, a woman has no one on whom to rely [for that training].[9]

Unperturbed, many of the nuns decide not to place their inspiration in the direct teachings of the Buddha but find inspiration instead in the story of the bodhisattva, Kuan Yin. In the biography of K'ang Ming-Kan, it relates how the young nun enquires of a monk to bestow upon her the fundamental Buddhist precepts:

He granted her request and also presented her with a copy of the bodhisattva Kuan Yin scripture, which she then practised chanting day and night without pause.[10]

Moreover, another nun, Fa-sheng is blessed with a vision of Kuan Yin, after falling seriously ill:

> The illness grew worse, and on the evening of the night of the new moon, the last day of the month, as she lay asleep [Amita Buddha] the Tathagata [who presides over the Western Paradise] appeared in the air together with his two bodhisattva attendants [Kuan Yin on the left and Ta-shih-chih on the right], with whom he discussed the two types of Buddhism [namely the Mahayana, or Great Vehicle, and the Hinayana, the Small Vehicle]. Suddenly [Amita Buddha] with his entire entourage soared over in a fragrant mist, descending to visit the sick woman. Rays of light gleamed, filling the whole convent for all to see. When everyone came to Fa-sheng to ask about the light, she explained what it was, and as soon as she had finished speaking, she died.[11]

The manner of dying is taken very seriously in Buddhism since an auspicious death signifies holiness. Rather alarmingly the practice of committing suicide by burning oneself alive was highly revered, and a nun would carry this out on the night of the changing phases of the moon, either the half-moon of the full moon. The biography of Shan-Miao is one particularly astonishing account. After wrapping herself in cloth soaked in oil and setting herself on fire, she summons her fellow nuns:

> 'Each of you must diligently make the effort to perfect your spiritual life because the cycle of birth and death is a fearsome thing. You must seek to escape it, taking heed not to fall into further transmigration. I have previously abandoned this body as a worship offering to the Buddha twenty-seven times, but it is only this time that I shall attain the first fruit [whereby I am no longer

liable to rebirth in the woeful destinies of hell, hungry ghosts or animals].[12]

One of the key practices for the Chinese nuns is meditation. In the life of Fa-hsiang, Shih Pao-ch'ang documents how she encourages another nun, Hui-su, to excel in her meditative discipline:

> Hui-su sat down in meditation with the rest of the assembly, but she did not get up again with the others. When they observed her they saw that she was rigid like wood or stone. When they tugged at her, she did not move. Some said that she had died, but three days later she got up and was her usual self. It was only then that the whole assembly recognized Hui-su's extraordinary accomplishment in meditation, and for the first time they became aware of Fa-hsiang's profound insight and ability [to recognize the spiritual capacities of others].[13]

And in the biography of Hui-hsü, whose nickname is Chou, Shih Pao-ch'ang writes of the only woman in his *Lives* to have composed her own verse. At a vegetarian meal prepared in her honour during the final days of her life, she picks up a brush and piece of paper and writes thus:

> *Worldly people who know me not*
> *Call me by my worldly name of old Chou.*
> *You invite me to a week-long feast of food,*
> *But the feast of meditation has no end.*[14]

As the early centuries of the first millennium CE passed, elements of both Chinese and then Japanese Buddhism would place greater and greater emphasis on meditation. In turn, specific esoteric practices also developed, known as *ch'an* in China and zen in Japan, with the final 'goal' being the state, or non-state, of *chien-hsing* or satori. Similarly, the dual aspects of the universe were also acknowledged: phenomenon and noumenon were respectively known as *nien* and *Hsin* in China and *nen* and *Kokoro* in Japan.

The key understanding to both teachings was that mystical knowledge was gained through transmission from master to pupil. This would either be through the imparting of verbal paradoxes and koans, the use of shock tactics such as being beaten with a stick, or simply through collective silence. Kuei-feng Tsung-mi, in his work, *The Complete Explanation of the Source of Ch'an*, observes how the sixth-century CE Indian teacher, Bodhidharma, tried to convey this point:

> When Bodhidharma came to China, he saw that most Chinese students did not grasp the truth of Buddhism. They merely sought it through interpretation of textual terminology, and thought of the changing phenomena all around them as real activity. Bodhidharma wished to make these eager students see that the finger pointing at the moon is not the moon itself. The real Truth is nothing but one's own mind. Thus he maintained that the real teaching must be transmitted directly from one mind to another, without the use of words.[15]

Inevitably, the mystical teaching that filtered into Japan, and eventually evolved into Shinto, developed its own esoteric mythology on the nature of reality and the birth of the cosmos. In the creation myth taken from the *Nihongi*, a collection of Japanese stories compiled in 720 CE, it relates the union of Heaven and Earth who give birth to four male and four female divine beings called *kami* as well as the first divine couple – the god Izanagi and goddess Izanami.

Moreover, in another collection of myths, entitled the *Kojiki* and compiled in 712 CE, the sacred feminine is personified in the form of the goddess Amaterasu meaning the 'Heavenly Shining Great Deity', who according to legend is born when Izanagi washes his left eye. She is given rulership over the heavens, whereas her brother, Susanowo, is given rulership over the underworld and the earth. Amaterasu and Izanagi bear children but later Amaterasu argues with Susanowo and runs away to hide in a cave. The world, devoid of her solar radiance, is therefore plunged into complete darkness during her departure.

Interestingly, in Japan, the goddess Amaterasu is worshipped as the sun and not the moon. Nevertheless, like all her mythological sisters, she represents the changing phases of nature as well as the primitive fear of solar eclipses, seen as omens of misfortune. The mid-winter ceremonies held in her honour re-enact the drama of coaxing her out of her cave in order to return light and life to earth, in the never-ending cycle of death and rebirth:

Immaculate as the sacred tree,
Her spirit pure and clear,
She lights the far corners
Of Heaven and earth –
The Great Kami of the Sun

This Way is the way
Of the Great Sun Kami,
Whose radiance from above
Lightens the very bounds
Of Heaven and earth.[16]

The feminine principle also finds expression in Confucianism. Confucius (551–479 BCE), or K'ung Fu-tzu in Chinese, founded his metaphysical principles on the concepts of relationship, hierarchy and harmony. He recognized that the universe was pervaded by a universal energy called *li* which manifested in the individual as ch'i, rather like the relationship between Brahman and atman. Moreover, he also believed that heaven (*ch'ien*) was male and the earth (*k'un*) was female. Although he stated that heaven rules over the earth, according to Confucius they exist in a harmonious relationship. In the *Chou Tun-yi* or 'An Explanation of the Diagram of the Great Ultimate', dating from the eleventh century CE, the beginning of creation is explained:

The Non-ultimate! And also the Great Ultimate (t'ai-chi). The Great Ultimate through movement generates the yang [male]. When its activity reaches its limit, it becomes tranquil. Through tranquillity the Great Ultimate generates the yin [female]. When tranquillity reaches its limit, activity begins again. Thus movement and tranquillity alternate and become the root of each other, giving rise to the distinction of yin and yang, and these two modes are thus established ...

The interaction of these two material forces engenders and transforms the myriad things. The myriad things produce and reproduce, resulting in an unending transformation.[17]

The male-female complement is further expounded in *The Book of Changes*, composed in the second millennium BCE, to which Confucius added his own commentary. Based on sixty-four figures of six horizontal lines, called hexagrams, they are used as a source of divination and prophesy. Moreover, 'The Creative' represents yang and 'The Receptive' represents yin; through their complementary opposition, they symbolize the manifest creation:

... the Receptive does not combat the Creative but completes it. It represents nature in contrast to spirit, earth in contrast to heaven, space as against time, the female-maternal as against the male-paternal ...

But strictly speaking there is no real dualism here, because there is a clearly defined hierarchical relationship between the two principles.[18]

Paradoxically, Confucius maintained his patriarchal view of the world, despite acknowledging male-female complementarity. In his *Analects*, Confucius makes quite clear his attitude towards the female species:

Women and people of low birth are very hard to deal with. If you are friendly with them, they get out of hand, and if you keep your distance, they resent it.[19]

Confucianism became the philosophical basis for the structure of Chinese society as we know it. As with all developing cultures, a patriarchal hierarchy became the norm. It has only been in recent times, however, with the opening up of the Asian continents to Western sociological influences, that women have finally been given the freedom and respect they rightfully deserve.

chapter nine

Rabi'a al-'Adawiyya

As the centuries were passing, many shades and nuances of the mystical teaching were appearing in different parts of the world – the impassioned reverence of the Indians, Egyptians and Mesopotamians, the insightful gnosis of the early Christians and the cool logic of the Buddhists. Now a new interpretation of the Truth would emerge in Arabia, revealed by the angel Gabriel to the Prophet Muhammed (570–632 CE) in his sacred book, the Quran:

> *Verily your God is One,*
> *The Lord of the heavens and the earth*
> *and all that lies between them …*[1]

Islam, the exoteric expression of the religion of the Muslim people, would draw on Jewish and Christian sources and develop into a distinct sophisticated lore, which had the effect of unifying a diversified collection of lawless tribes throughout the Arabian continent. Moreover, the esoteric message at the very heart of the Islamic teaching would speak of the Absolute, the unchanging omnipresent consciousness, accessible to those who earnestly sought the Beloved in the form of Allah, the Eternal Source:

> *God is the light of the heavens and the earth.*
> *The semblance of His light is that of a niche*

in which is a lamp, the flame within a glass,
the glass a glittering star as it were, lit with the oil
of a blessed tree, the olive, neither of the East
nor of the West, whose oil appears to light up
even though fire touches it not – light upon light.
God guides to His light whom He will.
So does God advance precepts of wisdom for men,
for God has knowledge of everything.[2]

In a time that saw the drowning of infant girls and the oppression of the fairer sex, Muhammed was revolutionary in re-establishing to a certain degree the equal rights of women, thus validating their dignity and independence. In fact, the Prophet makes perfectly clear in the Quran that he is addressing both men and women who have faith. Nevertheless, whilst acknowledging cosmic unity, Surah IV of the Quran entitled 'The Women' categorically states that women were made from the soul of men:

O men, fear your Lord
who created you from a single cell,
and from it created its mate,
and from the two of them dispersed men and women
(male and female) in multitudes.[3]

Like Christianity and Judaism, the Islamic faith believes in the creation myth of Adam and Eve. Interestingly, however, Eve is not to blame for humanity's transgression – it is Adam who takes responsibility for the Fall. Nevertheless, Muhammed, like the Buddha, still displayed a degree of prejudice against women and their capacity for religious commitment. One tradition of the Prophet even attests that:

Many men have been perfected, but of women only four; and the falling short of all other women was not due to their inherent nature but because of their acquired qualities (i.e. that for which they were themselves morally responsible). They are to be described also as wanting in intelligence and religion, and the explanation of their lack of religion is their neglect of prayer and fasting due to pride. Their lack of religion is in truth nothing but their neglect of prayer and fasting and the faith of Islam. For the practice of Islam and faith in it are one and the same thing to the one who realizes that good works come from faith.[4]

The four women who were believed to be the most perfected are Khadija, Muhammed's wife, who supported the Prophet during his own periods of religious doubt; Fatima, their youngest daughter, who carried on the legacy of the Islamic teaching after the Prophet's death; Mary, the mother of Jesus; and Jocheved, the mother of Moses. Interestingly, it is these women who form the very backbone of the three monotheist world faiths.

In time, the core Islamic teaching evolved into a purer, more profound expression known as Sufism. A number of explanations abide as to the word's derivative: first, the Arabic word, 'suf', meaning wool, refers to the coarse woollen mantles that Sufis wore to set themselves apart from the rest of the community; second, 'safa', meaning 'pure', relates to the purity of their minds and hearts; and third, 'saf', meaning 'rank', alludes to their status as the first rank of mortal beings in relation to God. Whatever the etymological root, the Sufi way is the path of love and the secret mysteries that are hidden in the human heart. Developing itself fully in the eighth century, the goal of Sufism is union with God, the knowledge that, 'Everything is perishing but His face.'[5] Having renounced the world and all its trappings, being purged of the ego and all its desires, the soul seeks a mystical marriage with the Divine.

One of the greatest exponents of Sufism the world has ever known is the poet, Ibn Arabi (1165–1240), who was born in Spain and lived out his life in Damascus. He outlined his vision of the Absolute through his vast collection of writings, differentiating between manifested nature (*Khalq*) and the all-pervading Self (*Haqq*). In his *Bezels of Wisdom*, which he intended to be a summary of his life's work, he readdresses the balance of the spiritual role of women and the nature of the sacred feminine:

> Thus it is that Muhammad's love for women derives from the divine love and because *God Gives to everything He has created* what is its due, essentially ...
>
> He places women first because they are the repository of passivity, just as the Universal Nature, by its form, comes before those things that derive their being from her. In reality, Nature is the Breath of the Merciful in which are unfolded the forms of the higher and lower Cosmos ...[6]

The first Sufis were lone individuals, seeking their Creator in isolation. And the most prominent woman Sufi, revered even above her male counterparts, was Rabiʿa al-ʿAdawiyya. Information about her life is scant, however, her story comes to us primarily through her thirteenth-century biographer, Attar, in his famous work, *Memoir of the Saints*, in a series of legends and anecdotes. Speaking of Rabiʿa, he says:

> That one set apart in the seclusion of holiness, that woman veiled with the veil of religious sincerity, that one on fire with love and longing, that one enamoured of the desire to approach her Lord and be consumed in His glory, that woman who lost herself in union with the Divine, that one accepted by men as a second spotless Mary — Rabiʿa al-ʿAdawiyya, may God have mercy upon her. If anyone were to say, 'Why have you made mention of her in the class of men?', I should say ... 'God does not look upon the outward forms ...'[7]

Born in Basra in 717 CE, she was the fourth daughter of a poor family and was hence given the name, Rabiʿa, meaning 'fourth'. At her birth, it said that the Prophet Muhammed appeared to her father in a dream, saying, '... this daughter who is born is a great saint, whose intercession will be desired by seventy thousand of my community.'[8] And yet despite such auspicious beginnings, a famine caused the death of her parents whilst she was still at a young age and she and her sisters were subsequently separated. Homeless and vulnerable, she was captured and sold into slavery.

Moreover, according to legend, a man tried to seduce her while she was out doing her daily chores. Running away from him, she tripped and dislocated her wrist. In utter despair, she implored her Maker: 'O Lord, I am a stranger and without mother and father, an orphan and a slave and I have fallen into bondage and my wrist is injured, [yet] I am not grieved by this, only [I desire] to satisfy Thee. I would fain know if Thou art satisfied [with me] or not.' A voice then replied: 'Be not sorrowful, for on the day of Resurrection thy rank shall be such that those who are nearest to God in Heaven shall envy thee.'[9]

At home, Rabi'a continued her labours in service of her master. One night, he awoke and saw her head bowed in worship, praying to God: 'O my Lord, Thou knowest that the desire of my heart is to obey Thee, and that the light of my eye is in the service of Thy court. If the matter rested with me, I should not cease for one hour from thy service, but Thou hast made me subject to a creature.'[10] Above her head, her master saw a lamp suspended in midair, the light from which flooded the entire house. Such was the radiance of the vision that, fearing the wrath of the Lord, he set her free the following morning. From thence, she journeyed to the desert and established herself in a cell for devotion and worship, possibly earning money as a flute player. But as her asceticism increased, she lived in holy poverty, isolated and alone in her complete renunciation of the world and absorption in the Self.

The moment when Rabi'a actually started to compose her poetry is only speculation and whether it is actually of her own hand or the stuff of folklore is also unclear. Nevertheless, the timeless quality of her work is imbued with the nondualist message of the mystics. In a syzygy of simple truth, she recounts the Beatific Vision:

O God,
Whenever I listen to the voice of anything You have made –
The rustling of the trees
The trickling of water

The cries of birds
The flickering of shadow
The roar of the wind
The song of the thunder,
I hear it saying:
    God is One!
    Nothing can be compared with God![11]

Multiplicity in unicity, many in the One. Rabiʻa's insight into the remembrance of God is the distillation of the exquisiteness of a moment, one which can so easily be unheard, unseen, unexperienced in the hubbub of life.

Indeed, the experience of the remembrance of God (*dhikr*) is both a practice and a mystical state. After the initial calling to embark on the journey to non-being, either through contact with a sheikh or through the grace of an inner voice, the progress of the seeker is charted by a series of stages or 'stations'. At each point, the soul acquires certain qualities, enabling it to ascend higher and higher to it its final goal – union with the Source. (The stages include repentance, surrender, voluntary poverty, patience, acceptance and gratitude.) Only when these attributes have been attained can the devotee move on to the next station of *gahd*, the dark night of the soul, a place of emptiness and despair where the ego struggles for its own existence. Without any sign of hope, the soul labours on, inspired only by its faith in the divine mystery and with its reward waiting in the final station, *mahabba* – the revelation of love.

Rabiʻa knew only too well the bittersweet taste of the journey and the rewarding fruit of love:

In love, nothing exists between breast and Breast.
Speech is born out of longing,
True description from the real taste.
The one who tastes, knows;
The one who explains, lies.

How can you describe the true form of Something
In whose presence you are blotted out?
And in whose being you still exist?
And who lives as a sign for your journey?[12]

Annihilation (*fana*) of the self is complete. After negation of the ego (or *nafs*), all is unveiled to be the loving totality of the Lord. *La ilaha il Allah* – 'There is no god but God'. Just like the Hindu practice *neti, neti* ('not this, not this'), there comes the realization that *Tat twam asi* ('Thou art That'):

Serving girl:
'It's Spring Rabi'a –
Why not come outside,
And look at all the beauty God has made!'

Rabi'a:
'Why not come inside instead, serving girl
And see the One who made it all –
Naked, without veil.'[13]

Throughout her long life, she was offered money, houses and proposals of marriage but she refused them all, citing the need for humble solitude:

My peace, brothers, is in my aloneness
Because my Beloved is alone with me there – always.
I've found nothing to equal His love,
That love which harrows the sands of my desert.
If I die of desire, and He is still unsatisfied –
That sorrow has no end.

To abandon all He has made
To hold in my hand
Proof that He loves me –
This is the name of my quest.[14]

And on the issue of becoming a man's wife:

> *Marriage has to do with being –*
> *But where can this being be found?*
> *I should belong to you? What makes you think*
> *I even belong to myself?*
> *I am His – His!*[15]

In a time when women's rights had deteriorated to the extent that the role of a wife was, to all intents and purposes, a slave to her husband, Rabi'a's words are particularly poignant. For her, the only interest in life is her love for the Divine – an exclusive, all-consuming passion that burns up every other earthly desire:

> *I have two ways of loving You:*
> *A selfish one*
> *And another way that is worthy of You.*
> *In my selfish love, I remember You and You alone.*
> *In that other love, You lift the veil*
> *And let me feast my eyes on Your Living Face.*
> *That I remember you always, or that I see You face-to-face –*
> *No credit to me in either:*
> *The credit is to You in both.*[16]

Only through the power of love can the veil of illusion reveal the Face of the Beloved. But this love must be for its own sake, with no thought given to hope of reward in heaven or fear of punishment in hell:

> *I carry a torch in one hand*
> *And a bucket of water in the other:*
> *With these things I am going to set fire to Heaven*
> *And put out the flames of Hell*
> *So that voyagers to God can rip the veils*
> *And see the real goal.*[17]

The allusion to the literal veil that hid a woman's face would not have been wasted on her female contemporaries.

Rabi'a was not, however, averse to male company. Many tales of her life refer to her friendship with the Sufi mystic, Hasan al-Basri (d. 728 CE), leader of a school of extreme asceticism. Although Rabi'a would have only been a young girl during their relationship, Attar relates Hasan's sentiments towards her:

> I passed a whole day and night with Rabi'a speaking of the Way and the Truth and it never passed through my mind that I was a man nor did it occur to her that she was a woman, and at the end when I looked at her, I saw myself a bankrupt [spiritually worth nothing] and Rabi'a as truly sincere.'[18]

It was said that Rabi'a would stay up all night long in prayer and silent meditation, long after her companions had gone to bed:

> *O God, the stars are shining;*
> *All eyes have closed in sleep:*
> *The kings have locked their doors.*
> *Each lover is alone, in secret, with the one he loves.*
> *And I am here too: alone, hidden from all of them –*
> *With You.*[19]

Rabi'a passed away in 801 CE, the owner of a reed mat, a screen, an earthenware jug and a bed of felt, which served also as a prayer mat. As is the case with many lives of the saints, friends and followers reported hearing her voice after her death, which is believed to have said, 'I have attained to that which I beheld.'

In spite of the fact that her physical body was no longer present, her memory lived on through her hagiographers and poems. Moreover, the Sufi teaching was gaining ground in its influence, attracting men and women to its mystical heart, and many sages would emerged to carry on its message.

One such Sufi was the poet and teacher Jalal al-Din Rumi

(1207–73), who is probably the most sublime writer of mystical love poetry the world has ever known. Founder of the Mevlevis, the Sufi order of whirling dervishes, he beautifully conveys the ecstatic yearning for union between lover and Beloved:

> When men and women become one, Thou art that One; when the units are wiped out, lo, Thou art that Unity.
>
> Thou didst contrive this 'I' and 'we' in order to play the game of worship with Thyself,
>
> That all 'I's and 'thou's might become one soul and at last be submerged in the Beloved.[20]

Drunk on love, all is One. And yet Rumi also understood the nature of the divine feminine:

> *The Prophet said that woman prevails over the wise …*
> *Woman is a ray of God; she is not just the earthly beloved.*
> *She is creative: you might say she is not created.*[21]

It is no wonder, then, that centuries later, Rabi'a is still referred to as the 'Doorkeeper of the Heart'. Transcending all earthly ties, her inner self annihilated in the Source, she gains immortal life:

> *O God,*
> *Another Night is passing away,*
> *Another Day is rising –*
> *Tell me that I have spent the Night well so I can be at peace,*
> *Or that I have wasted it, so I can mourn for what is lost.*
> *I swear that ever since the first day You brought me back to life,*
> *The day You became my Friend,*
> *I have not slept –*
> *And even if You drive me from your door,*
> *I swear again that we will never be separated –*
> *Because You are alive in my heart.*[22]

chapter ten

Yeshe Tsogyal

As well as the Greater and Lesser Vehicles of the Buddhist teaching, yet another school would emerge in northern India in the fifth century CE called Vajrayana or Tantric Buddhism, which included many shamanistic practices and goddess worship. Unlike the more purist approaches of Mahayana and Theravada, Tantra focuses on sensual activity as well as visionary experience as a means to realizing the Truth. Moreover, the cultivation of magical powers, called siddhis, is an essential component of the Tantric path.

Deriving from the Sanskrit root, '*tan*', meaning 'to expand', Tantra essentially is the union of the masculine and feminine – the Siva and Shakti, the yang and the yin. Despite the acknowledgement that all is One, experience of apparent duality takes centre stage. Thus unlike the *advaita* philosophy of the Upanishads, Tantra focuses on the expression of Reality through the direct utilization of emotion as well as the psychological energies of the body and mind.

According to the *Linga Purana*, an early Tantric text, Siva is perceived as the pure universal Absolute and Shakti as the creative force, both unified in the Self:

> In truth, there is no difference between Uma (Shakti) and Shankara (Siva); the One consists of two aspects; of this there is no doubt.[1]

Furthermore, individual Shakti resides in the physical body at the base of the spine as a coiled serpent of potential energy known as kundalini. *Sadhana* (spiritual practice), either through devotion or self-enquiry, hatha yoga or even specific sexual techniques can awaken this energy. When it does, it rises up through two main nerve-filaments, called *nadis*, either side of the spine, and passes through a series of chakras along the way. When the kundalini energy reaches the final chakra or *sahasrar* (the thousand-petalled lotus) at the crown of the head, the individual Shakti merges with universal Siva in a state of samadhi.

Indeed, the cultivation of Shakti is synonymous with the manifestation of inner wisdom, called Prajna. Buddhist texts known as the *Prajnaparamita*, used in both the Mahayana and Vajrayana schools, outline the need to focus on the perfection of wisdom as a prerequisite for enlightenment. Like Sophia, Maat and Me, wisdom is perceived as feminine and in the Tantra tradition, the female personification of Prajna is often referred to as the 'Mother of all Buddhas':

Homage to Thee, Perfect Wisdom,
Boundless, and transcending thought!
All thy limbs are without blemish,
Faultless those who Thee discern.

Spotless, unobstructed, silent,
Like the vast expanse of space;
Who in truth does really see Thee
The Tathagata perceives.

As the moonlight does not differ
From the moon, so also Thou
Who aboundst in holy virtues,
And the Teacher of the world …

To all heroes who of others
Have the welfare close at heart
Thou a mother, who does nourish,
Who gives birth, and who gives love.

Teachers of the world, the Buddhas
Are thine own compassionate sons;
Then art Thou, O Blessed Lady.
Grandam thus of beings all

All th'immaculate perfections
At all times encircle Thee,
As the stars surround the crescent,
O Thou blameless holy one!

Those in need of light considering,
The Tathagatas extol
Thee, O Single One, as many,
Multiformed and many-named.[2]

Moreover, in the Buddhist text, the *Ashtasahasrika*, one of the Buddha's wisest devotees, Sariputra, speaks of the nature of the sacred feminine:

The perfection of wisdom gives light, O lord. I pay homage to the perfection of wisdom! She is worthy of homage. She is unstained, and the entire world cannot stain her. She is a source of light, and from everyone in the triple world she removes darkness, and leads them away from the blinding darkness caused by defilements and wrong views. In her we can find shelter. Most excellent are her works. She makes us seek the safety of the wings of enlightenment.[3]

Another personification of the feminine principle in Buddhist teaching is the female bodhisattva, Tara, who is particularly popular in Tibet. In the *Tara Tantra*, written by Taranatha (b. 1575), who chronicled the history of Tibetan Buddhism, it speaks of Tara's previous incarnation as a woman and how she is offered the form of a man in reward for her spiritual rigour, to which she replies:

'In this life there is no such distinction as 'male' and 'female', neither of 'self-identity', a 'person' nor any perception [as such], and therefore attachment to ideas of 'male' and 'female' is quite worthless. Weak-minded worldlings are always deluded by this ... There are many who wish to gain enlightenment in a man's form, and there are but few who wish to work for the welfare of sentient beings in a female form. Therefore I may, in a female body, work for the welfare of beings right until samsara has been emptied.'[4]

Such is her commitment to helping others that she is awarded the title of Goddess Tara. Deriving from the Sanskrit root, 'tar', meaning 'to cross over', individuals paying homage to Tara are taken across the sea of samsara to the shore of immortality. Indeed, Tara governs the underworld, heaven and earth and represents the eternal wheel of life.

Like many of her goddess counterparts, Tara can take on many forms, the most popular being the Green Tara and the White Tara. The Green Tara is believed to be Mother Earth and is a fiercesome goddess, like Kali, who overcomes obstacles and danger. Emerald skinned, she sits in the lotus posture, holding the stem of a blue lotus in her left hand, which is raised up to her shoulder with the thumb and forefinger joined together (vitarka mudra, representing duality in unity). Her right hand, which rests on her knee palm upwards, makes the gesture of offering a boon (vara mudra). By praying to her, the Green Tara grants the wishes of her devotees as well as shields them from all suffering.

The White Tara, meanwhile, brings long life and everlasting happiness. Sitting in a similar posture to her sister, her skin is as luminous as the milky rays of the moon. Her right hand makes the gift-bestowing gesture and in her left hand, raised to her shoulder, she carries a white lotus. Indeed, the White Tara was born out of a lotus, blooming in the lake that formed from the first tear of the bodhisattva of compassion, Avalokitesvara, (whose human incarnation is the Dalai Lama). As his consort, the White Tara is still greatly revered in modern-day Tibet:

Lady whose eyes flash like lightning,
heroine, TARE TUTTARE,
born from the corolla of the lotus
of the Buddha's face: to you I bow.
Lady whose face is like the circle
of the full autumn moon,
lady who grasps a lotus flower
with the gift-bestowing gesture,
Homage to you!

From the age of this world TUTTARE!
Pacifying defilements with SVAHA!
With OM by your very essence
opening the gate of Brahma: to you I bow.
Protecting the entire world
from the eight terrors,
Blessed Lady, mother of all,
Homage to Tara, the mother![5]

There are twenty-one variations of Tara that exist in a myriad of colourful forms, including the Yellow Tara, representing bountiful-ness; the Blue Tara, representing wrath; the Black Tara, who subdues evil; and the Orange Tara, who helps with childbirth. In Tibetan temple banners, all the Taras are arranged in a group around a central Green Tara – green is believed to be the colour which embodies all the others of the spectrum. Moreover, as an intrinsic aspect of Tantric Buddhism, Tara mandalas are used as a form of visualization tech-nique, helping the devotee cultivate thoughts of loving kindness and attain spiritual enlightenment.

One of the greatest masters on the subject of Tantra was Padmasambhava (or Lotus Born), who took his Tantric Buddhism from India to Tibet in 747 CE upon the invitation of King Trisong Detsen, who wanted the sage to teach the Truth and build monas-teries throughout the land during a time of great political upheaval. Being of the Tantra school, Padmasambhava's teaching focused on the way in which oneness differentiates into duality and plays itself out in complementary opposites. Nevertheless, he never forgot the underlying unity of creation, and in his immortal work, *The Yoga of Knowing the Mind, and Seeing the Reality, which is called Self-Realization*, he writes:

> Although the wisdom of nirvana and the ignorance of samsara illusorily appear to be two things, they cannot truly be differentiated. It is an error to conceive them as other than one.[6]

King Trisong Detsen was married to a sixteen-year-old woman called Yeshe Tsogyal who was one of many wives living in his harem. However, having no interest in worldly affairs, she immediately sought the company of Padmasambhava in order to receive his spiritual training. In no time, Yeshe Tsogyal excelled to such an extent that she became his Tantric partner. Understandably, this precipitated a scandal within the King's palace and she was forced into exile.

The biography of Yeshe Tsogyal, the *Lady of the Lotus Born*, was composed as a *terma* or Dharma Treasure, spiritual texts concealed in sacred sites throughout Tibet to be discovered by future generations, thus preserving the lineage of the teaching. Written in old Tibetan symbolic script called *dayig*, Tsogyal dictated her story to Gyalwa Changchub and Namkhai Nyingpo, who wrote it down on sheets of yellow paper. They were then passed on to Tongyuk, the Black Water Lord, who sealed and hid them away, only to be rediscovered many years later by the treasure finder, or *tertön*, Taksham Samten Lingpa in the seventeenth century.

Yeshe Tsogyal, meaning 'Victorious Sea of Wisdom', was born in Tibet in 757 CE; at her birth, it is alleged that the sky was full of sweet music, rainbows and lotus blossoms. Moreover, her mother, Getso, had been visited nine months previously by a goddess, who announced to her, 'The Buddha has arisen, the Dharma and the sangha. Alala, this is a marvellous wonder!'[7]

Despite her auspicious entry into the world, Yeshe's early life was full of hardship and suffering. Recalling this period in her life, she says:

> I am a timid woman and of scant ability; of lowly condition, the butt of everyone. If I go for alms, I am set upon by dogs; if food and riches come my way, I am the prey of thieves; since I am beautiful, I am the quarry of every lecherous knave; if I am busy with much to do, the country folk accuse me; if I don't do what they think I should, the people criticize; if I put a foot wrong, everyone detests me. I have to worry about everything I do. That is what it is like to be a woman! How can a woman possibly gain accomplishment in Dharma? Just managing to survive is already hard enough![8]

Her fears and experience were not unique. Despite the teaching expounding the equality of the masculine and feminine principles, everyday life was permeated with the only too familiar patriarchal practice, with the incidence of female lamas and teachers during this time being most rare.

Meanwhile, Padmasambhava had been reflecting upon how to help propagate the Buddhist teachings; being trained in the manner of Tantra, he knew he must take a consort. At the court of King Trisong Detsen and the sight of Yeshe Tsogyal, he exclaims:

> Emaho!
> *The Secret mantra is called 'secret'*
> *Not because it harbours any defect.*
> *But rather it is hid*
> *From narrow minds upon the lower paths ...*
>
> *By sensual desire I am utterly unstained,*
> *The fault of carnal longing is unknown to me.*
> *But in the practice of the Secret Mantra*
> *The presence of a woman is required.*
> *She must be faithful and of good lineage,*
> *And pure in her* samaya *[commitment to the Tantric guru].*

She must be fair and excellently wise,
Skilled, and graced with qualities of mercy,
Unreserved in open-handed giving,
A perfect wisdom dakini indeed.[9]

Thus, Padmasambhava initiated Yeshe Tsogyal into Vajrayana Buddhism. Throughout her long life, she would travel throughout Tibet and Nepal, staying in caves and monasteries and helping those wanting spiritual perfection. Such was her holiness that she is accredited with raising the dead, defeating demons and controlling even the elements of nature. Of her master, the Guru Rimpoche, she says:

All the teachings of the Buddha were present in the precious Master Padmasambhava. He was like a vessel filled to overflowing. And after I had served him long in the three ways pleasing to a teacher, all that he possessed he gave me, the woman Yeshe Tsogyal. He poured it out as from one vase to another. My mind at ease in Dharma, I understood the differences between the nine vehicles and was able to distinguish true doctrine from false. Knowing the secret of the karmic law of cause and fruit, I conceived a desire for that truly unsurpassable teaching that totally transcends karma.[10]

And of Yeshe Tsogyal, Padmasambhava is also in no doubt of her perfected wisdom:

In the supreme body of a woman you have gained accomplishment;
Your mind itself is Lord; request him for empowerment and blessing.
There is no other regent of the Lotus Guru.[11]

Moreover, he goes on to praise Yeshe's accomplishments:

Yogini seasoned in the Secret Mantra!
The ground of Liberation
Is this human frame, this lowly human form –
And here distinctions, male or female,

Have no consequence.
And yet if bodhichitta [*the desire to attain Buddhahood*] *graces it,*
*A woman's form indeed will be supreme!*12

The importance of finding an authentic teacher is an important element in Tibetan Buddhism and it is for this reason that Yeshe Tsogyal speaks at length about the relationship between her and Padmasambhava (whom she also calls Guru Rimpoche). When it is time for Padmasambhava to leave the mortal realm, Yeshe is beside herself with grief. But the Master is having none of it and initiates her into the highest level of insight:

Nothing will surpass this, Mistress Tsogyal!
Padmasambhava's compassion neither ebbs nor flows;
The rays of my compassion for Tibet cannot be severed.
There I am in front of anyone who prays to me –
*Never will I separate from those who have faith.*13

As all the last remaining veils of illusion fall away, Yeshe stands stupefied:

It was like waking in the morning from a dream … Thereupon I gained a fearless confidence: the nest of hope and fears fell to nothing, and the torment of defiled emotions was cleared away. I experienced directly that the Teacher was inseparable from myself …14

Yeshe Tsogyal was entrusted with carrying on the work of spreading the Tantric teaching. She attracted many followers and established monasteries and lay communities. But her mission was not always easy. On retreat in a cave in the Tibetan mountains, she was attacked and raped by a gang of reprobates; however, instead of admonishing them of their misdemeanour, she took the opportunity to initiate them into the Dharma.

When it comes to her own departure from the world, she passes on the wisdom that she first received from her own teacher:

Meditate upon the Teacher as the glow of your awareness.
When you melt and mingle mutually together,
Taste that vast expanse of nonduality.
There remain.

And if you know me, Yeshe Tsogyal,
Mistress of samsara and nirvana,
You will find me dwelling in the heart of every being.
The elements and senses are my emanations,
And emanated thence, I am the twelvefold chain of co-production:
Thus primordially we never separate.

I seem a separate entity
Because you do not know me.
Therefore find my source and root!
And from within, awareness will arise;
The great and primal Wisdom will be all-pervading.
Bliss of the natural state will gather like a lake,
And Higher Insight, fishes' eyes of gold, will grow and spread.
Nurture this production of experience and bliss,
And on the wings of such perfected virtuosity,
You will make the crossing to the other shore.[15]

In *Lady of the Lotus Born*, Yeshe Tsogyal speaks of her encounter with another one of Padmasambhava's consorts, Dungmen Gyalmo, also known as Princess Mandarava. A *dakini* or wisdom goddess from India, Yeshe asks her to initiate her into the highest teaching but Princess Mandarava reassures her thus:

Accomplished in the Secret Mantra,
Dancer in the sky,
Wonder-worker who dissolved her impure form
Into the sphere of purity,
You drank the nectar of the teachings
Of the Lotus Born

And gathered all their essence –
Great Mother, Wisdom that has gone beyond,
Is this not yourself?

Entering the path wherein the truth
Of all phenomena is seen,
You utterly forsook the eight preoccupations of this life
And, practising austerities, lived upon essential substance,
Overcoming all phenomenal existence.
Tsogyal, ever-young, immaculate, to you I bow![16]

Indeed, Buddhist art often depicts Padmasambhava with Princess Mandarava and Yeshe Tsogyal at either side as his two principal consorts.

It is believed that Yeshe Tsogyal reincarnated as Machig Lapdron who lived during the twelfth century (1055–1145). She is best known for creating the Cöd ritual, a Tantric technique in which practitioners mentally cut up pieces of their body and offer it to the Buddhist deities, used as an aid in transcending attachment to the physical form. In *The Dedication of the Illusory Body in Sacrifice*, she writes:

This illusory body, which I have held to be so precious,
I dedicate [in sacrifice] as a heaped-up offering,
Without the least regard for it, to all the deities that constitute the
    visualized assembly;
May the very root of self be cut asunder.[17]

Moreover, in another text, *The Yogic Dance which Destroyeth Erroneous Beliefs*, Machig Lapdron encourages her devotees to empower themselves with the sacred feminine:

Now visualize thyself as having become, instantaneously,
The Goddess of the All-Fulfilling Wisdom,
Possessed of the power of enlarging thyself to the vastness of the Universe,
And endowed with all the beauties of perfection;

[Then] blow the human thigh-bone trumpet loudly,
And dance the Dance which Destroyeth Erroneous Beliefs.[18]

The spread of Buddhism and Tantra throughout the West in modern times is almost unprecedented in an age when religious faith is on the decline. Paradoxically, it is the plight of the Tibetan people that has given new life to stories of the *dakinis* and female lamas, inspiring women today of all faiths from around the world.

chapter eleven

Andal

Meanwhile, in India, a new class of writing was emerging which would convey the unified vision of *advaita* Vedanta in a more accessible format. Unlike the directly revealed Truth of the Vedas and Upanishads, referred to as *sruti*, meaning 'heard', this new body of orally-transmitted literature is known as *smriti*, meaning 'remembered'. The most important texts of this period are the *Puranas*, written as a means to popularize the teachings through concrete example, such as myths and legends and the lives of great saints within the context of historical events. Moreover, stories of the Hindu goddesses and gods are central.

Composed by a variety of sages and poets between approximately 400 CE and a millennium later, there are eighteen principal *Puranas*. In the *Devi Mahatmya* section of the *Markandeya Purana*, the goddess figure is eulogized in her immanent form:

> O Goddess, you are insight, knowing the essence of all scripture, you are Durga, a vessel upon the ocean of life [that is so] hard to cross, devoid of attachments.
>
> [You are] Sri, whose sole abode is in the heart of Kaitabha's foe [Vishnu], you are Gauri, whose abode is made with the one who is crowned with the moon [Siva].
>
> Slightly smiling, spotless, like the orb of the full moon, as pleasing as the lustre of the finest gold [is your face].[1]

Other goddesses are honoured throughout the *Puranas*. One of the most famous is Durga, who is created by the gods to slay the buffalo demon, Mahisa. Like the warrior aspect of her Greek counterpart, Athena, she is the powerful goddess of war and rides a lion and wields many weapons. Also known as Chandi, she wears a garland of skulls, whilst holding a severed head in one hand and a lotus in the other, symbolizing the opposing forces of good and evil in the universe. In the *Devi Mahatmya*, Durga gives birth to Kali from the spot between her eyebrows, right in the midst of battle. As a goddess of terrifying demeanour (and often interchangeable with Durga in other myths), Kali's mission is to save the world:

> In such a way, then, does the divine goddess, although eternal, take birth again and again to protect creation. This world is deluded by her; it is begotten by her; it is she who gives knowledge when prayed to and prosperity when pleased. By Mahakali is this entire egg of Brahma pervaded, lord of men.[2]

The Hindu *trimurti* – Brahma, the creator, Vishnu, the preserver and Siva, the destroyer – are graced by the presence of their goddess consorts. Saraswati reappears once again during the Puranic era along with her consort, Brahma – in the *Rig Veda*, she is the sacred embodiment of the River Ganges; in the *Puranas*, however, Saraswati is the embodiment of wisdom ('*Sara*' means 'one who gives the essence', '*swa*' 'of our own Self').

Pictorially, Saraswati is represented as sitting on a lotus. She holds the sacred scripture in one hand (representing *jnana* yoga) and a lotus blossom in the other. With her third and fourth hands, she plays the vina or Indian lute (representing bhakti yoga). She always wears white, as a symbol of her purity, and the swan is her vehicle. Moreover, her four hands are also representative of the four aspects of the inner personality, namely *manas* (mind), *buddhi* (intellect), *ahamkara* (ego) and *chitta* (heart). In the *Padma Purana*, the goddess of wisdom is praised:

Devi Saraswati, the protectoress of the universe, seated on a white lotus and adorned with white flowers, wears a white apparel.

The Eternal One is besmeared with white sweet-scented pastes and has a white rosary in Her hands, is anointed with white sandal paste and holds a white vina.

The white coloured One is adorned with white jewels, to Her Siddhas, Gandharvas, gods and demons offer their salutations as also the sages and Her praise the Rishis always sing.

Whoever chants this hymn to Devi Saraswati, the sustainer of the universe, at dawn, noon and at dusk attains all knowledge.[3]

The second god of the Hindu trinity is Lord Vishnu, the preserver of the universe: in order for society to function properly, there must be wealth. Hence, he is married to Laksmi, the goddess of good fortune and prosperity. Also known as Sri, she has skin the colour of a red lotus, is seated on a red lotus and has a garland of red lotuses around her neck. She is also, not surprisingly, referred to as the goddess of the lotus, Padma. Paradoxically, accumulation of material wealth is not what is to be striven after – it is the cultivation of moral and ethical values which are the goal. In the myth of the 'Churning of the Ocean Milk' told in the *Vishnu Purana*, Laksmi emerges from the sea, which represents the *sattvic* mind, wreathed in lotuses. Of Vishnu's and Laksmi's relationship, the Purana says:

The eternal Sri, loyal to Vishnu, is the mother of the world. Just as Vishnu pervades the universe, O excellent Brahmin, so does she. Vishnu is meaning; Sri is speech. She is conduct; Hari [Vishnu] is behaviour. Vishnu is knowledge; she is insight. He is Dharma; she is virtuous action.

Vishnu is the creator; Sri is creation. She is the earth and Hari earth's upholder. The eternal Laksmi is contentment, O Maitreya; the blessed lord is satisfaction.[4]

As with many Hindu deities, she has a bifurcated history in that she also represents the legacy of the great Mother Earth, in particular the autumn harvest, and as such is worshipped on the day of the autumnal full moon.

The final goddess of the trinity is Parvati, meaning 'she who dwells in the mountains' (the Himalayas), who is married to Siva, Lord of destruction. Also known as Uma (a variant spelling of *Om*), she represents manifested matter. Of unsurpassed beauty, Parvati represents the true celebration of womanhood. She is usually depicted in bright-coloured saris, drenched in garlands and holding lotuses in her hands.

Initially born into the world in order to seduce Siva, she also symbolizes the nourishing life-giving Source as a complement to her ascetic and reclusive husband. However, she does not win him over through her feminine wiles but through her devotion to spiritual practice. Disguising himself as a matted-haired ascetic, Siva decides to test Parvati until he is satisfied by her purity and steadfastness:

'I have tested you, blameless woman, and find you firmly devoted to me. I came to you in the form of a *brahmacarin* and said to you many things, all out of desire for your own welfare. I am profoundly pleased with your special devotion. Tell me what your heart desires! There is nothing you do not deserve! Because of your *tapas*, I shall be your servant from this moment on. Due to your loveliness, each instant without you lasts an age. Cast off your modesty! Become my wife forevermore! Come, beloved. I shall go to my mountain at once, together with you.'

Parvati became overjoyed at hearing these words of the lord of the gods and abandoned immediately all the hardships of *tapas*. Trembling at the sight of Siva's celestial form, Parvati kept her face modestly turned down and replied respectfully to the lord, 'If you are pleased with me and if you have compassion for me, then be my husband, O lord of the gods.'

Thus addressed by Parvati, Siva took her hand according to the custom and went to Mount Kailasha with her. Having won her husband, the mountain-born girl performed the divine offices for the gods.[v]

After their marriage, Siva and Parvati depart for Mount Kailasha in Tibet, Siva's favourite dwelling place, where their lovemaking is so intense that it shakes the very foundations of the cosmos. Over the course of time, they have three children, including the elephant god, Ganesha. It is said that Siva and Parvati represent the balance between the way of the renunciate and the way of the householder. Moreover, Parvati symbolizes created matter and Siva the immanent spirit of the universe, just like the dyads of Prakriti and Purusha, yin and yang, Yahweh and Shekhinah. Thus Parvati and Siva not only complement each other, they are in fact each other's completion.

The hermaphroditic image of Siva and Parvati, known as the Ardhanareshwara, is a familiar symbol in India, with the right side representing Siva, complete with trident and serpent, and the left side Parvati, adorned with jewellery and flowers. Images of the lingam (the male principle) and the yoni (the female principle) are also familiar objects in temples, as is the practice of dabbing a white dot on the forehead (*shweta bindu*), to represent semen, and the red dot (*shona bindu*), menstrual blood.

The union of two perfected lovers finds expression in much of Hindu literature and none can be more powerful and beguiling as the *Ramayana*, composed around the second century BCE by the sage, Valmiki. It is the famous tale of Rama and Sita, who are incarnations of Vishnu and Laksmi. Rama is heir apparent to his father, King of Ayodhya. He wins the hand of Sita, who is from a neighbouring kingdom, by stringing Siva's bow (in a similar manner to Odysseus proving his identity to Penelope in Homer's *Odyssey*). Court intrigue and scandal force Rama and Sita into exile for fourteen years, whereupon they have many adventures, including the famous episode where Sita is kidnapped by the demon, Ravana, and taken to his kingdom in Lanka. Rama enlists the help of the monkey god, Hanuman, and between them they eventually manage to liberate Sita.

When Rama and Sita return to the kingdom of Ayodhya, Sita's faithfulness during her year's captivity is brought into question. As a test of her purity, she is commanded to undergo an ordeal by fire. Accepting her fate, she steps into the flames but Agni, the god of fire, extinguishes it and addresses Rama thus:

> 'Here is Vaidehi [Sita], O Rama, there is no sin in her! Neither by word, feeling or glance has thy lovely consort shown herself to be unworthy of thy noble qualities. Separated from thee, that unfortunate one was borne away against her will in the lonely forest by Ravana, who had grown proud on account of his power. Though imprisoned and closely guarded by titan women in the inner apartments, thou was ever the focus of her thoughts and her supreme hope. Surrounded by hideous and sinister women, though tempted and threatened, [Sita] never gave place in her heart to a single thought for that titan and was solely absorbed in thee. She is pure and without taint ...; it is my command that she should not suffer reproach in any way.[6]

The *Ramayana* is in every way an analogy of the human condition and Rama and Sita are representative of the ideal couple – Rama is the strong, discerning hero; Sita is the loyal, beautiful wife.

Because the direct experience of Reality is rare, the wise use myth and story to communicate their esoteric message. And none could be more compelling than another masterpiece, the *Mahabharata*, the Hindu epic written by an unknown poet sometime between the tenth and fifth centuries BCE. Again similar to Homer's *Odyssey* in its panoramic scope, it recounts the story of a great war between two rival clans living in ancient India. Underpinning the many tales and adventures is the teaching of the Hindu sage, Kapila and the philosophy of *Samkhya* – the knowledge that the drama of life is merely the play of maya.

Many women feature in the *Mahabharata* but it is Draupadi who is the most central female character – indeed, it is an argument over her virtue and reasoning abilities that precipitates the war between the Pandavas and the Kauravas. Later in a game of dice, the eldest of the five Pandava brothers, Yudhishthira, gambles away himself, his brothers and their joint wife, Draupadi. The victor of the game, the king's son, Duryodhana, demands that Draupadi be brought before him, dragged by the hair. But she is no ordinary wife and displays a highly developed understanding of the Dharma. She reasons that if Yudhishthira had gambled himself away, he would no longer be a free man and, therefore, had no right to decide the fate of her and her other husbands.

In a fit of anger upon hearing the obvious truth, Duryodhana orders that Draupadi and her husbands be stripped of their clothing. As one of King Dhritarashtra's sons pulls at Draupadi's sari, it miraculously continues to unravel unendingly, thus protecting her honour. As a devotee of the Lord Sri Krishna, eighth incarnation of Lord Vishnu, her virtue is saved by her guru's grace:

> Of all the women of mankind, famous for their beauty, of whom we have heard, no one have we heard accomplished such a deed! While the Parthas and the Dhartarastras are raging beyond measure, Krishna Draupadi has become the salvation of the Pandavas! When they were sinking, boatless and drowning, in the plumbless ocean, the Pancali [Draupadi] became the Pandavas' boat, to set them ashore![7]

Draupadi and Lord Krishna share a very special relationship. Draupadi always considers him to be her *sakha* or beloved friend and Krishna addresses her as *sakhi*, in recognition of the platonic love between them. Speaking of her humiliation in the court of King Dhritarashtra, Krishna tells Draupadi that he is most impressed by her steadfast belief in the Dharma and in return, promises to bring about the complete annihilation of the house of the Kauravas.

Thus, the battle of Kurukshetra sees the destruction of the Kaurava dynasty and forms one of the most famous passages in the *Mahabharata*, being more commonly known as the *Bhagavad Gita*, meaning 'The Song of God'. Attributed to the sage Vyasa, and seen essentially as a separate work in its own right, it is the most definitive treatise on *Samkya* philosophy ever composed. The *Bhagavad Gita* opens with Arjuna, one of Draupadi's husbands, and Krishna, his chariot driver, facing the impending task of entering into battle against the Kauravas. Despite the enmity that exists between both families, Arjuna is overwhelmed and utterly despondent by the drama which is about to unfold. But Krishna, acting as a personification of the Self, reminds him of his immortal being. He goes on to point out that the universe is merely the play of opposites, the perennial battle of existence. Through an understanding of the Dharma and by knowing the phenomenal world to be all but an illusion, the individual can be set free from the bondage of ignorance and the chains of mortality.

Krishna discriminates between Purusha and Prakriti, between the Absolute and maya, between the real and the unreal. He then reveals to Arjuna the four paths to liberation – devotion (bhakti yoga), action (karma yoga), knowledge (*jnana* yoga) and contemplation (*raja* yoga, the 'royal road' and highest path). Whichever path we choose, however, all ultimately lead to the one Self:

> He who realizes the divine truth concerning My birth and life, is not born again; and when he leaves his body, he becomes one with Me.
>
> Many have merged their existence in Mine, being freed from desire, fear and anger, filled always with Me, and purified by the illuminating flame of self-abnegation.
>
> Howsoever men try to worship Me, so do I welcome them. By whatever path they travel, it leads to Me at last.[8]

Moreover, the practice of meditation and the one-pointed focus on the Self will lead the devotee to everlasting bliss:

> When the volatile and wavering mind would wander, let him restrain it, and bring it again to its allegiance to the Self.
>
> Supreme Bliss is the lot of the sage, whose mind attains Peace,

whose passions subside, who is without sin, and who becomes one with the Absolute.

Thus, free from sin, abiding always in the Eternal, the saint enjoys without effort the Bliss which flows from realization of the Infinite.[9]

The *Bhagavad Gita* is one of the most profound texts on the nature of nonduality in existence, in that it synthesizes living in the world and performing one's duty, all the while concentrating one's heart on the supreme Absolute:

> … the Great Souls, O Arjuna! Filled with My Divine Spirit, they worship Me, they fix their minds on Me and on Me alone, for they know that I am the imperishable Source of being.
>
> Always extolling Me, strenuous, firm in their vows, prostrating themselves before Me, they worship Me continually with concentrated devotion.
>
> Others worship Me with full consciousness, as the One, the Manifold, the Omnipresent, the Universal.
>
> I am the Oblation, the Sacrifice, and the Worship; I am the Fuel and the Chant, I am the Butter offered to the fire, I am the Fire itself; and I am the Act of Offering.
>
> I am the Father of the universe and its Mother; I am its Nourisher and its Grandfather; I am the Knowable and the Pure; I am *Om*; and I am the Sacred Scriptures.
>
> I am the Goal, the Sustainer, the Lord, the Witness, the Home, the Shelter, the Lover and the Origin; I am Life and Death; I am the Fountain and the Seed Imperishable.
>
> I am the Heat of the Sun. I release and hold back the Rains. I am Death and immortality; I am Being and Not-Being.[10]

The *Bhagavad Gita* very quickly became the Bible of Hinduism since it espoused the *advaita* Vedanta doctrine in a practical format. Nevertheless, other great sages would go on to reveal the mystical teachings in a unique way – for example Patanjali, the sage of the early centuries CE in his *Yoga Sutras*; Shankara, in the seventh century CE, in his classic work *Vivekachudamani* or 'The Crest Jewel of Wisdom', and Dattatreya in the tenth century, in his *Avadhut Gita*.

The *Bhagavad Gita* also precipitated the cult of bhakti in the form of Krishna worship. As the eighth incarnation of Vishnu, Krishna is the male embodiment of the Self and many sacred texts have been composed in his honour. Whereas the *Mahabharata* focuses on his wise counsel in the battle towards the Pandavas, it is the *Bhagavata Purana* or the *Srimad Bhagavatam* that recounts his adventurous adolescence and his amorous exploits with the *gopis* (cowherdesses) in Vrindavan.

It is said that Krishna was the lover of 16,000 gopis, who all leave their household cares behind to lose themselves in the *rasa lila*, the circular dance of the soul. Through the beguiling tunes of his magic flute, Krishna lulls the women into a trance of devotion and ecstasy. He says to them:

'I know what is in your minds and I have accepted your devotion to me. Believe me, devotion to me has never gone unrewarded. You have given me your hearts and your minds and there is nothing in your minds except love for me. Listen to me. The love which is lodged in your hearts is so pure that it can never become lust of the type which lies in the human heart. The seed of a plant will give forth new shoots when planted in the earth. But if it is fried or baked, then it will not be able to sprout again. Even so, love of a human type which is for human beings will give birth to further involvements with this world. But love which is directed towards me will be an end in itself and it will never make you earth-bound. Go home with the assurance from me that your efforts will not go unrewarded.[11]

Despite treating all his women alike, one in particular was his eternal consort and supreme devotee and her name was Radha. Believed to be the embodiment of Laksmi, Radha was a strikingly beautiful and discerning young woman. And like Rama and Sita before them, Radha and Krishna are the epitome of the divine pair, united in their love.

The bhakti movement would continue to grow throughout India, inspiring many sages and poets. One in particular was Narada, living sometime during the first few centuries of the first millenium. Little is known of his life but his *Bhakti Sutras* are beautiful expositions on the nature of love:

> Now, in a spirit of auspiciousness, we shall commence to expound on bhakti – spiritual devotion.
>
> The nature of spiritual devotion is the supreme love.
>
> And its essence is the nectar of immortality.
>
> Obtaining spiritual devotion, a person becomes a siddha, a perfected one, beyond death and fully satisfied.
>
> Achieving spiritual devotion, one becomes completely desireless – grieving not, hating not, not rejoicing in fleeting happiness, without passion for personal concerns.
>
> With a realization of spiritual devotion one becomes spiritually intoxicated; one becomes overwhelmed; one comes to rejoice in the Self.[12]

And in the manner of Rumi, Narada attempts to define the indefinable:

> The essential nature of love is inexpressible.
>
> Like taste for one who is mute.
>
> Love is manifest where there is an able vessel.
>
> This love takes the form of an intimate experience of exquisite subtlety – devoid of the influence of the three modes of nature, devoid of desire – a boundless, perpetual expansion.
>
> Achieving that experience one sees only love, hears only love, speaks only of love, and thinks of love alone.[13]

For Narada, the highest bliss, the everlasting joy of eternal peace, is not through the attainment of wisdom but through the simple act of loving itself:

Some assert that spiritual devotion can be developed solely by wisdom.

Some assert that wisdom and devotion are both necessary.

According to the son of Brahma, Narada, spiritual devotion is its own fruit.[14]

And the fruit of devotion is union with God:

Spiritual devotion is singular, though it manifests as eleven forms: cherishing the glorious qualities of God; cherishing the spiritual forms; cherishing ritual worship; cherishing constant remembrance; cherishing service; cherishing God as a dear friend; cherishing God with parental affection; cherishing God like a loving wife; cherishing knowledge of the Self; cherishing oneness with God; cherishing the supreme separation.[15]

The cult of bhakti continued to dominate Hindu society through the centuries. Moreover, Krishna worship became the main focus for the expression of devotees' love. Many poets have written about their love for Krishna but one in particular stands above all others – the female Tamil saint from the middle of the seventh century, Andal.

Legend has it that Andal was discovered under a basil brush (the herb sacred to Vishnu) as a baby in Srivilliputtur by the Brahman priest Periyalvar, who raised her as his own daughter. He initially called her Kodai, meaning 'she who is born of Mother Earth'. As a child, she became so totally devoted to Krishna that she would wear garlands prepared by her father intended for his honour in the temple. Indeed, her only wish was that she would one day become Krishna's bride. Her father, catching Kodai admiring herself in the mirror covered in the garlands, reprimanded her but Vishnu allegedly appeared to him later that night in a dream. He commanded her father that only the garlands that had been worn by Kodai could be used in offering, since they were drenched in the sweet fragrance of her pure being.

Periyalvar realized the holiness of his devoted daughter and renamed her Andal, meaning 'she who dives deep into the ocean of divine love'.

Such were her longings for Krishna that Andal imagined herself to be one of the gopi girls, pining for the presence of her Lord. Thus inspired, Andal composed the *Tiruppavai*, or 'Song Divine' as a record of her intense and passionate experience. A poem of thirty stanzas, it recounts the ecstatic longing of the young Vrindavan women for their divine lover, Lord Krishna. The overall effect is not the sackcloth and ashes of the Christian mystics but an erotically charged exaltation of love:

> *Favouring January's full moon is here –*
> *Maidens bejewelled, keen on bathing, come out!*
> *Darling girls of the cowherd clan*
> *Whose hamlet brims over with beauty and wealth;*
> *That cruel sharp spear Nanda's son,*
> *Young lion of Yasoda [Krishna's foster mother] with her love-filled eyes*
> *Cloud-hued, red-orbed, sun and moon for his face*
> *Narayana [Vishnu] himself has offered his gracious drum all for us*
> *To sing his praise and gain the world's.*[16]

Krishna's love is all the women require:

> *In morning's small hours we came to adore*
> *Those golden lotuses, your feet: why?*
> *Born are we in the cowherd caste*
> *But you must take us in your own employ.*
> *Not only for today do we seek your drum*
> *But for ever and ever, seven times seven births!*
> *Would be one with you, work only for you –*
> *Change all our other wishes, Lord!*[17]

Their love is total and yet similarly available to anyone who sincerely desires it:

> *There thirty stanzas in chaste Tamil*
> *In honour of Him who churned the sea,*
> *Were composed by Kodai the daughter*

Of that Prince of Brahmin priests
With his garland fresh and cool,
Of the lovely village, Srivilliputtur.
Maids bejewelled, their face the moon
Seeking Kesava ['beautiful haired'] got his grace
As narrated in these lines.

Whoever will chant them without fail
Will be looked after by the Lord
His four shoulders high as hills,
Eyes red, face comely and benign:
Will gain his grace wherever they go
And be happy evermore![18]

The poem is still sung daily in temples throughout southern India today.

Andal's literary talent continued to flourish – her 'Sacred Utterances' or *Nacchiyar Tirumozhi*, explores in greater length her devotion to Krishna. In rapturous exaltations of ecstasy and anguish in a sequence of fourteen poems similar in its eroticism to the *Song of Songs*, Andal describes her yearning for Krishna:

O famed and expert God of Love,
Take note of the penance I undergo –
My body unwashed, my hair unbound,
My lips without colour, one meal a day.
One thing I have to say, my Lord,
That my womanhood may not be a waste
Grant me this, my life's aim,
That I become Kesava's servant-maid.[19]

Her yearning is intense and she begs Krishna to reveal himself to her:

O lovely Koel [Krishna], through my greed to embrace
The one on the milky sea,

My surging breasts in their ecstasy
Melt and distress my soul.
What do you gain by hiding yourself?
If you will coo and bring to me
The one with the discus, conch and mace
You will get a place in heaven.[20]

The sixth poem, 'A Dream Wedding', is the culmination of Andal's hopes and imaginations – she becomes the bride of Krishna:

My friend, I dreamt that numerous priests
Brought water for holy sprinkling
From the four corners of the earth
And raising Vedic chants,
Knotted the guardian string round my wrist
That I may wed Kannan [Krishna] the pure.[21]

The marriage customs observed in Andal's time – the bridegroom coming in procession the night before the wedding, their going around the sacred bridal fire and then proceeding through the streets in the evening – are all observed today in southern India, chanted to Andal's song of the 'Dream Wedding'.

Later in the poem, she speaks of losing herself in her love:

Fair mothers, my sweet ambrosia
Of Srirangam
With his lovely hair, his lovely mouth
His lovely eyes
And the lovely lotus from his belly button –
My husband –
Has my loose bangle
Made me lose indeed!

My Lord of Srirangam,
Rich and righteous,

Who owns this sea-swept earth entire
And the sky
Has made his possessions
Now complete
With the bangle which I wore
On my hand![22]

Throughout her short life, Andal refused to marry any mortal man – Krishna was the sole object of her affection. It is said that Vishnu, supremely pleased with her devotion, appeared to Periyalvar once more in a dream, instructing him to bring Andal to the holy shrine at Srirangam, on the banks of the Cauvery in southern India. Legend says that the moment that she entered the sanctum of the temple, she was surrounded by a blaze of light and was absorbed into the image of Vishnu. She was only fifteen years old.

When and where Andal composed her verses is not clear but she is keen to impart the knowledge that it is she who is authoress of her immortal words. Indeed, throughout her verse, Andal teaches us that love for the divine Beloved can set us free:

Kodai whose brow no brow can match
Putter Vishnuchittan's [Periyalvar's] daughter
Made these verses in her passion
For that jewelled lamp of the cowherd clan
Who wrought mischief with his pranks.
Those who can recite them well
Shall never struggle in the sea of sorrows.[23]

chapter twelve

Hildegard of Bingen

Europe would have to wait until the early Middle Ages for a substantial body of mystical writings to emerge. Indeed, such was the associated expansion in human endeavour in all fields of artistic and intellectual expression that scholars have termed this period in history the early Renaissance. However, much of the literary outpouring is steeped in Christian theology making the nondualist vision all the more elusive. Nevertheless, a handful of writers persevered in their expression of the Oneness of God.

One important writer who lived many centuries earlier in Rome and who was to have a profound effect upon metaphysical thought during this time was Boethius (480–524 CE). A brilliant philosopher in his own right, he translated the works of Plato from Greek into Latin. Despite the respect he gained in his lifetime, he fell out with the Emperor Theodoric, who sentenced him to death. Boethius's famous *Consolation of Philosophy* was composed during his internment in prison in Pavia and before his impending execution. It is the account of a vision, in which he is visited by a woman, who reveals herself to be Sophia (also known as Sapientia):

> While I was pondering thus in silence, and using my pen to set down so tearful a complaint, there appeared standing over my head a woman's form, whose countenance was full of majesty, whose eyes shone as with fire and in power of insight surpassed the eyes of

men, whose colour was full of life, whose strength was yet intact though she was so full of years that none would ever think that she was subject to such age as ours. One could but doubt her varying stature, for at one moment she repressed it to the common measure of a man, at another she seemed to touch with her crown the very heavens: and when she had raised higher her head, it pierced even the sky and baffled the sight of those who would look upon it. Her clothing was wrought of the finest thread by subtle workmanship brought to an indivisible piece. This she had woven with her own hands, as I afterwards did learn by her own showing. Their beauty was somewhat dimmed by the dullness of long neglect, as is seen in the smoke-grimed masks of our ancestors. On the border below was inwoven the Greek letter Pi, on that above was to be read the Greek letter Theta. And between the two letters there could be marked degrees, by which, as by the rungs of a ladder, ascent might be made from the lower principle to the higher. Yet the hands of rough men had torn this garment and snatched such morsels as they could therefrom. In her right hand she carried books, in her left was a sceptre brandished.[1]

Over the course of several days, their discourse leads Boethius to a greater understanding of the world and its meaning. Sophia points out to him that it is peace of mind which is truly sought by the wise:

Thus there is nothing wretched unless you think it to be so: and in like manner he who bears all with a calm mind finds his lot wholly blessed. Who is so happy but would wish to change his estate, if he yields to impatience of his lot? With how much bitterness is the sweetness of man's life mingled! For even though its enjoyment seem pleasant, yet it may not be surely kept from departing when it will. It is plain then how wretched is the happiness of mortal life which neither endures for ever with men of calm mind, nor ever wholly delights the care-ridden. Wherefore, then, O mortal men, seek ye that happiness without, which lies within yourselves? Ye are confounded by error and ignorance. I will show you as shortly as I may, the pole on which turns the highest happiness. Is there aught that you value more highly than your own self? You will answer that there is nothing. If then you are master of yourself, you will be in possession of that which you will never wish to lose, and which Fortune will never be able to take from you.[2]

Indeed, peace comes from within. Moreover, the entire manifested world is cradled in the One:

> This universe would never have been suitably put together into one form from such various and opposite parts, unless there were some One who joined such different parts together; and when joined, the very variety of their natures, so discordant among themselves, would break their harmony and tear them asunder unless the One held together what it wove into one whole. Such a fixed order of nature could not continue its course, could not develop motions taking such various directions in place, time, operation, space, and attributes, unless there were One who, being immutable, had the disposal of these various changes. And this cause of their remaining fixed and their moving, I call God, according to the name familiar to all.[3]

Such was the influence of Boethius's *Consolation of Philosophy* that it undoubtedly inspired the later twelfth-century Italian writer, Dante Alighieri (1265–1321), to compose his *La Vita Nuova* ('The New Life'). Composed of canzoni woven together with a prose commentary, it narrates Dante's love for a young woman called Beatrice (whom he only saw by sight three times), his premonition of her death in a dream, her actual death at the young age of twenty, and his ultimate resolve to write a work that would be a worthy monument to her memory. Thus, it is upon his seeing Beatrice for the first time that Dante knows that his fate is sealed:

> At that moment, I say most truly that the spirit of life, which hath its dwelling in the secretest chamber of the heart, began to tremble

so violently that the least pulses of my body shook therewith; and in trembling it said these words: 'Here is a deity stronger than I; who coming, shall rule over me.' At that moment the animate spirit, which dwelleth in the lofty chamber whither all sense carry their perceptions, was filled with wonder, and speaking more especially unto the spirits of the eyes, said these words: 'Your beatitude hath now been made manifest unto you.' At that moment the natural spirit, which dwelleth there where our nourishment is administered, began to weep, and in weeping said these words: 'Alas! How often shall I be disturbed from this time forth.' I say that, from that time forward, Love quite governed my soul …[4]

Beatrice continues to dominate Dante's work, including his famous *La Divina Commedia*, in which she is the guiding image of wisdom and is exalted as the symbol of divine grace. And in a similar vein, the Italian poet, Francesco Petrarch (1304-1374) was also inspired by the unrequited love of a woman called Laura. His *Canzoniere* or 'Songbook' comprises sonnets and odes, detailing the elevation of the human soul from earthly passion to fulfilment through God.

Dante's and Petrarch's poetry belong to the tradition of courtly love, the code of behaviour defining romantic aristocratic relationships. Deriving from the ideas set out by Ovid in his *Ars Amatoria* ('The Art of Loving'), various rules were elaborated through the songs and poems of troubadours and minstrels. Courtly love, usually between a knight or nobleman and a lady of high birth, was effectively akin to a form of sanctioned adultery, since many status marriages of the period were merely business contracts. Paradoxically, infidelity between lovers was considered more of an act of infidelity than an extra marital affair.

The *Roman de la Rose*, the epic French dream allegory composed by Guillaume de Lorris and Jean de Meun, is an exquisite example of this type of literature. It tells the tale of the poet's love for a young girl, who is represented in his dreams as a rosebud growing in a garden. The rose is the familiar symbol of love and divine knowledge, and its gathering is its consummation and union. Such was the poem's impact that the writer Geoffrey Chaucer (1343–1400) would translate some of its verse into Middle English.

The legends of the Holy Grail also fall under the genre of courtly love. Popularized through the works of the twelfth-century French poet, Chrétien de Troyes and the fifteenth-century English writer, Sir Thomas Malory, the Grail quest became synonymous with the Gnostic search to discover the Kingdom of Heaven within. Moreover, Christ's chalice, from which he drank at the Last Supper, became a symbol of his unwavering love and salvation. The search for this relic, therefore, became the inspiration for the legendary knights of the Court of King Arthur and the symbol of their inner spiritual journey.

Moreover, worship of the sacred feminine, with emphasis on the Virgin Mary and Mary Magdalene, starts to re-emerge, particularly within specialist Medieval cults: Alchemy and the Hermetic Arts; the Knights Templar, a religious and military order formed to protect pilgrims visiting Palestine; and the Cathar Church, a nondualist sect who took their philosophical guidance from the Gnostic text, *The Apocrypha of John*. Interestingly, Bernard of Clairvaux, who championed the Cistercian Order, was directed by Pope Eugenius III to eradicate the Cathars' influence but was unable to find fault in their doctrinal theories, despite the fact that they were later suppressed. In fact, Bernard dedicated all his Cistercian abbeys to 'Notre Dame', showing that he, at least, was sympathetic to the sacred feminine.

Indeed, Bernard of Clairvaux was highly respected and wielded great political influence. One woman who sought his counsel was the German Benedictine nun, Hildegard of Bingen. In 1146, he received a letter from her in which she outlined how she had been blessed with a series of visions that had propelled her to write and compose music. Nevertheless, Hildegard was plagued with doubt about the relative merits of her work. In her letter, she explains:

I am very concerned by this vision which has appeared to me in the spirit of mystery, for I have never seen it with the external eyes of the flesh. I who am miserable and more than miserable in my womanly existence have seen great wonders since I was a child. And my tongue could not express them, if God's Spirit did not teach me to believe.[5]

Indeed, she craved approval from Bernard to sanction her spiritual creativity. So impressed was he by her letter that he discussed the matter with Pope Eugenius and papal authority was given for the publication of her works. Within a few years, Hildegard became one of the most renowned female writers and spiritual advisors of Europe, being referred to as the 'Sybil of the Rhine'.

Hildegard of Bingen was born at Bermersheim in Germany in 1098 into a well-established noble family. The tenth and youngest child, she was given as an 'oblate' or offering to the Church at the age of eight, a not uncommon practice. Rather than being placed immediately into a convent, she was put under the care of Jutta of Spanheim. A couple of years later she and Hildegard joined the monastery of Disibodenberg, which housed both monks and nuns, whereupon she took the veil. Upon Jutta's death in 1136, Hildegard succeeded her as abbess.

Hildegard experienced many visions throughout her life. In her autobiographical notes, she recalls her childhood and how she felt called to the voice of prophecy from the Divine:

Wisdom teaches in the light of love, and bids me tell how I was brought into this my gift of vision ... 'Hear these words, human creature, and tell them not according to yourself but according to me, and, taught by me, speak of yourself like this.' In my first formation, when in my mother's womb, God raised me up with the breath of life, he fixed this vision in my soul ... And in the third year of my life I saw so great a brightness that my soul trembled: yet because of my infant condition I could express nothing of it. But in my eighth year I was offered to God, given over to a spiritual way of life, and till my fifteenth year I saw many things, speaking of a number of them in a simple way, so that those who heard me wondered from where they might have come or from whom they may be.[6]

It was not until her fortieth year that she finally felt compelled to share her visions, encouraged by her lifelong and trusted friend, the monk, Volmar, schoolmaster of the monastery. Hildegard was keen to stress that her insights were nothing to do with dreams or hallucinations or trance – her experience was viewed with her inner eye whilst she remained perfectly lucid throughout. Nevertheless, Hildegard suffered intense sickness during and after her visions whereupon her body was pervaded by 'aerial torments' and her womb was consumed with an 'aerial fire'. Reflecting on her life in her seventies, Hildegard said:

> Since my infancy, however, when I was not yet strong in my bones and nerves and veins, I have always seen this vision in my soul, even till now, when I am more than seventy years old. And as God wills, in this vision my spirit mounts upwards, into the height of the firmament and into changing air, and dilates itself among different nations, even though they are far-off regions and places remote from me. And because I see these things in such a manner, for this reason I also behold them in changing forms of clouds and other created things. But I hear them not with my physical ears, not with my heart's thoughts, nor do I perceive them by bringing any of my five senses to bear – but only in my soul, my physical eyes open, so that I never suffer their failing in loss of consciousness [*extasis*]; no, I see these wakefully, day and night. And I am constantly oppressed by illness, and so enmeshed in physical pains that they threaten to bring on my death; but so far God has stayed me.[7]

In 1150, inspired by yet another vision, Hildegard decided to leave Disibodenberg to establish her own independent nunnery at Rupertsberg on the Rhine, near the town of Bingen, where she was elected abbess. With a group of twenty or so nuns, physical life initially was intolerable, with little material comforts. Many nuns subsequently abandoned the newly formed monastery, including Hildegard's closest female confidante and protégée, Richardis of Stade, which caused her to suffer intense feelings of loss and betrayal.

Nonetheless, as the years passed, Hildegard's inner life took on new strength. She undertook preaching tours and engaged in correspondence with all the major thinkers and theologians of her time. Most importantly, she embarked on a writing project of encyclopaedic proportions to systematize her experiences of God. The many visions she had witnessed throughout her life were thus recorded and arranged into a sequence of three interconnected books written in Latin: *Know the Way* (completed 1151); *The Book of Life's Merits* (1163); and *The Book of Divine Works* (1173). Within the framework of the books, Hildegard also addressed subjects as diverse as the nature of the cosmos, the meaning of the Trinity as well as various ethical and social issues. She also compiled non-mystical texts, in particular two prose works entitled *Causes and Cures* and *Physica*, which focus on the natural world and medicine.

In 'Know the Way' or *Scivias*, her major religious work taking ten years to complete and comprising twenty-six visions, the third vision is an allegorical representation of the universe. In it she describes a 'cosmic egg', consisting of a series of concentric ovals – the outermost being a ring of bright flames; the next, a layer of dark violent fire; and then a star-filled region surrounding a circle of moisture. At the centre of the egg is a globe within which is a mountain. She writes:

> I saw a huge form, rounded and shadowy, and shaped like an egg;
> it was pointed at the top, wide in the middle and narrower at the
> bottom. The large form which you see represents, on the level of
> faith, the omnipotent God, incomprehensible in its majesty, incon-
> ceivable in his mysteries, the hope of all the faithful.[8]

Despite Hildegard's vision being steeped in Christian theology, she is intimately aware of the underlying unity of the universe. Moreover, in a radical departure from her theological contemporaries, she places repeated emphasis on the sacred feminine by outlining in the fourth vision the relationship between God and the mother of humankind:

Then I saw a most great and serene splendour, flaming, as it were, with many eyes, with four corners pointing towards the four parts of the world, which was manifest to me in the greatest mystery to show me the secret of the Supernal Creator; and in it appeared another splendour like the dawn, containing in itself a brightness of purple lightning. And behold! I saw on the earth people carrying milk in earthen vessels and making cheeses from it; and one part was thick, and from it strong cheeses were made; and one part was thin, and from it weak cheeses were curdled; and one part was mixed with corruption, and from it bitter cheeses were formed. And I saw the image of a woman who had a perfect human form in her womb. And behold! By the secret design of the Supernal Creator that form moved with vital motion, so that a fiery globe that had no human lineaments possessed the heart of that and touched its brain and spread itself through all its members.

But then this human form, in this way vivified, came forth from the woman's womb and changed its colour according to the movement the globe made in that form ...[9]

In the fifth vision, Hildegard focuses on Synagogue, an enormous female figure 'like the tower of a city':

... you see the image of a woman, pale from her head to her navel; she is the Synagogue, which is the mother of the Incarnation of the Son of God. From the time her children began to be born until their full strength she foresaw in the shadows the secrets of God but did not fully reveal them ...[10]

And describing the way in which the soul rules over the body, she uses another familiar metaphor, again in the fourth vision:

The soul in the body is like sap in a tree, and the soul's powers are like the form of the tree. How? The intellect in the soul is like the greenery of the tree's branches and leaves, the will like its flowers, the mind like its bursting first fruits, the reason like the perfected mature fruit, and the sense like its size and shape. And so a person's body is strengthened and sustained by the soul. Hence, O human, understand what you are in your soul …[11]

Greenness and greenery are recurrent themes in Hildegard's prose. Associated with the moist pastures of paradise, it continues the theme of the divine spirit pervading the entire created world as an eternal life-giving force. Indeed, one of the most breathtaking features of *Scivias* is the fact that the text was illuminated by a contemporary monk or nun in order to enhance and embellish Hildegard's visionary message. In a psychedelic epiphany of colour and form, each vision has an accompanying illustration. Unfortunately, the original Rupertsberg manuscript vanished in the bombing of Dresden and has not been seen since 1945. Nevertheless, a hand-painted facsimile on parchment made by the nuns of Eibingen provides an accurate copy.

The Book of Life's Merits, the second volume in Hildegard's great trilogy, develops the sequence of her visions, concentrating this time on the ethical and moral position of the human race within the divinely ordered cosmos. It is her final text, *The Book of Divine Works*, however, which is the crowning glory of her work. Again written over a period of ten years, it comprises ten visions and centres on the opening passage from the Gospel of St John, 'In the beginning was the word …' Most importantly in this work, she uses once again a female figure to convey her mystical message by opening the first vision with the image of a beautiful woman. Reminiscent to Sophia appearing to Boethius, Hildegard's literary powers are in their zenith:

And I saw amid the airs of the South in the mystery of God a beautiful and marvellous image of a human figure; her face was of such beauty and brightness that I could more easily have stared at the sun. On her head she had a broad band of gold. And in that golden band above her head there appeared a second face, like an old man, whose chin and beard touched the top of the first head. Wings protruded from behind the neck of the figure on either side, and rising up clear of the golden band their tips met and joined overhead. On the right, above the sweep of the wing, was an image of an eagle's head, and I saw it had eyes of fire in which there appeared the brilliance of angels as in a mirror. On the left, above the sweep of the wing, was the image of a human face, which shone like the brightness of the stars. Their faces were turned towards the East … 12

And in a remarkable passage, she utters one of the most exquisite nondualist passages ever written. In the manner of an excerpt from one of the *Gnostic Gospels* or the Upanishads, Hildegard describes the mystical vision:

The figure spoke: I am the supreme fire and energy. I have kindled all the sparks of the living, and I have breathed out no mortal things, for I judge them as they are. I have properly ordained the cosmos, flying about the circling circle with my upper wings, that is with wisdom. I am the fiery life of divine substance, I blaze above the beauty of the fields, I shine in the waters, I burn in sun, moon and stars. And I awaken all to life with every wind of the air, as with invisible life that sustains everything. For the air lives in greenness and fecundity. The waters flow as though they were alive. The sun also lives in its own light, and when the moon has waned it is rekindled by the light of the sun and thus lives again; and the stars shine out of their own light as though they are alive …

Thus I am concealed in things as fiery energy. They are ablaze through me, like the breath that ceaselessly enlivens the human being, or like the wind-tossed flame in a fire. All these things live in their essence, and there is no death in them, for I am life. I also am rationality, who holds the breath of the resonant word by which the whole of creation was created; and I have breathed life into everything, so that nothing by its nature may be mortal, for I am life.

And I am life: not the life struck from stone, or blossoming from branches, or rooted in man's fertility, but life in its fullness, for all living things have their roots in me. Reason is the root, through which the resonant word flourishes.13

Everything in the creation is holy to Hildegard – even the sexual act, dismissed as 'sinful' by so many of her contemporary theologians, is heralded as a wonderful expression of the Divine. In her medical notes, she writes:

> When a woman is making love with a man, a sense of heat in her brain, which brings forth with its sensual delight, communicates the taste of that delight during the act and summons forth the emission of the man's seed …[14]

Indeed, for a virgin, Hildegard displays a surprising and yet intuitive understanding of the sexual feelings between men and women:

> The man's love compared with the woman's, is a heat of ardour like a fire on blazing mountains, which can hardly be put out, whilst hers is a wood fire that is easily quenched; but the woman's love, compared with the man's is like a sweet warmth proceeding from the sun, which brings forth fruits …[15]

As well as being blessed with the power of the pen, Hildegard also had the gift of composing music, 'the sacred sound through which all creation resounds'.[16] For her, the soul was 'symphonic' and resonated with the rhythms and harmonies of the universe. Although she had no musical training, she composed choral music for the liturgy, written as texts with nuems (medieval musical notation), which are collected together in the *Symphony of the Harmony of Celestial Revelations*. Again, Hildegard uses her musical voice to praise the sacred feminine in a song entitled 'O Virtus Sapientiae':

> *Power of Wisdom,*
> *circling all things,*
> *comprehending all things,*
> *on one path, which has life.*

Three wings:
one soars in the height,
one exudes from the earth,
one soars everywhere.
Praise to you, as befits you, Wisdom.[17]

Modern recordings of her songs reveal a haunting sophistication, often with melancholic undertones, more prevalent with more modern polyphony than medieval plainsong.

Hildegard of Bingen lived a long life and her creative output is almost unsurpassed. Before she died, a scandal erupted in the nunnery at Rupertsberg involving the burial of a young nobleman (believed by the Church to have been excommunicated) in the convent cemetery. The upshot of the affair was that the nuns were forbidden to take part in communion or to sing the liturgy. Although the situation was finally resolved by much pleading on Hildegard's part, it left a bitter taste. After all, how could a respected abbess be subject to petty protocol after a lifetime's service to God?

Hildegard died in 1179, aged eighty-one. Hers was a life imbued with courage and determination in the face of ongoing religious and political misogyny. Moreover, her feisty persona gave her the strength not only to manage a thriving convent but channel her spiritual visions into some of the most beautiful celestial music and prose ever to be produced.

chapter thirteen

Sun Bu-er

Meanwhile, back in the East in China, yet another distinct philosophical system founded in the mystical teaching was emerging and came to be known as Taoism. However, prior to its systemization, the age-old beliefs of Chinese shamanism placed worship of the universal Mother Goddess at its very core. One of the most popular female deities whose legacy was absorbed into the Taoist faith was the Queen Mother of the West, who lived in the mythological Garden of Paradise. Within the garden was an immense and magical tree, laden with luscious peaches. It is said that whoever eats the fruit of the tree will gain immortality (in the same manner as the Gnostic text, *The Reality of the Rulers*). As her story becomes assimilated into the Taoist tradition during the Han Dynasty, a legend arises of her meeting King Father of the East, as beautifully described in the *Han Wu ku-shih*, composed by a Taoist sage sometime between the second and sixth centuries CE:

> That night, at the seventh division of the clock, there was not a cloud in the sky; it was dark, as if one might hear the sound of thunder, and stretching to the edge of the heavens there was a purple glow. By and by the Queen Mother arrived. She rode in a purple carriage, with the daughters of jade riding on each side; she wore the sevenfold crown upon her head; the sandals on her feet were black and glistening, embellished with the design of a

phoenix; and the energies of new growth were like a cloud. There were two green birds, like crows, attending on either side of the Mother.

When she alighted from her carriage the emperor greeted her and bowed down, and invited her to be seated. He asked for the drug of deathlessness, and the Queen said, 'Of the drugs of long, long ago, there were those such as the Purple Honey of the Blossoms of the centre; the Scarlet honey of the Mountains of the clouds; or the Golden juice of the fluid of jade ... But the emperor harbours his desires and will not let them go, and there are many things for which his heart still yearns; he may not yet attain the drug of deathlessness.'

Then the Queen drew out seven peaches; two she ate herself and five she gave to the emperor ... She stayed with him until the fifth watch, and although she discussed matters of this world, she was not willing to talk of ghosts or spirits; and with a rustle she disappeared ...[1]

Other women who are honoured by the Taoist tradition form part of the Eight Immortals, a group of male and female sages renowned for their holiness and wisdom. Their tales and biographies are told by Huai Nan Tsu (d. 122 BCE), grandson of Emperor Kao Tsu and founder of the Han Dynasty. In his *History of the Great Light*, which also expounds the teachings of the Tao, he speaks of the lives of two important women, revered to this very day. The first is Lan Ts'ai Ho, a strolling minstrel, who sings of the unreality of the world and its sensual pleasures. Dressed in a blue robe, she reputedly only wore one shoe. It is said that at the end of her life, she disappeared into a cloud. Pictorially, she is represented by a basket of flowers and is the patron saint of florists.

The second woman, and of greater importance, is Ho Hsien Ku, the Immortal Maiden. In a story of tremendous courage and steadfastness, the young maiden is the servant girl to a bitter and miserly old woman. When Ho Hsien Ku feeds seven starving beggars, she is severely reprimanded by her mistress for wasting her food, who demands that Ho Hsien Ku goes and finds the beggars so that they can vomit back up that which they have taken:

> She pushed the tearful and frightened Ho Hsien Ku to the floor and the helpless girl was forced to put a handful of the vomited noodles in her mouth. As soon as the noodles touched her tongue she felt her body become lighter and lighter. She felt her legs rise from the ground and her body began to float away from the spiteful old woman, away from the home where she had suffered so miserably.
>
> The old woman began to panic and turned round to demand an explanation from the beggars but they too had risen high above the house. She caught a last glimpse of the beggars before they disappeared into the clouds and her servant, Ho Hsien Ku, was in their midst.
>
> The Seven Immortals had come to earth to test the young girl's character and she had proved herself worthy of her immortality. Because she had endured suffering without complaint and given to the poor without thought for herself, she could work alongside the Immortals for eternity.[2]

It is said that Ho Hsien Ku lived in the mountains eating mother-of-pearl and moonbeams and is represented pictorially standing on a lotus flower.

Taoism is one of the traditional religions of China, along with Buddhism, and its mystical roots can be traced to sages living as far back as 3000 BCE, taking many of its precepts from the Chinese text, the *I Ching* or 'Book of Changes'. However, it wasn't until the sixth century BCE that the maxims of Taoism were recorded in written form by the Old Master, Lao Tsu (b. 601 BCE), in his spiritual masterpiece, the *Tao Te Ching*.

Literally, the Tao is the eternal Spirit, the undifferentiated consciousness that permeates the entire universe (rather like Purusha or Siva); *Te* is manifest phenomena, differentiated matter in all its myriad forms and designs (Prakriti or Shakti); and *Ching* simply means book. The story goes that after a lifetime's service as the Curator of the

Imperial Library at K'au, Lao Tsu decided to withdraw from the world and all its worries and retire to the country. En route, he rested at the pass of Hsien-ku where he stayed with its keeper, Yin Hsi. A spiritual seeker, he persuaded Lao Tsu to write down his philosophical insights, which we now know as the *Tao Te Ching*. In eighty-one short chapters, its perennial wisdom is as profound today as it was then:

> *The Tao that can be told is not the eternal Tao.*
> *The name that can be named is not the eternal name.*
> *The nameless is the beginning of heaven and earth.*
> *The named is the mother of ten thousand things.*
> *Ever desireless, one can see the mystery.*
> *Ever desiring, one sees the manifestations.*
> *These two spring from the same source but differ in name; this appears*
>   *as darkness.*
> *Darkness within darkness.*
> *The gate to all mystery.*[3]

Interestingly, Lao Tsu was one of those rare sages who gives great emphasis to the sacred feminine. He appreciates that it is an intrinsic aspect of creation:

> *The valley spirit never dies;*
> *It is the woman, primal mother.*
> *Her gateway is the root of heaven and earth.*
> *It is like a veil barely seen.*
> *Use it; it will never fail.*[4]

Understanding all the subtleties of the universe, he exquisitely recounts the understanding of the mystics:

> *Give up learning, and put an end to your troubles.*
>
> *Is there a difference between yes and no?*
> *Is there a difference between good and evil?*

Must I fear what others fear? What nonsense!
Other people are contented, enjoying the sacrificial feast of the ox.
In spring some go to the park, and climb the terrace,
But I alone am drifting, not knowing where I am.
Like a newborn babe before it learns to smile,
I am alone, without a place to go.

Others have more than they need, but I alone have nothing.
I am a fool. Oh yes! I am confused.
Others are clear and bright,
But I alone am dim and weak.
Others are sharp and clever,
But I alone am dull and stupid.
Oh, I drift like the waves of the sea,
Without direction, like the restless wind.

Everyone else is busy,
But I alone am aimless and depressed.
I am different.
I am nourished by the great mother.[5]

Another great exponent of Taoism was the venerable Chuang Tsu, who, like Lao Tsu, had tasted the Infinite. Living in the third century BCE, his written accounts of the Tao, collated in the *Book of Chuang Tsu* were, by contrast, much longer, often allegorical, expositions. Legend has it that he lived in the kingdom of Wei and, owing to his wise reputation, was asked by the King to come and work for him, to which he replied that he would rather work in a filthy ditch than be subject to the restrictions and hypocrisy of a court. A man of supreme sagacity, Chuang Tsu says:

I guard my awareness of the One and rest in harmony with exter-nals ... My light is the light of the Sun and the moon. My life is the life of heaven and earth. Before me is the undifferentiated [*Te*] and behind me is the Unknowable [Tao]. Men may die but I will endure forever.[6]

Both Lao Tsu and Chuang Tsu also recognized that within the *Te* is the dance of the complementary forces – the yang, the positive, and sometimes referred to as masculine; and the yin, the negative, and sometimes referred as feminine. Like the Hindu *gunas* of *rajas* and *tamas* respectively, the balancing of these forces yields the natural, *sattvic*, state. As Chuang Tsu writes:

> In the beginning, even nothing did not exist. There was only the Tao. Then something unnamed which did not yet have form came into existence from the Tao. This is *Te*, from which all the world came into being. Things had not received their forms, but the division of the yang and the yin Principles, which are intimately related, had already appeared. This vibratory motion constitutes all creation. When the yang and the yin become active, all things come into being. It is in this way that *Te* created all forms.[7]

The ritualization of Taoism through the centuries saw, just as with all religious institutions, a patriarchal structure emerge in the officiating of ceremonies and duties. Nevertheless, owing to the fact that the feminine principle, the yin, is an intrinsic element of the Tao itself, the sacred feminine is highly honoured. Indeed, despite the majority of texts written by and for men, there is the repeated emphasis on the need to discover the female energy within. Many alchemical practices were cultivated by Taoist adepts, including the visualization of the Jade Woman, a celestial guardian of immortality, in an act of lovemaking:

> ... actualize a young woman as present within the sun or the moon. A purple cap is placed on her head, and she has a cloak and skirt of vermilion damask. She calls herself the Jade Woman of the Cinnabar Aurora of the Highest Mysteries of the Greatest Mystery ...

From her mouth she exhales a red pneuma which fills the space between the light-rays from sun or moon completely. It combines with them until rays and auroral glow are both used up, then gushes into one's own mouth. One masters it and gulps it down. Actualize the woman also as exhaling it in sequence; activate it nine times ten. After these have been gulped down, actualize a conscious command to the phosphor of the sun or moon to press intimately close upon one's face, and command the Jade Woman's mouth press a kiss upon your own mouth, causing the liquor of the pneuma to come down into the mouth … This done, actualize the salival liquid from the mouth of the Jade Woman, commanding it to gush into one's own mouth. Then, having rinsed it with the liquor, proceed to swallow it …

Perform these things for five years and the Jade Woman of Greatest Mystery will come down to you, and lie down to take her ease with you … This is the ultimate in accumulating resonance, in knotting germinal essences together, in transmuting life …[8]

One of the greatest women Taoist sages is immortalized in the anonymous sixteenth-century text, *Seven Taoist Masters*. Like Yeshe Tsogyal, Sun Bu-er's story is a blend of fact and fiction but her biography gives an insight into a woman possessing profound mystical knowledge. Meaning 'peerless', Sun Bu-er (and also written as Sun Pu-erh) was born in 1124 CE in Shantung, China. She had three children and her husband, Ma Tan-yang, was a devotee of the well-known Taoist teacher, Wang Ch'ung-yang, from whom she too wanted to receive instruction.

Nevertheless, Wang Ch'ung-yang was not satisfied as to whether she was committed enough to understand the message of the Tao. Moreover, in order to receive the proper training, she would need to travel to the city of Loyang, over a thousand miles away – the journey would be long and, owing to her physical beauty, she would be risking molestation along the way. But Sun Bu-er was undeterred. Immediately she went to the kitchen and heated a wok full of oil. She then poured in cold water causing the oil to spit and sizzle. Closing her eyes, she let the burning liquid splatter her face, causing the skin to blister and burn. She then returned to Wang Ch'ung-yang and asked him again if she could receive spiritual instruction – this time, impressed by her sacrificial act, he agreed.

After teaching her the methods of internal alchemy, Wang Ch'ung-yang showed Sun Bu-er how to unite yin and yang within. When he was satisfied that she had progressed enough, he speaks to her thus:

> 'Remember, hide your knowledge. Do not let people know you are a seeker of the Tao. After you have finished the Great Alchemical Work, then you may reveal yourself and teach others. In the meantime, let your face heal. Do not even let your servants know of your plans. Leave as soon as you are ready. You need not come to say farewell to me. We shall meet again soon at the celebration of the ripening of the immortal peach.'9

Feigning madness, she ran away from her husband and set off, at the age of fifty-one, for Loyang, living in caves and begging for food along the way. After twelve years of seclusion and spiritual practice in the city, she achieved immortality. Desiring to instruct her fellow townsfolk of her new-found wisdom, it is said that she transformed two branches into a man and woman and bid them to cavort shamelessly through the streets. Causing a public outcry, the community gathered one day to burn the illustrious couple. A fire was lit and then suddenly, Sun Bu-er allegedly appeared seated on a cloud, saying:

> 'I have finally attained the Tao and today I shall be carried into the heavens by fire and smoke. I transformed two branches into a man and a woman so that circumstances would lead you here to witness the mystery and the powers of the Tao. In return for your kindness and hospitality to me through the years I shall give you this couple. They will be your guardians, and I shall see to it that your harvests will be plentiful and your city protected from plagues and natural disasters.'10

For the next five years, it is said that Loyang enjoyed great wealth and prosperity. Meanwhile, Sun Bu-er returned to the home of her husband only to be disappointed by his comparatively small spiritual progress. Reprimanded thus by his wife for his overly comfortable lifestyle, Ma Tan-yang immediately renounced his material possessions and set off for the city of Loyang.

Owing to her supreme knowledge of the Tao, Sun Bu-er was given the honorary title of Immortal Sister. She collected many devotees over the years, as well as recorded her spiritual understanding in a collection of poetry and prose. It is not clear exactly when her *Fourteen Verses* were composed, however, they form a sequence of exquisite aphorisms upon which the earnest seeker can meditate:

> *Before our energy existed,*
> *One energy was already there.*
> *Like jade, more lustrous as it's polished,*
> *Like gold, brighter as it's refined.*
> *Sweep clear the ocean of birth and death,*
> *Stay firm by the door of total mastery.*
> *A particle at the point of open awareness,*
> *The gentle firing is warm.*[11]

This is Sun Bu-er's invocation to proceed along the Way of the Tao, to sweep away the sea of samsara and to remain vigilant at all times. (The 'door of total mastery' refers to what Lao Tsu called the Mysterious Pass, the place where yang and yin are in harmony.)

Only through controlling the breath and reining in thought, can the spiritual aspirant be restored to the elixir of the Tao and the secret of immortal life:

> *If you want the elixir to form quickly,*
> *First get rid of illusory states.*
> *Attentively guard the spiritual medicine;*
> *With every breath return to the beginning of the creative.*

The energy returns, coursing through the three islands;
The spirit, forgetting, unites with the ultimate.
Coming this way and going this way,
No place is not truly so.[12]

This process can take a moment to realize or the length of one's entire life. Either way, practice must be sincere and sustained:

All things finished,
You sit still in a little niche.
The light body rides on violet energy,
The tranquil nature washes on a pure pond.
Original energy is unified, yin and yang are one;
The spirit is the same as the universe.
When the work is done, you pay court to the Jade Palace;
A long whistle gusts a misty gale.[13]

As well as the *Fourteen Verses*, Sun Bu-er recorded three 'secret texts' that were revealed to her through the words of contemporary Taoist adepts and, supposedly, beings from higher levels of existence. The first text, *Unexcelled True Scripture of Inner Experiences of Jadelike Purity*, handed down by the 'Celestial Mother of Violet Light', recounts the beginning of the universe and the creation of human beings:

The Primal Ultimately Real Sacred One produced life and opened up the heavens, used the power of great spiritual capacities and great intelligence to form the world, pair yin and yang, and set forth evolution.

First, in the occult space of the real heaven of great purity, It produced external images to represent internal experiences. It separated the energy of nine to make the colour of wood essence of the east, forming an ideal person of the energy of nine to rule it ...

The true director of the infinity of the two mysteries of the right and left disseminates our Way among celestials and humans, inducing them to abandon deeds that cause impermanence and enter the subtlety of true unity, neither ageing nor dying, peacefully existing forever.

The Primal Revered One emanated great light from Its seven openings, illuminating infinite lands, twelve thousand heavens and a hundred billion human worlds, each of which used its own power to scatter scents and shower flowers as offerings. All were delighted, and all came to understand the original mind.[14]

She then goes on to point to the way in which human beings can rekindle their inner vitality and a level of deeper awareness:

> *One mind produces right concentration,*
> *Myriad forms are spontaneously arrayed,*
> *Five energies are distributed through the quarters.*
> *The five energies are pregnant with one spirit,*
> *The one spirit pervades transformations,*
> *Crystallizing and refining the original reality.*
> *The original reality is not something with form:*
> *It is neither existent nor nonexistent.*
> *If people can penetrate this principle,*
> *Then they'll understand the pearl that unifies sense experience.*[15]

The second text, *True Scripture on Inner Nourishment of the Embryonic Basis of Judelike Purity*, revealed by the 'Real Leader of the Original Terrace of the Jewel Spirit', recounts the tale of The Great Exalted One, the Old Master Lao Tsu, who pays a visit to The High Lord of the Original Beginning and who is told of the Way of the Tao:

> I have given you the sublime Tao of the embryonic basis – combine the outer mysterious female with the inner mysterious female, use the outer true spirit to augment the inner true energy. Gather the myriad treasures of heaven, nurture the basic vitality of your embryo, causing the spirit to live in the embryo and the energy to

cleave the spirit. The mind-ruler subtlety controls the energy, and the breathing is tuned evenly. Then myriad spirits will honour you, and all demons will disappear.[16]

The Great Exalted One then produces countless incarnations, who together all sing of his praise:

The supreme spiritual father,
Revealing a great expedient,
Has commanded the Great Exalted One
And the Celestial Mother of the Violet Light
To produce incarnations in the lower regions
To liberate multitudes of us.

By discipline and concentration
We all attain higher birth,
Gain mentally produced bodies,
And realize the unexcelled Tao.

We magically produce
Millions of bodies,
Eternally celebrating mystic virtues
Forever inexhaustible.

Those magnificent virtues
Cannot be fully comprehended.
We believe in them –
How shall we ever repay?

We promise to make great vows
That last for ever more.
Also to liberate sentient beings –
This intention alone
Is called requiting virtue.[17]

As ever, of utmost importance in Sun Bu-er's writings is the theme of disciplining the mind through the practice of self-enquiry, which leads to a discovery of the 'real source'. The third text, *Precious Treatise on Preservation of Unity on the Great Way or The Mind-Mirror of the Mystic Pearl*, also advocates the necessity of self knowledge. Reminiscent in style to the cryptic teachings of Lao Tsu, it was revealed to her by the 'Realized One of Mount Heng', (Mount Heng being one of the five holy mountains of China):

> *The Tao is uncontrived, yet there is nothing it does not do.*
> *It can be witnessed by the mind, not known by knowledge.*
> *What is 'knowing'? What is 'witness'?*
> *Knowledge dismisses knowledge.*

> *(This means that after you know, you should dismiss knowledge, hide your tracks, and conceal your light.)*

Witness openly responds.

(This means when you keep empty and open, without contrivance, eventually there is spiritual effect, like en echo responding to a sound.)

Response comes from nowhere.

(This means it is spontaneous.)

Mind then penetrates.

(When the mind is empty, without contrivance, eventually it understands the Tao; understanding the Tao, spirit penetrates.)

Penetrate the One, and all tasks are undone. The One is the root.

(The One is the root of the Tao.)

The task is the door.

(*Attaining the basis of the One is the mind seal of the Great Exalted One. This is what is called the task.*)

When the task returns to One, the One is ever present.

(*This refers to the task of keeping to the One; when the work is done, you return to one energy, whereupon the body and open selfishness naturally are formless and one energy is ever present.*)

The presence should not be reified;
provisionally we speak of keeping to it.

(*This means that the one energy is ever present, and we should not reify the energy in our own bodies – to speak of preserving the One or keeping to the One is only a provisional expression.*)

Keep open selflessness and naturally be eternal.

(*This means just preserve open selflessness, and your spirit and body will naturally endure forever with the Tao.*)[18]

Sun Bu-er not only understood the nature of the sacred feminine but also knew it to be an intrinsic aspect of the One, a vital partner in the dance of the Tao. Indeed, interest in modern times in the teachings of Taoism is testament to the need for harmony between yin and yang and the appreciation of their complementarity in the universe and our daily lives.

chapter fourteen

The Beguines

In 1225, Thomas Aquinas was born, one of the most influential thinkers of medieval Europe. Greatly affected by Aristotle, his greatest work, the *Summa Theologica*, is a survey of Catholic theology, whose legacy can be felt even to this day. Despite his impressive reasoning acumen, drawing on biblical and classical sources, Aquinas held the then common belief that women were inferior to men. Although he conceded that the female form was necessary for procreation, he was adamant as to her position in the cosmos:

> I answer that, when all things were first formed, it was more suitable for the woman to be made from the man than [for the female to be from the male] in other animals. First, in order thus to give the first man a certain dignity consisting in this, that as God is the principle of the whole universe, so the first man, in likeness to God, was the principle of the whole human race ... each has his or her particular duty, and in which the man is the head of the woman. Wherefore it was suitable for the woman to be made out of man, as out of his principle.[1]

Interestingly, in the year before his death, Aquinas had a complete realization of the unity of God. On 6th December 1273, after a lifetime's research into the nature of Reality, he was sitting in Mass and, without warning, was permeated with the timeless wisdom of the mystics. Describing the experience, he wrote, 'All that I have written seems to me like straw compared to what has now been revealed to me.'[2] He died four months later without writing another single word.

A near contemporary of Aquinas living in Germany was also writing about the Divine – the scholar Johannes Eckhart (1260–1328). After joining the Dominican priory in Erfurt at fifteen years old, he quickly excelled in his religious studies, eventually earning a place at the University of Paris. There he was made 'Master in Sacred Theology' and was referred to thereafter as Meister Eckhart. His major works include *The Talks of Instruction*, *The Book of Divine Consolation* and *On the Noble Man*, as well as innumerable sermons written in both Latin and German.

In a synthesis of Greek and Christian thinking, Meister Eckhart's writings are essentially grounded in the concept of unicity or oneness, from which all of creation emanates and to which it all ultimately returns:

> God is infinite in his simplicity and simple in his infinity. Therefore he is everywhere and is everywhere complete. He is everywhere on account of his infinity, and is everywhere complete on account of his simplicity. Only God flows into all things, their very essences. Nothing else flows into something else. God is in the innermost part of each and every thing, only in its innermost part, and he alone is One.[3]

Also reminiscent to the teachings from the Upanishads, Eckhart heralds the Beatific Vision:

> One with One, one from One, one in One and one in One in all eternity.[4]

Moreover, although he makes no issue over gender, seeing both men and women as aspects of the One, he is keen to demonstrate how oneness differentiates itself in relation to the created world. In similar fashion to the concepts of Purusha and Prakriti, Siva and Shakti,

Eckhart elucidates the difference between the Godhead (*Gottheit*) and God (*Gott*):

> God and the Godhead are as different from each other as heaven and earth … Creatures speak of God – but why do they not mention the Godhead? Because there is only unity in the Godhead and there is nothing to talk about. God acts. The Godhead does not … The difference between God and the Godhead is the difference between action and non-action.[5]

Sadly, as with so many sages of the past, Eckhart's nondualist teachings did not sit well within the orthodox Catholic Church. He was officially charged with heresy and, in 1327, was summoned to the Papal Court in Cologne, where he skilfully answered all accusations against him, managing to escape the death penalty. Despite being the thorn in the side of the Church, his writings have survived as testament to the eternal Truth. Indeed, his nondualist philosophy has influenced many modern-day German thinkers, including the monist philosopher, Arthur Schopenhauer (1788–1860).

One other important theme that Eckhart expounds in his work is the concept of nothingness, the total annihilation of the ego in the Self. In one of his most famous sermons, the *Beati Pauperes Spiritu*, he points to the place beyond time and space, to a place even beyond God:

> When I stood in my first cause, I then had no 'God' and then I was my own cause. I wanted nothing, I longed for nothing, for I was an empty being, and the only truth in which I rejoiced was in the knowledge of myself. Then it was myself I wanted and nothing else. What I wanted I was, and what I was I wanted; and so I stood empty of everything …
>
> Therefore I am the cause of myself in the order of my being, which is eternal and not in the order of my becoming, which is temporal. And therefore I am unborn and in the manner in which I am unborn I can never die. In my unborn manner I have been eternally, and am now, and shall eternally remain.[6]

And it is this theme of nothingness and abandonment in the face of the Eternal that permeates the writings produced by a group of women mystics living between the twelfth and fourteenth centuries around north-western Europe, collectively known as the beguines. Although they lived an essentially communal life, often attached to nearby Franciscan, Cistercian or Dominican communities, they were different from more conventional nuns in that they did not take permanent vows, promising instead to care for the sick, engage in manual labour and not to marry as long as they lived in the beguinage. As well as offering spiritual sustenance, beguine communities were also refuges for women left widowed or unmarried by the large numbers of men either killed or absent in the Crusades. Whatever their reasons for living in such a way, they strove to live an unworldly life whilst living in the world – the middle way between the ascetic and the householder.

The first communities of beguines (men living in the same manner were called beghards) seem to have been organized around 1170 by the revivalist priest Lambert le Bègue in Liège. Owing to the fact that their lives were simple and devoid of more orthodox doctrine and supervision, there naturally arose a purer appreciation of the Gospels and a desire to infiltrate the very heart of Christ's teachings. Indeed, what set them apart from their contemporaries was the belief that the imitation of Christ was not just a means of joining together with him in mystical marriage (*unio spiritus*), but a means of actually becoming *one* with him (*unio indistinctionis*). It was inevitable, therefore, that as the centuries passed, the beguines were subject to increasing suspicion from the established Church with subsequent charges of heresy.

One such beguine was Marguerite Porete. Believed to have been born in Hainault in north-eastern France (formerly in the Flanders region), nothing is known of her exact date of birth or early life. However, sometime between 1296 and 1306, she wrote one of the most important documents detailing the mystical life ever to be written: *The Mirror of Simple Souls*. Indeed, such was its profound effect that the Church authorities, threatened by its powerful wisdom, ordered Marguerite to be burnt at the stake. Unlike Meister Eckhart, she did not argue an effective defence but chose to remain silent throughout the proceedings. She died on 1st June 1310 in the Place de Grève in Paris, becoming the first heretic to be torched to death at the hands of the French Inquisition.

Although all copies of the text were banned by the Church, a number of facsimile editions, translated into Latin, Italian, and Middle English, were distributed to various theologians and scholars across Europe, thus ensuring its survival. One such scholar, upon whom *The Mirror* had a considerable influence was none other than Meister Eckhart. Indeed, there is ample evidence to suggest that whilst Eckhart was on a trip to Paris, he was privy to the unauthorized text.

Written in Old French and addressed to a female audience, the manuscript extends to over 60,000 words and is a dialogue in the manner of troubadour love poetry between *Dame Amour* (Lady Love), and *Raison* (Reason), concerning the conduct of *Ame* (the Soul). Unlike Hildegard, Marguerite makes no apology for writing such a work – her words are imbued with a dazzling self-confidence unique to her time. Indeed, the opening of *The Mirror* immediately sets the tone:

You who would read this book,
If you indeed wish to grasp it,
Think about what you say,
For it is very difficult to comprehend;
Humility, who is keeper of the treasury of Knowledge
And the mother of the other Virtues,
Must overtake you.

Theologians and other clerks,
You will not have the intellect for it,
No matter how brilliant your abilities,
If you do not proceed humbly.
And may Love and Faith, together,
Cause you to rise above Reason,
[Since] they are ladies of the house ...[7]

As a spiritual handbook, Marguerite outlines the 'seven states of grace' along the spiritual path leading to annihilation in the Self. With an intimate knowledge of human psychology, she expounds the soul's ascent towards a oneness of being between lover and Beloved, merging into love itself.

The lower three stages, which, according to Marguerite the soul must go through, include all outward signs of religious practice and moral virtue; the soul must also experience two deaths, namely of 'sin' and of 'nature' in order to move onto the next stage. The fourth stage is where the soul is drenched in love, owing to her repeated contemplation, meditation and ecstasies of prayer. However, according to Marguerite, this is where most spiritual aspirants falter for there still remains an individual soul, exerting an independent will.

It is the fifth stage where the soul must undergo yet another death – that of the individual 'spirit' – in order that the fullness of divine love can flood unimpeded through the being, annihilating and reducing the soul to nothing:

> Now such a soul is nothing, for she sees her nothingness by means of the abundance of divine Understanding, which makes her nothing and places her in nothingness ... Therefore she wills only one thing: the Spouse of her youth, who is only One ... Now she is All, and so she is Nothing, for her Beloved makes her One.[8]

Here, the liberated soul is no longer subject to the more conventional acts of the sacrament of Holy Church. Now, she can list where she wants, free from all religious and ideological restraints. And yet there are still two more states of grace through which she must pass. At the sixth stage, the soul no longer has a separate identity and is merged into everything that is God:

> ... the Soul does not see herself on account of such an abyss of humility which she has within her. Nor does she see God on account of the highest goodness which He has. But God sees Himself in her by His divine majesty, who clarifies this Soul with Himself, so that

she sees only that there is nothing except God Himself who is, from whom all things are. And He who is, is God Himself.[9]

Here we hear the Old Testament psalm echoing once again: 'Be still and know that I am God.'[10] Similarly, willing nothing, being nothing, annihilating oneself in God is the message of Meister Eckhart – indeed the parallels between the two are strikingly similar in theme:

> Ah, Love, says this Soul, the meaning of what is said makes me nothing, and the nothingness of this alone has placed me in an abyss below less than nothingness without measure. And the understanding of my nothingness, says this Soul, has given me the All, and the nothingness of this All, says the Soul, has taken from me prayer, and I pray nothing.[11]

All and nothing – two diametrically opposed states and yet simultaneously coexisting in the One. This is the paradox of mysticism; through the renunciation of the individual 'spirit', the universal soul is attained:

> I shall completely repose in peace, says this Soul, alone and nothing … It is the goal of my work, says this Soul, always to will nothing. For as long as I will nothing, says this Soul, I am alone in Him without myself, completely unencumbered. And if I should will something, she says, I am with myself, and therefore I have lost freeness. But when I will nothing I have lost everything beyond my will, therefore nothing is lacking to me. To be unencumbered is my conduct. I would will nothing at all.[12]

Like the nondualist message of the Upanishads, all that remains is silent awe. Moreover, the seventh and final stage, Marguerite declares, is only knowable when the soul has left the body.

Towards the end of *The Mirror of Simple Souls*, the character of Truth makes an appearance and praises the soul who has reached the sixth stage:

O emerald and precious gem,
True diamond, queen and empress,
You give everything from your fine nobility,
Without asking from Love her riches,
Except the willing of her divine pleasure
Thus is this right by righteousness,
For it is the true path
Of Fine Love, whoever wishes to remain on it.
O deepest spring and fountain sealed,
Where the sun is subtly hidden,
You send your rays, says Truth, through divine knowledge;
We know it through true Wisdom:
Her splendour makes us completely luminous.[13]

The soul answers with a song in praise of herself and of the accomplishment of her spiritual journey. First, she acknowledges her former encumbered state:

I used to be enclosed
In the servitude of captivity,
When desire imprisoned me
In the will of affection.
There the light of ardour
From divine love found me,
Who quickly killed my desire,
My will and affection,
Which impeded in me the enterprise
Of the fullness of divine love ...[14]

However, all attachments and identification have fallen away in the face of the Beloved:

And Divine Love tells me
That she has entered within me,
And so she can do,

Whatever she wills,
Such strength she has given me,
From One Lover whom I possess in Love,
To whom I am betrothed,
Who wills what He loves,
And for this I will love Him.

I have said that I will love Him.
I lie, for I am not.
It is He alone who loves me:
He is, and I am not;
And nothing more is necessary to me
Than what He wills,
And that He is worthy.
He is fullness,
And by this am I impregnated.
This is the divine seed and Loyal Love.[15]

What Marguerite offers is a book that acts as a mirror revealing God's luminosity and fullness – a vision which is ultimately known to be a reflection of oneself. But it was also a vision that was at the expense of her own life.

Another important beguine, of whom we know very little, is Mechthild of Magdeburg (1210–1297), who was born to an aristocratic family living in Saxony. At twenty-three, she decided to leave the comforts of her noble life and become a beguine in the nearby town of Magdeburg. In around 1250, at the age of forty, she confided in her confessor, the Dominican Heinrich of Halle, that she had been experiencing mystical phenomena throughout her life. He urged her to write them down and then later helped her to collate the subsequent manuscript. Thus, over the following twenty years, Mechthild composed the first six books of her spiritual masterpiece, *The Flowing Light of the Godhead*, (written in Middle Low German but given the Latin title *Lux Divinitatis*). Then after moving to the Cistercian community at Helfta where she became gravely ill and almost blind, she dictated the seventh and final book before her death.

The Flowing Light of the Godhead is an intensely powerful treatise on the nature of divine love. She employs many literary genres in the composition of her work – visions, sermons, poetry, allegorical dialogues between Lady Love and Lady Knowledge – in an attempt to convey the immediacy of her mystical life. Her first encounter with the Divine, which occurred in her early twenties, is described in raw intimacy as she recounts the journey of her soul up towards the Creator:

> God's true greeting, coming from the heavenly flood out of the spring of the flowing Trinity, has such force that it takes away all the body's strength and reveals the soul to herself, so that she sees herself resembling the saints, and she takes on a divine radiance. Then the soul leaves the body, taking all her power, wisdom, love and longing. Just the tiniest bit of her life force remains with the body as in a sweet sleep. Then she sees one complete God in three Persons and knows the three Persons in one God undivided.[16]

In the same manner as Hildegard, Mechthild immediately sanctions her writing with God's authority:

> 'Ah, Lord God, who made this book?'
> 'I made it in my powerlessness, for I cannot restrain myself as to my gifts.'
> 'Well then, Lord, what shall the title of the book be, which is to your glory alone?
> 'It shall be called a flowing light of my Godhead into all hearts that live free of hypocrisy.'[17]

Indeed, it is the relationship between the heart of humankind and the heart of God that consumes Mechthild's spiritual quest. It is the agony and ecstasy of two souls involved in the erotic dance of courtship, ultimately merging and dissolving in their mutual love:

'Stay, Lady Soul.'
'What do you bid me, Lord?'
'Take off your clothes.'
'Lord, what will happen to me then?'
'Lady Soul, you are so utterly formed to my nature
That not the slightest thing can be between you and me.
Never was an angel so glorious
That to him was granted for one hour
What is given to you for eternity.
And so you must cast off from you
Both fear and shame and all external virtues.
Rather, those alone that you carry within yourself
Shall you foster forever.
These are your noble longing
And your boundless desire.
These I shall fulfil forever
With my limitless lavishness.'

'Lord, now I am a naked soul
And you in yourself are a well-adorned God.
Our shared lot is eternal life
Without death.'

Then a blessed stillness
That both desire comes over them.
He surrenders himself to her,
And she surrenders herself to him.
What happens to her then – she knows –
And that is fine with me.
But this cannot last long.
When two lovers meet secretly,
They must often part from one another inseparably.[18]

In poetry reminiscent to the *Song of Songs*, Mechthild is lost in her rapture for her Lord. He speaks to her through his 'loving Mouth':

'You are the feelings of love in my desire.
You are a sweet cooling for my breast.
You are a passionate kiss for my mouth.
You are a blissful joy of my discovery.
I am in you
And you are in me.
We could not be closer,
For we two have flowed into one
And have been poured into one mould.
Thus shall we remain forever content.'[19]

Like Marguerite, she renounces all earthly ties and dies unto herself:

Thus you become full of the fire of love.
This makes you here utterly happy.
You can no longer teach me anything.
I cannot turn away from love.
I must be its captive.
Otherwise, I cannot go on living.
Where it dwells, there I must remain,
Both in death and in life.
This is the folly of fools
Who live free of anguish.[20]

Like so many poems in praise of the God, Mechthild understands the paradoxical nature of liberation:

Under this immense force she loses herself.
In this most dazzling light she becomes blind in herself.
And in this blindness she sees most clearly.
In this pure clarity she is both dead and living.

The longer she is dead, the more blissfully she lives.
The more blissfully she lives, the more she experiences.
The less she becomes, the more flows to her ...[21]

So radical was Mechthild's vision that many of her more conservative contemporaries sought to burn its contents. Asking for help, God inspires her thus:

'My dear One, do not be overly troubled.
No one can burn the truth.
For someone to take this book out of my hand,
He must be mightier than I …

'The words symbolize my marvellous Godhead.
It flows continuously
Into your soul from my divine mouth.
The sound of the words is a sign of my living spirit
And through it achieves genuine truth.'[22]

Mechthild inspired many of her contemporary nuns at Helfta to impart their own mystical experiences, including Mechthild of Hackeborn (1241–1298) in *The Book of Special Grace* and Gertrude the Great (1256–1302) in *The Herald of Divine Love*. Unfortunately, *The Flowing Light of the Godhead* fell into oblivion after Mechthild's death – it wasn't until the nineteenth century that any serious interest in her book was shown and an English translation had to wait until 1953.

Another great female mystic of the thirteenth century was the Flemish woman, Hadewijch of Brabant (near Antwerp). Nothing is really known about who she was and exactly when she lived – eleven women living in roughly the same period have been identified with the same name. However, like Marguerite and Mechthild, Hadewijch was a beguine. Most scholars are of the opinion that she lived in a community but was evicted for her radical position – that one's life must be an expression of the oneness of divine love. Indeed, all her works are infused with the passion and abandonment of a lover in the throws of mystical ecstasy.

Recorded in a Brabantine dialect, she composed poetry and a series of letters as well as a sequence of fourteen visions. At the

beginning of Vision Seven, 'Oneness in the Eucharist', she unequiv-
ocally states:

> On a certain Pentecost Sunday I had a vision at dawn. Matins
> were being sung in the church and I was present. My heart and
> my veins and all my limbs trembled and quivered with eager
> desire and, as often occurred with me, such madness and fear
> beset my mind that it seemed to me that if I did not content my
> Beloved, and my Beloved did not fulfil my desire, so that dying I
> must go mad, and going mad I must die. On that day my mind
> was beset so fearfully and so painfully by desirous love that all my
> separate limbs threatened to break, and all my separate veins
> were in travail.[23]

Hadewijch also displays the same nondualist vision as her contemporary beguines. In the letter, 'He in Me and I in Him', she speaks of
the soul manifesting in the One:

> May God make known to you, dear chid, who he is and how he
> deals with his servants and especially with his handmaids – and may
> he submerge you in him!
>   Where the abyss of his wisdom is, he will teach you what he is,
> and with what wondrous sweetness the loved one and the Beloved
> dwell one in the other, and how they penetrate each other in such
> a way that neither of the two distinguishes himself from the other.
> But they abide in one another in fruition, mouth in mouth, heart in
> heart, body in body, and soul in soul, while one sweet *divine Nature*
> flows through them both, and they are both one thing through
> each other, but at the same time remain two different selves – yes,
> remain so forever.[24]

Hadewijch employs the language of courtly love to describe her feelings. Moreover, the bittersweet taste of the lover is a theme that
fascinates Hadewijch, no more beautifully composed in the poem,
'Paradoxes of Love':

The storming of love is what is sweetest within her,
Her deepest abyss is her most beautiful form,
To lose our way in her is to arrive,
To hunger for her is to feed and to taste,
Her despairing is sureness of faith,
Her worst wounding is to become whole again,
To waste away for her is to endure,
Her hiding is to find her at all times,
To be tormented for her is to be in good health,
In her concealment she is revealed.

What she withholds, she gives,
Her finest speech is without words,
Her imprisonment is freedom,
Her most painful blow is her sweetest consolation,
Her giving is her taking away,
Her going away is her coming near,
Her deepest silence is her highest song,
Her greatest wrath is her warmest thanks,
Her greatest threatening is remaining true,
Her sadness is the healing of all sorrow.[25]

Despite having a profound effect on the great Dutch mystic, Jan van Ruusbroec (1293–1381) and in all probability, Beatrice of Nazareth (1200–1268), the Flemish author of the mystical treatise, *On the Seven Manners of Loving*, Hadewijch's work unfortunately fell into oblivion. It was not until the nineteenth century that her manuscripts were uncovered in the British Library of Brussels and the light of her wisdom was revealed once again.

In 1312, the Council of Vienne decreed that the way of life of the beguines and beghards be forbidden. But worse was yet to come. In the middle of the fifteenth century, two Dominican Inquisitor priests, Heinrich Kramer and James Sprenger, composed a handbook outlining the evil nature of women and practices deemed as witch-craft. Known as the *Malleus Maleficarum*, ('The Hammer of

Witches'), it became the authoritative text used to flush out perceived female dissenters for the following three hundred years. Continuing in the same vein as Augustine, women were perceived as inferior, substandard human beings. According to the *Malleus Maleficarum*:

> And it should be noted that there was a defect in the formation of the first woman, since she was formed from a bent rib, that is, a rib of the breast, which is bent as it were in a contrary direction to a man. And since through this defect she is an imperfect animal, she always deceives ... And all this is indicated by the etymology of the word; for *Femina* comes from *Fe* and *Minus* ...[26]

Moreover, Kramer and Sprenger believed women to be sex-obsessed consorts of the devil:

> All witchcraft comes from carnal lust, which is in women insatiable. There are three things that are never satisfied [infidelity, ambition, lust], yea a fourth thing which says not 'It is enough' that is the mouth of the womb. Wherefore for the sake of fulfilling their lusts they consort even with devils ...
>
> Now there are, as it is said in the Papal Bull, seven methods by which they infect with witchcraft the venereal act and the conception of the womb: first, by inclining the minds of men to inordinate passion; second, by obstructing their generative force; third, by removing the members accommodated to that act; fourth, by changing men into beasts by their magic art; fifth, by destroying the generative force in women; sixth, by procuring abortion; seventh, by offering children to devils, besides other animals and fruits of the earth with which they work much harm.[27]

Unfortunately, the specific reference to childbirth put the lives of many women acting as midwives in jeopardy, owing to their specific knowledge of birth control, abortion and the use of medicinal herbs. Thus, the burning of 'witches' became pandemic throughout medieval Europe and its practice carried on well into the eighteenth century. Estimates of the number of women who died at the hands of the Catholic Church place the figure as high as four million.

The most illustrious victim of such heinous female victimization is the French woman, Joan of Arc (1412–1431). Inspired by voices and visions of God, she helped the French drive out the British from France during a bloody international war. Nevertheless, she was captured by the enemy and tried as a witch and a heretic. She was accused of three crimes – first, that the voices she heard were in fact those of evil spirits; two, that she had refused to submit to the authority of the Church, claiming she only obeyed a higher power; and three, that as a woman, she should never dress in men's clothing. Guilty as charged, Joan was burnt at the stake on 30th May 1431.

How is it possible for such an horrific holocaust against the female species to have lasted so long? Why did so many misogynistic concepts prevail without redress? Why was the sacred feminine mercilessly sabotaged to the point of its virtual annihilation?

Perhaps the lesson to be learnt is not to dwell on a painful past but to look to the present age in the hope that such acts of barbarity and violence against women will one day be completely obliterated.

chapter fifteen

Julian of Norwich

As the Catholic Church continued to debate the minutiae of Christian theology, many men and women were turning their attention to a more profound and personal experience of the oneness of God. Indeed, Meister Eckhart's legacy set the tone for the next wave of mystical writings that would continue to flourish throughout mainland Europe. One such work was *The Imitation of Christ*, composed by the German monk, Thomas à Kempis (1380–1471). As one of the most moving and exuberant outpourings of one man's love of God, he pays particular attention to the mystical relationship between lover and Beloved:

> He who is thus a spiritual lover knows well what his voice means which says: 'Thou, Lord God, art my whole love and my desire! Thou art all mine and I all Thine! Spread my heart into Thy love that I may know how sweet it is to serve Thee, and to be as though I were entirely melted into Thy love.' O I am immersed in love and go far above myself for the great fervour that I feel of Thy unspeakable goodness! I shall sing to Thee the song of love; and my soul shall never be weary to praise Thee with the joyful song of love that I shall sing to Thee. I shall love Thee more than myself, and not myself but for Thee.[1]

England also witnessed its own period of spiritual testament. In 1390, the first complete edition of the Bible was translated into vernacular

Middle English by the Lollards. More importantly, the anonymous fourteenth-century classic, *The Cloud of Unknowing*, would provide one of the most beautiful expositions of the nature of the mystical life: separated by a 'cloud of unknowing' from God, the individual can taste divine love through the use of a single-word prayer, rather like a mantra, eradicating all extraneous thought:

> ... take thee but a little word of one syllable: for so it is better than of two, for ever the shorter it is the better it accordeth with the work of the Spirit. And such a word is this word GOD or this word LOVE ... And fasten this word to thine heart, so that it never go thence for thing that befalleth.
>
> This word shall be thy shield and thy spear, whether thou ridest on peace or on war. With this word, thou shalt beat on this cloud and this darkness above thee. With this word, thou shalt smite down all manner of thought under the cloud of forgetting.[2]

Just like the method of transcendental meditation in the East, repetition of LOVE or GOD is a technique bringing the individual in touch with the Divine.

Other writers of the period include the fourteenth-century hermit, Richard Rolle of Hampole, in Yorkshire (1300–1349). As a spiritual counsellor, he composed many of his later works specifically for women, despite starting life as a staunch misogynist. In his *Form of Living*, written specifically for Margaret Kirkby, a member of the Cistercian community at Hampole, Rolle asks the question, 'What is love?' to which he expounds:

> Love is an ardent yearning for God, with a wonderful delight and security ... Love is one life, coupling together the one loving and the one beloved ... Love is the beauty of all virtues ... , a device through which God loves us and we God and each of us one another. Love is the desire of the heart ... a yearning between two people ... a stirring of the soul to love God for himself and all other things for God ... Truth may exist without love, but it cannot be of

any use without it. Love is the perfection of scholarship, the strength of prophecy, the fruit of truth, the spiritual strength of the sacraments, the confirming of intellect and knowledge, the wealth of the poor, the life of the dying.[3]

Life for women in medieval Britain was particularly harsh. Like their European counterparts, they were in the main restricted to the home – patriarchal and Church establishments prevented them from participating in any form of public life. With a population that also had a surplus of unmarried women, it is little wonder, therefore, that many women sought the seclusion of religious orders as an escape from the material world in preparation for the promise of a glorious existence in Heaven.

One specific text, composed towards the end of the twelfth century by an anonymous male author, was a guide for nuns called the *Ancrene Riwle* (or sometimes the *Ancrene Wisse*) meaning 'The Nun's Rule'. Written in eight parts in a West Midlands dialect, it outlines specific behaviour to be adopted by the nun in her quest for purity and perfection. Once again, the notion of the female gender being the weaker sex, carrying the sinful legacy of Eve, forms the subtext of the *Rule*. Believed to be morally defective, it is for her own good that she must succumb to religious instruction. It is only through the redemptive power of her love of God where the nun's salvation lies. Her relationship with Christ must, therefore, become the focus of her heart:

> Therefore, my dear sisters, over everything else, be energetic about having a pure heart. What is a pure heart? I have said it before: that is, that you wish nothing, and love nothing, and love nothing except God alone – and those things, for God's sake, which help you towards him.[4]

The *Ancrene Riwle* joins a cluster of similar texts, collectively known as the Katherine Group, which comprises the lives of three female saints – St Katherine, for whom the group is named, St Margaret and

St Juliana. Each story focuses on the need for chastity as a prerequisite for the spiritual life, with Christ as the nun's exclusive lover. Other texts include the *Sawles Warde* ('The Protection of the Soul'), which likens the body to a castle of the soul and the senses to its gates, guarded by Wit and Will; *Holy Maidenhood*, which advocates the virtues of virginity; and *The Wooing of our Lord*, an emotional address to the crucified Christ.

All these diverse texts relating to the specific salvation of women were composed by their male contemporaries. It was only a matter of time, therefore, before the voice of a woman would emerge, defending her feminine right to express her experience of God and her name was Julian of Norwich. Although well known in her day, very little of her life has been preserved. Indeed, even her name is elusive – the title, 'Julian of Norwich' is taken from the church where she lived in Norwich. (The original church was destroyed by the Germans in 1942, however, it has subsequently been rebuilt.)

Of what we do know, Julian was born in December 1342 into a wealthy family in Norwich and educated at a boarding school attached to Carrow Abbey nunnery. It is not clear when she took ecclesiastical orders but she chose to live her life as an anchoress (deriving from the Greek word meaning 'to retire') whereby she was literally entombed in a sealed cell attached to the church. Although her daily needs, such as food and firewood, would have been attended to by a servant, she effectively had chosen to die unto the world, in order to focus her attention exclusively on her interior life.

In her early thirties she was struck down by an acute illness, lasting for nearly a week, which brought her to the brink of death. During this harrowing time, she received a total of sixteen 'showings' or visions of Christ and his Passion. After a miraculous recovery, she set about recording her visions as the *Revelations of Divine Love*. Some twenty years later, she rewrote the entire text, expanding the narrative and adding commentary and theological reflection. Thus, the Short Text was composed in 1373 and the Long Text in roughly 1393:

And when I was thirty-and-a-half years old, God sent me a bodily sickness in which I lay for three days and three nights; and on the fourth night I received all the rites of Holy Church and did not believe that I would live until morning. And after this I lingered on for two days and two nights. And on the third night I often thought that I was dying, and so did those who were with me. But at this time I was very sorry and reluctant to die, not because there was anything on earth that I wanted to live for nor because I feared anything, for I trusted in God, but because I wanted to live so as to love God better and for longer, so that through the grace of longer life I might know and love God better in the bliss of heaven.[5]

But all is well and Julian makes a full recovery:

Then I truly believed that I was at the point of death. And at this moment all my suffering suddenly left me, and I was as completely well, especially in the upper part of my body, as ever I was before or after. I marvelled at this change, for it seemed to me a mysterious work of God, not a natural one.[6]

A woman of her times, Julian would have been acutely aware of the misogynistic message of her male clerical colleagues as well as the legacy of St Paul. Despite proclaiming how uneducated and humble she is, she defiantly defends her right to speak:

God forbid that you should say or assume that I am a teacher, for that is not what I mean, nor did I ever mean it; for I am a woman, ignorant and frail … Just because I am a woman, must I therefore believe that I must not tell you about the goodness of God, when I saw at the same time both his goodness and his wish that it should be known?[7]

Once again, Julian writes with the familiar metaphor of divine lovers in an attempt to convey her feelings of devotion and awe. As the embodiment of love, Christ is Julian's beloved – through their divine marriage, the two become One:

> And in this binding and union he is a real and true bridegroom, and me his loved bride and his fair maiden, a bride with whom he is never displeased; for he says, 'I love you and you love me, and our love shall never be divided.'[8]

Moreover, Julian chooses to develop a different form of relationship, one that is arguably more profound – that between mother and child. Indeed, what is of great significance in the *Revelations of Divine Love* is the way in which she not only expounds the concept of God the Father but also introduces the theme of Christ the Mother. Appearing only in the Long Text, when she presumably had more time to develop the idea, she cleverly juxtaposes the authoritarian portrayal of Father God, more associated with fear and punishment, against the protective personification of Mother Christ, all nurturing and all forgiving:

> And so our Mother, in whom our parts are kept unparted, works in us in various ways; for in our Mother, Christ, we profit and grow, and in mercy he reforms and restores us, and through the power of his Passion and his death and rising again, he unites us to our essential being. This is how our Mother mercifully acts to all his children who are submissive and obedient to him.[9]

As Christ's children, we return to his 'motherhood' for our support and sustenance. Indeed, Julian is also reinforcing the Middle Ages idea that milk was reprocessed blood. Christ's bleeding on the Cross is, therefore, seen as the nourishing love of the Mother's milk – feeding us, sustaining us and uniting us in his love.

Like Hildegard, Julian is also blessed with a vision of the universe. And like all the mystics before her, she is made to understand that everything that exists is a manifestation of the Self:

And in this vision he showed me a little thing, the size of a hazelnut, lying in the palm of my hand, and to my mind's eye it was as round as any ball. I looked at it and thought, 'What can this be?' And the answer came to me, 'It is all that is made.' I wondered how it could last, for it was so small I thought it might suddenly disappear. And the answer in my mind was, 'It lasts and will last forever because God loves it; and in the same everything exists through the love of God.' In this little thing I saw three attributes: the first is that God made it, the second is that he loves it, the third is that God cares for it. But what does this mean to me? Truly, the maker, the lover, the carer; for until I become one substance with him, I can never have love, rest or true bliss; that is to say, until I am so bound to him that there may be no created thing between my God and me.[10]

What is striking about Julian is her capacity to rationalize her visions into a comprehensive philosophical argument. Despite this nondual explanation of the cosmos, it still perplexes her; contemplating this paradox, she asks her Lord how could sin exist if he were responsible for all that was made. Echoing the *Gospel of Mary Magdalene*, Julian writes:

And after this I saw God in an instant, that is to say, in my under-standing, and in seeing this I saw that he is in everything. I looked attentively, knowing and recognizing in this vision that he does all that is done. I marvelled at this sight with quiet awe, and I thought, 'What is sin?' For I saw that God does everything, no matter how small. And I saw that truly nothing happens by accident or luck, but by the eternal providence of God's wisdom. Therefore I was obliged to accept that everything which is done is well done, and I was sure that God never sins. Therefore it seemed to me that sin is nothing, for all this vision no sin appeared.[11]

She explains further that God compels us to suffer in order to test our love and make us humble. But, as her Lord reiterates, everything is as it should be, and in what has become one of her most immortal lines, quoted centuries later by TS Eliot in his beautiful poem, 'The Four Quartets', she writes:

> It is true that sin is the cause of all this suffering, but all shall be well, and all shall be well, and all manner of things shall be well.[12]

The theme of oneness also permeates all of Julian's writings. More reminiscent to an Indian Upanishad, she boldly asserts her radical message:

> God is our mother as truly as he is our father; and he showed this in everything, and especially in the sweet words where he says, 'It is I,' that is to say, 'It is I: the power and goodness of fatherhood. It is I: the wisdom of motherhood. It is I: the light and grace which is all blessed love. It is I: the unity. I am the sovereign goodness of all manner of things. It is I that make you love. It is I that make you long. It is I: the eternal fulfilment of all true desires.'[13]

This is the final truth: 'It is I who am highest; it is I who am lowest; it is I who am all.'[14] God is omniscient, omnipresent, omnipotent. And knowledge of this fact is most important:

> ... all men and women who wish to lead the contemplative life need to have knowledge of it; they should choose to set at nothing everything that is made so as to have the love of God who is unmade. This is why those who choose to occupy themselves with earthly business and are always pursuing worldly success have nothing here of God in their hearts and souls: because they love and seek their rest in this little thing where there is no rest, and know nothing of God, who is almighty, all wise and all good, for he is true rest. God wishes to be known, and is pleased that we should rest in him; for all that is below him does nothing to satisfy us. And this is why, until all that is made seems as nothing, no soul can be at rest. When a soul sets all at nothing for love, to have

him who is everything that is good, then it is able to receive spiritual rest.[15]

It is highly unlikely that Julian would have been familiar with the writings of the beguines but once again, we hear the common theme of rendering oneself unto nothing in order to become everything and all with God:

> For if I look solely at myself, I am really nothing; but as one of mankind in general, I am in oneness of love with all my fellow Christians; for upon this oneness of love depends the life of all who shall be saved; for God is all that is good, and God has made all that is made, and God loves all that he has made.[16]

Everything that God wills for us is owing to his love. And this is what Julian finally comes to understand some fifteen years later after the initial sequence of showings in one final revelation, a few years prior to composing the Long Text:

> 'Do you want to know what your Lord meant? Know well that love was what he meant. Who showed you this? Love. What did he show? Love. Why did he show it to you? For Love. Hold fast to this and you will know and understand more of the same; but you will never understand or know from it anything else for all eternity.' This is how I was taught that our Lord's meaning was love.[17]

Without doubt, her showings of Divine Love are one of the most profound and impassioned revelations written by a woman. Through her intellectual rigour and poetic expression, she joins the canon of sacred female literature. Julian lived until her mid-seventies although the date of her death is unknown. Similarly, her burial place is also a mystery.

The Middle Ages were a time when the outpourings of the Christian mystics were at their zenith and in particular, the writings of women. On the continent, other famous nuns of the period included Clare of

Assisi (1193–1254), Catherine of Siena (1347–80), Angela of Foligno (1248–1309), Margaret Ebner (1291–1351), Bridget of Sweden (1303–73), Catherine of Bologna (1413–63) and Catherine of Genoa (1447–1510). Indeed, it is a period unmatched in the history of spiritual literature in its exploration of the sacred feminine within the context of the Christian teaching.

chapter sixteen

Mirabai

As the sacred feminine struggled against political and ecclesiastic prejudice in Europe, her worship continued unimpeded throughout the Indian continent. Many sages and poets continued to reveal the mystical doctrine of *advaita* and amongst them was Jnaneshvar (1271–1296). Born in northern India, he understood at a very young age the perennial wisdom. Although he is best known for his *Jnaneshvari*, a commentary on the *Bhagavad Gita*, it is his *Amritanubhav*, 'The Nectar of Mystical Experience', which details the passionate relationship between Siva and Shakti – the divine lovers inseparably bound:

> *I offer obeisance to the God and Goddess,*
> *The limitless primal parents of the universe.*
>
> *The lover, out of boundless love,*
> *Has become the Beloved.*
> *Both are made of the same substance*
> *And share the same food.*
>
> *Out of love for each other, they merge;*
> *And again they separate for the pleasure of being two …*
>
> *Two lutes: one note.*
> *Two flowers: one fragrance.*
> *Two lamps: one light.*

Two lips: one word.
Two eyes: one sight.
These two: one universe ...

In the same way, the duality of Siva and Shakti
Vanishes, when their essential unity is seen.[1]

One particular scripture that was to emerge during this period that further eulogized the immanence of Shakti was the *Devi Gita*, 'The Song of the Goddess'. Similar in overall structure and theme to the *Bhagavad Gita*, the fifty-seven verses of the *Devi Gita* constitute the last ten chapters of the seventh book of the *Devi Bhagavata Purana*, the chief Puranic text of Shakti worshippers. Composed in Sanskrit *shlokas* sometime between the thirteenth and sixteenth centuries CE, the Goddess offers wise counsel to her special devotee, the Mountain King Himalaya, in front of an assembly of gods. Expounding an esoteric blend of *advaitic* and Tantric philosophy, the Goddess proclaims that all phenomenal existence is supported in the eternal Self – the only difference here is that this eternal oneness of being is feminine.

Manifesting as a blinding flash of light, the three-eyed, four-armed Goddess, Mother of the World, emerges before the Mountain King:

She was exceedingly beautiful of limb, a maiden in the freshness of youth.
Her full, upraised breast put to shame the swelling buds of the lotus.
Her girdle and anklets jingled with clusters of tinkling bells.
She was adorned with necklace, armlets and bracelets of gold ...

The Mother's kindly face, so gracious, displayed a tender smile on the
  lotus mouth.
This embodiment of unfeigned compassion the gods beheld in their
  presence.
Seeing her, the embodiment of compassion, the entire host of gods
  bowed low,

Unable to speak, choking on tears in silence.
Struggling to regain their composure, their necks bending in devotion,
Their eyes brimming with tears of loving joy, they glorified the World
    Mother with hymns.[2]

The Goddess then reveals her mystical knowledge:

May all the gods attend to what I have to say.
By merely hearing these words of mine, one attains my essential nature.
I alone existed in the beginning; there was nothing else at all,
    O Mountain King.
My true Self is known as pure consciousness, the highest intelligence, the
    one supreme Brahman.
It is beyond reason, indescribable, incompatible, incorruptible.
From out of itself evolves a certain power renowned as Maya.

Neither real nor unreal is this Maya, nor is it both, for that would be
    incongruous.
Lacking such characteristics, this indefinite entity has always subsisted.
As heat inheres in fire, as brilliance in the sun,
As cool light in the moon, just as this Maya inheres firmly in me.
Into that Maya the actions of souls, the souls themselves, and the ages
    eventually
Dissolve without distinctions, as worldly concerns disappear in deep sleep.
By uniting with this inherent power of mine, I become the cosmic seed.[3]

And echoing the *Gnostic Gospels* as well as Hildegard's vision of the
cosmos, the Goddess knows that ultimately she pervades everything,
that paradoxical state where all possibilities are contained:

I am the sun and the stars, and I am the Lord of the stars.
I am the various species of beasts and birds; I am also the outcaste and
    thief.
I am the evildoer and the wicked deed; I am the righteous person and
    the virtuous deed.

I am certainly female and male, and asexual as well.
And whatever thing, anywhere, you see or hear,
That entire thing I pervade, ever abiding inside it and outside.
There is nothing at all, moving or unmoving, that is devoid of me …[4]

Worship of the goddess and the cultivation of ecstatic yearning for the Divine continued to flourish through the bhakti movements that proliferated throughout India. Most groups, however, tended to focus on male deities such as Siva and Krishna, inspiring musicians and poets to compose exquisite songs and poetry, as in the manner of Andal. Another greatly loved poetess who wrote verse still popular today was Lalla, meaning 'darling'.

Born in Kashmir in a village called Pandrenthan in approximately 1320, she was also known as Lal Ded, Lal Diddi or Lalleshwari. Very little is known of her life except that she was married at twelve but was mistreated by her cruel husband and jealous mother-in-law. Abandoning her home at the age of twenty-four, she became a student of the Hindu teacher, Sed Bayu as well as the Sufi master, Ali Hamadani. As Lalla fell more and more in love with God, she lost all concern for her worldly existence and lived a life dancing naked through the streets and villages in a state of ecstatic trance.

One such legend of her life tells of the time when Lalla was ridiculed for her state of undress. Obtaining cloth from a merchant, she divided it equally into two strips and then placed a strip on each shoulder. Throughout the day, when she received praise, she would tie a knot in one strip, and when she received criticism, she tied a knot in the other. At the end of the day, she asked the cloth merchant to weigh the strips – of course, they were still of equal weight. Lalla then pointed out that praise and criticism are of equal measure and should be greeted with equanimity, for they are both part of the fabric of existence.

Written in an old Kashmiri dialect, Lalla's poetry is outwardly sparse and yet suffused with metaphor and intense emotion. Speaking of life in the world compared to the mystic path, she says:

Loosen the load of sweetness I'm carrying.
The sling-knot is biting into my shoulder.

This day has been so meaningless.
I feel I can't go on.

When I was with my teacher, I heard a truth
that hurt my heart like a blister,

the tender pang of seeing
something I loved as an illusion.

The flocks I tended are gone.
I am a shepherd without even a memory

of what that means, climbing this mountain.
I feel so lost.

This is my inward way, until I came
into the presence of a Moon, this new knowledge

of how likenesses unite. Good Friend,
Everything is you, I see only God.

Now the delightful forms and motions
are transparent. I look through them

and see myself as the Absolute. And here's
the answer to the riddle of this dream:

You leave, so that we two
can do One Dance.[5]

As a devotee of Siva, her verse also explores the passionate and erotic infatuation she has for her Lord, where lover and Beloved become One:

I, Lalla, entered the jasmine garden,
where Siva and Shakti were making love.

I dissolved into them,
and what is this
to me, now?

I seem to be here,
but really I'm walking
in the jasmine garden.[6]

Moreover, as a believer of the *advaita* Vedanta doctrine, her words are steeped in the knowledge that the purpose of life is to merge with the universal Self, echoing the Upanishadic maxim, *Tat tvam asi*:

Everything is new now for me.
My mind is new, the moon, the sun.
The whole world looks rinsed with water,
washed in the rain of I am That.

Lalla leaps and dances inside the energy
that creates and sustains the universe.[7]

And as she dances and sings, there is the realization that she must die unto herself, in order for her to attain immortal life:

Self inside self, You are nothing but me.
Self inside self, I am only You.

What we are together
will never die.

The why and how of this?
What does it matter?[8]

Lalla died in 1391 after a lifetime's wandering and teaching – her poetry is, nonetheless, as arresting as the day it was composed.

Many other beautiful poems and songs were written during this period, including the famous *Gita Govinda*, the erotic love song of Radha and Krishna. Written by the wandering mendicant and poet, Jayadeva, in the twelfth century, its popularity spread throughout the subcontinent and is still sung in temples today. Recalling the same intense passion of the *Song of Songs*, the explicit eroticism of the *Gita Govinda* weaves its way through the psychology of courtship, the delight and delirium of two lovers ultimately merging in their love of each other and their love of God.

Up until Jayadeva's classic work, Radha had little place in Indian literature, only being referred to in selected passages. Now, she takes centre stage – she is the proud and passionate, intense and solitary woman who absorbs Krishna's attention. Pleading and begging, he starts to woo her:

> *You are my ornament, my life,*
> *My jewel in the sea of existence.*
> *Be yielding to me forever,*
> *My heart fervently pleads!*
> *Radha, cherished love,*
> *Abandon your baseless pride!*
> *Love's fire burns my heart –*
> *Bring wine in your lotus mouth!*[9]

Teasing and testing Krishna, fascinating him, eluding him and finally triumphing over him in an act of ecstatic lovemaking, Radha yields to her lover:

> *Displaying her passion*
> *In loveplay as the battle began,*
> *She launched a bold offensive*
> *Above him*

And triumphed over her lover.
Her hips were still,
Her vine-like arm was slack,
Her chest was heaving,
Her eyes were closed.
Why does a mood of manly force
Succeed for women in love?

Then, as he idled after passionate love,
Radha, wanting him to ornament her,
Freely told her lover,
Secure in her power over him.[10]

Many women were inspired by Radha's example, wanting to be Krishna's supreme and exclusive lover. The Rajasthani poetess, Mirabai, was no exception, and her verse has made her one of the best-loved woman saints in northern India. She was born in 1498 in the village of Chaukari in the Merta District of Rajasthan into a Rajput clan during a time of intense political unrest under the ruling Afghan Empire. Legend recounts how the young and beautiful princess answered the palace gate to give food to a sadhu, who in return thrust into her palm a tiny statue of Krishna, which she continued to treasure all her life. Indeed, at that moment she resolved that she would marry Krishna, whom she addressed by the name of Shyam, the Dark One.

Unfortunately, as was the custom, she was forced into an arranged marriage with Prince Bhoj Raj, the son of a great warrior of the Sisodiya clan. Knowing herself to be already betrothed to her beloved Shyam, she refused to consummate her marriage, thus causing great enmity between herself, her husband and her interfering mother-in-law. Chance took a turn and her husband lost his life soon after on the battlefield, leaving Mirabai to devote herself exclusively to her Lord. However, fuelled by grief and anger, her husband's family attempted to kill her – first, by a draft of poison; next, a poisonous snake; and finally, a bed of razor-sharp spikes.

Needless to say this was all too much for Mirabai to bear so she quickly departed, spending the rest of her days wandering the forests, roads and temples of northern India, ending up in Vrindavan in her quest to find Krishna.

Composed in Marwari, a dialect of Hindi, Mirabai's poetry joins the canon of great bhakti literature – similar in theme to Lalla's spiritual eroticism, Mirabai's style is, however, much more expressive in its rollercoaster of emotion and heartache. Speaking of the conflict between her outer and inner life, she writes:

> My friend, I went to the market and bought the Dark One.
> You claim by night, I claim by day.
> Actually, I was beating a drum all the time I was buying him.
> You say I gave too much; I say too little.
> Actually, I put him on a scale before I bought him.
> What I paid was my social body, my town body, my family body, and all
>   my inherited jewels.
> Mirabai says: The Dark One is my husband now.
> Be with me when I lie down; you promised me this in an earlier life.[11]

Once again, Krishna is presented as a bewitching and beguiling lover, just out of reach and seemingly always in the arms of another. But then, just when all hope is fading, a glimpse is enough to restore her faith:

> Another night
> sleepless;
> tossing in bed,
> reaching for someone not there.
> Tossed darkness
> life wasted
> a tossed mind convulsing all night.
> Another night sleepless and then,
> the bright dawn.[12]

After the dark night of the soul, release finally comes:

> *What do I care for the words of the world?*
> *The name of the Dark One has entered my heart.*
> *Those who praise, those who blame,*
> *Those who say I am crazy, wicked, an uncontrollable fire –*
> *All ignorant fools, caught in their senses.*
> *It is true, Mira has no sense: she is lost in the sweetness.*
> *To take this path is to walk the edge of the sword;*
> *Then the noose of birth and death is suddenly cut.*
> *Mira lives now beyond Mira.*
> *She swims, deep mind and deep body, in Shyam's ocean.*[13]

Mirabai was acutely conscious of her female status in the world – on the one hand, it meant subjugation to the rules of patriarchs and the men in her life; on the other it licensed her to a lover's relationship with *Shyam*. But ultimately, it is all spume on the sea of samsara:

> *Why life,*
> *why again,*
> *and what reason birth as a woman?*
> *Good deeds in former lives they say.*
> *But –*
> *growth, cut, cut, decline –*
> *life disappears second by second*
> *and never comes back,*
> *a leaf torn from its branch*
> *twists away.*
> *Look at this raging ocean of life forms,*
> *swift, unappeasable,*
> *everything caught in its tide.*
> *O beloved, take this raft quickly*
> *and lead it to shore.*[14]

Mirabai died in 1565, the author of some 1,400 verses, set in various ragas or musical compositions. It is even thought that she wrote a commentary on the *Gita Govinda* though no such text is traceable. It is also believed that during her lifetime, she had a handmaiden who followed her into exile, transcribing songs and poetry into a large notebook, but which is thought to have vanished sometime in the seventeenth century. Nevertheless, so famous has Mirabai's legacy become that her story has been turned into at least ten contemporary Indian films.

Of course, the most famous treatise to come out of India celebrating the nature of love between a man and a woman is the *Kama Sutra* or 'Aphorisms of Love'– commonly viewed as a manual on the art of lovemaking but conceived originally to aid spiritual development, in the same manner as Tantra. Composed by Vatsyayana sometime between the first and sixth century CE, it contains approximately 1,250 *shlokas* guiding the aspirant in his or her perfection of sexual and emotional intimacy:

> Kama is the enjoyment of appropriate objects by the five senses of hearing, feeling, seeing, tasting and smelling, assisted by mind together with the soul. The ingredient in this is a peculiar contact between the organ of sense and its object, and the consciousness of pleasure which arises from that contact is called Kama ...[15]

Later texts, the 'The Art of Love' (*Ananga Ranga*), written by the Indian poet Kalyan, and *The Perfumed Garden* by the Muslim poet, Shaykh Umar ibn Muhammed al-Nefzawi, both in the sixteenth century, also give advice for choosing the best lover, sexual positions and the most auspicious times of the month for having the most satisfying intercourse.

The overall attitude in the East during the medieval period regarding spiritual sensuality is wholly positive – it is seen as a path to the Absolute. What a contrast it is to the perverseness of the West, where the body is seen predominantly as a shackle of stinking flesh, fit only for defilement and pain. No wonder the sacred texts of India, and in particular those associated with sexual pleasure, would ultimately find homes in the western continents during the modern age.

chapter seventeen

Teresa of Avila

After the scholasticism of the Middle Ages in the West, the next period in history would see a rebirth of the classical values associated with ancient Greece and Rome. The Renaissance, starting in fourteenth-century Italy and continuing throughout Europe for the following three centuries, saw yet again another profound shift in the level of human consciousness. Drawing much on the philosophical ideas of Plato, Renaissance humanism advocated that mankind was essentially at the centre of the universe, untainted by original sin, controlling his or her own destiny.

One such body of writing that had considerable influence on Renaissance thinking was the *Corpus Hermeticum*, believed to be written by Hermes Trismegistus (a contemporary of Moses) and brought to Florence in roughly 1460 by a monk from Macedonia. Belonging to a non-Christian lineage of Hellenistic Gnosticism, it was translated from the Greek by Marsilio Ficino (1433–99) at the behest of Cosimo de Medici. The books of the *Corpus Hermeticum* deal with the subject of the individual's relationship with the Divine and, more specifically, the way in which the universe is a manifestation of the masculine and feminine principles, all the while cradled in the All:

> Look upon things through me and contemplate the Kosmos as it lies before your eyes, that body which no harm can touch, the most ancient of all things, yet ever in its prime and ever new. See too the

seven subject worlds, marshalled in everlasting order, and filling up the measure of everlasting time as they run their diverse course. And all things are filled with light ... and the Sun is the begetter of all good, the ruler of all ordered movement, and the governor of the seven worlds. Look at the Moon, who outstrips all the other planets in her course, the instrument by which birth and growth are wrought, the worker of change in here below. Look at the earth, firm-seated at the centre; the foundation of this goodly universe, the feeder and nurse of all terrestrial creatures ... And all are filled with soul, and all are in movement, immortals in heaven and mortals in earth ...

God is the All; and there is nothing that is not included in the All ... and the All permeates all things, and has to do with all things.[1]

Neoplatonism reached many shores, including the court of Queen Elizabeth I (1533–1603). A keen patron of the arts, the radical ideas from the continent blossomed under her reign. Indeed, in a time when women had little say in public life, she was able to utilize her femininity to its full effect. One particular poet who attended the court circle of the Virgin Queen was Edmund Spencer (1552–1599). In honour of his sovereign, he composed the epic lyrical poem, *The Faerie Queene*, an allegory of the human soul. Set in the court of Gloriana, it is also a celebration of Elizabeth, one of the greatest monarchs England has ever known:

> ... *O Goddess heavenly bright,*
> *Mirror of grace and majesty divine,*
> *Great Lady of the greatest isle, whose light*
> *Like Phoebus' lamp throughout the world doth shine,*
> *Shed thy fair beams into my feeble eye,*
> *And raise my thoughts too humble and too vile,*
> *To think of that true glorious type of thine* ...[2]

In an age that saw the triumph of reason over religious superstition, Elizabeth becomes the personification of the Mother Goddess.

Moreover, portraits commissioned by her make use of the traditional symbols always associated with a female deity – the Tudor rose and fleur-de-lis, the serpent and sword, and branches of the olive tree.

The most important writer of Elizabeth's court was, however, the illustrious William Shakespeare (1564–1616), probably the greatest poet and dramatist ever to have lived. He was also deeply passionate about the contemporary Neoplatonist philosophy and embodied his beliefs in his masterpiece, *The Tempest* – again, an allegory of the human soul and its yearning for love and self-knowledge. Speaking of the fragile nature of human existence, Prospero (based on the contemporary magus, Doctor John Dee) declares:

> *Our revels are now ended. These our actors,*
> *As I foretold you, were all spirits, and*
> *Are melted into air, into thin air:*
> *And, like the baseless fabric of this vision,*
> *The cloud-capped towers, the gorgeous palaces,*
> *The solemn temples, the great globe itself,*
> *Yea, all which it inherit, shall dissolve,*
> *And, like this insubstantial pageant faded,*
> *Leave not a rack behind. We are such stuff*
> *As dreams are made on; and our little life*
> *Is rounded with a sleep.*[3]

Time and transience, love and loss, were common themes within much of the literary output during this period, in particular a contemporary group of writers known as the Metaphysical Poets, which included John Donne (1572–1631), George Herbert (1593–1633), Andrew Marvell (1621–1678), Henry Vaughan (1622–1695) and Thomas Traherne (1637–1674). In many ways, the mystical vision of the English Christian mystics of the Middle Ages was picked up and distilled in the conceits of the Metaphysical Poets of the Renaissance.

In Andrew Marvell's 'The Garden', extolling the paradisal state of nature, the poet recalls a moment of transcendent ecstasy:

What wondrous life is this I lead!
Ripe apples drop about my head;
The luscious clusters of the vine
Upon my mouth do crush their wine;
The nectarene, and curious peach,
Into my hands themselves do reach;
Stumbling on melons, as I pass,
Ensnared with flowers, I fall on grass.

Meanwhile the mind, from pleasures less,
Withdraws into its happiness:
The mind, that ocean where each kind
Does straight its own resemblance find,
Yet it creates, transcending these,
Far other worlds, and other seas,
Annihilating all that's made
To a green thought in a green shade.[4]

Here the idea of greenness is reminiscent of Hildegard's own mystical vision of the natural world and the immanence of God.

Back in mainland Europe, scholars and monks were describing the nondual message in the more conventional format of autobiographical prose and dialogue. One such mystic was Nicholas of Cusa (1401–64). Born in the Rhineland, he grew up with an insatiable appetite for the mystical writings of philosophers such as Plato and Meister Eckhart. At twenty-eight, he experienced the complete realization of God and thereafter spent the rest of his life writing about the spiritual path. In his book, *De Sapientia*, 'On Wisdom', Nicholas outlines the difference between knowledge obtainable through intellectual learning and that obtainable from direct experience. Written as a dialogue between a teacher and pupil, he says that true wisdom is only attainable through love and grace:

Wisdom is not to be found in the art of oratory or in great books but in a withdrawal from these sensible things and in turning to the most simple and infinite forms. You will learn how to receive it into a temple purged from all vice, and by fervent love to cling to it until you may taste it and see how sweet That is which is all sweetness. Once this has been tasted, all things which you now consider as important will appear as vile and you will be so humbled that no arrogance or other vice will remain in you. Once having tasted this wisdom, you will inseparably adhere to it with a chaste and pure heart. You will choose rather to forsake this world and all else that is not of this wisdom, and living with unspeakable happiness you will die. After death, you will rest eternally in that fond embrace which the eternally blessed wisdom of God himself vouchsafed to grant both to you and to me.[5]

And yet despite trying to make the case for direct experience, various schisms and political upheavals focusing on the minutiae of interpretation of Christ's teachings were rocking the Catholic Church. The Renaissance may have freed men's minds but as with any break with tradition, its repercussions had both positive and negative consequences.

In an attempt to expose the corrupt practices in the Roman Catholic Church, the German theologian, Martin Luther, issued his famous *Ninety-Five Theses* (1517), which in turn precipitated the Protestant Reformation. And yet despite his desire for change, Luther still clung on to his misogynist ideas with regard to the position of women. In a series of lectures given on Genesis, he still emphasised the inferiority of the female gender owing to Eve's transgression:

> Hence it follows that if the woman had not been deceived by the serpent and had not sinned, she would have been the equal of Adam in all respects. For the punishment, that she is now subjected to the man, was imposed on her after sin and because of sin, just as the other hardships and dangers were: travail, pain, and countless other vexations.[6]

Moreover, on the issue of sex, Luther has an extraordinary take on being able to condemn women, on the one hand, for being wanton temptresses and yet exonerate men's lustful desire for them on the other:

And so, in the case of the woman, we must think not only of the managing of the household which she does, but also of the medicine which she is. In this respect, Paul says [I Cor. 7:2]: 'Because of fornication let each one have his own wife.' And the Master of the Sentences declares learnedly that matrimony was established in Paradise as a duty but after sin also as an antidote. Therefore we are compelled to make use of this sex in order to avoid sin. It is almost shameful to say this, but nevertheless it is true. For there are very few who marry solely as a matter of duty.[7]

Luther's cake-and-eat-it philosophy beggars belief. Furthermore, his French contemporary, John Calvin (1509–64) in his *Institutes of the Christian Religion* was also an advocate of the importance of marriage for men as a means of avoiding the 'sin' of fornication.

Luther's and Calvin's stance produced a retaliatory revolution within the Catholic Church itself, known as the Counter Reformation, in an attempt to oppose the effects of Protestantism. Central to the enforcement of this movement were the Roman Inquisitors, originally established by the papacy in the Middle Ages, who were now responsible for flushing out perceived Protestant traitors throughout Europe. Moreover, in Spain, the Inquisition effortlessly shifted its focus from recent ethnic cleansing of Muslims and Jews onto more general dissenters against the Catholic faith. Indeed, the infamous Inquisitor-General, Tomas de Torquemada, would torture and murder hundreds of thousands of heretics, all in the name of Christ.

Into such a climate was born one of the most famous mystics of all time – Juan de la Cruz (1542–91). More commonly known as John of the Cross, he was born Juan de Yepes y Alvarez in Fontiveros, a small village just outside Avila in Old Castille. He was sent to a church orphanage at a young age, where he quickly showed a calling for the priesthood. Thus, at the age of twenty-five, he was ordained.

It was around this time that Juan met the nun, Teresa of Avila, who had already founded a reformed Order of Carmelite nuns, called the Discalced (barefoot) Carmelites. She had been searching for a number of monks to serve as confessors to the sisters in a convent in Medina to which Juan readily agreed. Indeed, the more ascetic approach to the contemplative life offered by Teresa greatly appealed to him. Similarly, despite his small physical stature, Juan was a great inspiration and guide to both the sisters and indeed all those who came into contact with him.

Nevertheless, the ecclesiastical authorities were less impressed – mounting jealousies and suspicions culminated in Juan's imprisonment by the Inquisition. Entombed in a small stone privy-closet for nine months, he eventually managed to escape, and, despite the physical ordeal, it inspired him to compose his famous 'Dark Night of the Soul', one of the most beautiful allegories describing the anguish of the soul for its Beloved:

On a dark night, Kindled in love with yearnings – oh, happy chance! –
I went forth without being observed, my house being now at rest.

In darkness and secure, by the secret ladder, disguised – oh, happy chance! –
In darkness and in concealment, my house being now at rest.

In the happy night, in secret, when none saw me,
Nor I beheld aught, without light or guide, save that which burned in
my heart.

This light guided me more surely than the light of noonday
To the place where he (well I knew who!) was awaiting me – a place
where none appeared.

Oh, night that guided me, oh, night more lovely than the dawn,
Oh, night that joined Beloved with lover, lover transformed in the
Beloved!

Upon my flowery breast, kept wholly for himself alone,
There he stayed sleeping, and I caressed him, and the fanning of the
cedars made a breeze.

The breeze blew from the turret as I parted his locks;
With his gentle hand he wounded my neck and caused all my senses to
  be suspended.

I remained, lost in oblivion; my face I reclined on the Beloved.
All ceased and I abandoned myself, leaving my cares forgotten among
  the lilies.[8]

Moreover, in the same manner as the beguines, Juan implores seekers to renounce all worldly attachments, in order to denude the soul of its cravings and desires. In another of his profound works, *The Ascent of Mount Carmel*, he says:

> To reach satisfaction in all, desire its possession in nothing. To come to possess all, desire the possession of nothing. To arrive at being all, desire to be nothing. To come to the knowledge of all, desire the knowledge of nothing. To come to the pleasure you have not, you must go by a way of no pleasure. To come to the knowledge you have not, you must go by a way of unknowing. To come to the possession you have not, you must go by way of poverty. To come to be what you are not, you must go by a way of non-existence.[9]

Juan de la Cruz remained friends with Teresa of Avila until her death in 1582. Both had a profound influence on the other and yet they led very different lives. Teresa Sanchez de Cepeda y Ahumada was born on 28th March in 1515 in Avila and was one of ten children. Of mixed Jewish and Christian blood, her mother died when she was only twelve. At sixteen, she was placed in a girls' boarding school, run by Augustinian nuns whereupon she decided she wanted to take the veil herself. She thus entered the Carmelite Monastery of the Incarnation in Avila at the age of twenty-one.

Two years later, Teresa was struck down by an illness so severe that it rendered her in a coma for almost four days. It left her almost completely paralyzed for the following three years with the effect that she could only get about by crawling on her hands and knees.

Indeed, her acute suffering remained well up to her late thirties. To add to her difficulties, she inwardly struggled between a life drawn in one direction towards God and contemplation and the other towards the world. But then in 1554 two experiences reconfirmed her allegiance to the cloistered life. The image of a statue of Christ, wounded and bleeding, compelled her to throw herself on the ground in an act of utter humility, accompanied by wailing and floods of tears. And shortly afterwards, whilst reading the *Confessions* of St Augustine and of his hearing the voice of God calling him home, she too felt a similar presence beckoning her from within. It is from this time on, she would later write, that a new life for her began.

This precipitated a sequence of mystical visions and intellectual insights. In an attempt to make any sense of them, Teresa thus embarked on a literary career. Her autobiography, *Life*, was composed in 1562 and immediately attracted praise for its depth of spiritual understanding, executed with breathtaking honesty. Indeed, as with all her Christian sisters before her, she was at pains to excuse her 'wretched' female state, indicating that she only wrote her experiences at the behest of her confessors. Writing in basic Spanish, with little punctuation and peculiar syntax, she repeatedly declares her outcast state:

> For I am not learned nor have I led a good life, and I have neither a scholar nor anyone else to guide me. Only those who have commanded me to write this know that I am doing so and they are not here at present. I have almost to steal the time for writing, and that with difficulty, because it hinders me from spinning, and I am living in a poor house where there is a great deal to do. If the Lord had given me greater skill and a better memory, I might have profited by what I have heard and read. But I have very little of either. So if anything I have said is right, it is because the Lord has willed it for some good purpose of His own …[10]

This was not as self deprecatory as it first appears – the Spanish Inquisition would have been hot on the heels of anyone offering anything other than an orthodox interpretation of Christ's message.

Thus by renouncing all responsibility for authorship, Teresa was effectively protecting herself and her sister flock.

Later that year, Teresa founded a new monastery of St Joseph in Avila. In contrast to the 180 nuns living in the Incarnation, only twelve sisters shared the new convent. Despite the physical hardships, the project was a great success. Life focused predominantly on contemplative prayer, which suited Teresa's temperament. By 1567, so inspired by her initiative, she had her fateful meeting with Juan de la Cruz, who helped her go on to establish further Carmel monasteries throughout Spain.

She spent the rest of her life travelling, meeting the rich and poor, the learned and unlettered, in an attempt to popularize her unique way of devotion to God. Her avails were not without resistance, however, and the many hardships and ecclesiastical resistance she had to endure, particularly as a woman in her twilight years, were testament to her strength and courage. By the time of her death in 1582 in Alba, still out on the road dispensing her Godly advice, she had established fourteen Carmelite monasteries as well as amassing a voluminous correspondence with some of the most famous personages of her day, including King Philip II of Spain.

Throughout her life, she also managed to produce some beautiful and profound mystical expression, combining theoretical teaching with personal experience. Never pausing to reflect upon what she had just written, she once surmised that she wished she could write with both hands, in order to get down her thoughts onto paper more quickly.

In her *Life*, she speaks of her early years, her severe illnesses and spiritual struggles. A keen user of metaphor, she also outlines the stages on the spiritual path in terms of irrigating a garden, in her analogy of the 'four waters'. The soul, Teresa explains, is a garden, formed on barren soil and full of weeds. 'His Majesty' pulls out the weeds and then plants good seeds. However, it is the individual's responsibility, the gardener, to water the garden – and the four methods of irrigation described represent the stages of prayer through which the soul must pass.

The first stage is extremely hard, owing to the inexperience of the individual, and in order to demonstrate this, Teresa uses the analogy of drawing water from a well. The second stage is still difficult and is exemplified through the turning of the crank of a waterwheel and using a system of aqueducts. The third stage is where God starts to help in the process and Teresa describes this as using water that comes straight from a river or spring. The fourth and final stage is where the analogous garden is watered by the sweet rain from the heavens above:

> I am now speaking of that rain that comes down abundantly from heaven to soak and saturate the whole garden. If the Lord never ceased to send it whenever it was needed, the gardener would certainly have leisure; and if there were no winter but always a temperate climate, there would never be a shortage of fruit and flowers, and the gardener would clearly be delighted. But this is impossible while we live, for we must always be looking out for one water when another fails. The heavenly rain very often comes down when the gardener least expects it. Yet it is true that at the beginning it almost comes after long mental prayer.[11]

The Lord then speaks to Teresa about the nature of the soul upon the blossoming of the garden:

> 'It dissolves utterly, my daughter, to rest more and more on Me. It is no longer itself that lives: it is I. As it cannot comprehend what it understands, it understands by not understanding.'[12]

Her next major text, written for her sisters in the convent and completed in 1569 was *The Way of Perfection*, a treatise on the power of prayer. In it, she insists that peace of the soul is the prerequisite for inner contemplation, fostered by humility, love of one's neighbour and detachment:

> Once we have detached ourselves from the world, and from our kinsfolk, and are cloistered here, in the conditions already

described, it must look as if we have done everything and there is nothing left with which we have to contend. But, oh my sisters, do not feel secure and fall asleep, or you will be like a man who goes to bed quite peacefully, after bolting all his doors for fear of thieves, when the thieves are already in the house. And you know there is no worse thief *than one who lives in the house.* We ourselves are always the same; unless we take great care and each of us looks well to it that she renounces her self-will, which is the most important business of all, there will be many things to deprive us of the holy freedom of spirit *which our souls seek* in order to soar to their Master unburdened by the leaden weight of the earth.[13]

Nevertheless, this does mean that one should cultivate a sterile heart. Just like the replenishing rain, each sister's soul needs constant love and reassurance, the nourishment of a mother's milk:

The soul is like an infant still at its mother's breast: such is the mother's care for it that she gives it its milk without its having to ask for it so much as by moving its lips. That is what happens here. The will simply loves, and no effort needs to be made by the understanding, for it is the Lord's pleasure that, without exercising its thought, the soul should realize that it is in His company, and should merely drink the milk which His Majesty puts into its mouth and enjoy its sweetness.[14]

Without doubt, however, Teresa's masterpiece is *The Interior Castle*, written some ten years later when she was in her early sixties. The most extraordinary fact concerning its composition is that it fell under the shadow of the Inquisition and in particular the encroaching presence of Tomas de Torquemada. Rumours abounded that he was on his way to Avila to quash Teresa's work and the Carmelite Order, however, a Spanish papal nuncio who favoured her efforts was able to divert his attention elsewhere.

Thus it was in the midst of such political machinations that she was able to write the most sublime allegory on the human soul. Immediately, Teresa sets the scene in her work:

> ... there came to my mind what I shall now speak about, that which will provide us with a basis to begin with. It is that we consider our soul to be like a castle made entirely out of a diamond or of very clear crystal in which there are many rooms, just as in heaven there are many dwelling places.[15]

There are seven dwelling places in total – the first three representing the stages of human effort, principally through prayer and the ordinary help of grace; the remaining four deal with the mystical aspects of the spiritual path. Teresa is quick to point out, however, the underlying paradox of her analogy:

> It seems I'm saying something foolish. For if this castle is the soul, clearly one doesn't have to enter it since it is in oneself. How foolish it would seem were we to tell someone to enter a room he is already in. But you must understand that there is a great difference in the ways one may be inside the castle. For there are many souls who are in the outer courtyard – which is where the guards stay – and don't care at all about entering the castle, nor do they know what lies within that most precious place, nor who is within, nor even how many rooms it has. You have already heard in some books on prayer that the soul is advised to enter within itself. Well, that's the very thing I'm advising.[16]

In the fifth dwelling place, Teresa uses the analogy of a silkworm to describe the soul's metamorphosis, spinning itself a cocoon:

> Therefore, courage, my daughters! Let's be quick to do this work and weave this little cocoon by taking away our self-love and self-will, our attachment to any earthly thing ... Let it die; let this silkworm die, as it does in completing what it was created to do!

And you will see how we see God, as well as ourselves placed inside His grandeur, as this little silkworm within its cocoon ...

When the soul is, in this prayer, truly dead to the world, a little white butterfly comes forth ... Truly, I tell you that the soul doesn't recognize itself. Look at the difference there is between an ugly worm and a little white butterfly.[17]

But this is not the end of the journey. Despite its new-found freedom, the butterfly cannot find rest, alighting hither and thither. It is in the sixth dwelling place that union with God must take place, and here Teresa switches to the familiar metaphor of the mystical relationship. Here the gifts of humility and self-knowledge are the love tokens between lover and Beloved. But still there is one last stage, the seventh dwelling place, where there is total absorption in God and the two are joined in marriage:

The spiritual betrothal is different, for the two often separate. And the union is also different because, even though it is the joining of two things into one, in the end the two can be separated and each remains by itself ... Let us say that the union is like the joining of two wax candles to such an extent that the flame coming from them is but one, or that the wick, the flame, and the wax are all one. But afterward one candle can be easily separated from the other and there are two candles; the same holds for the wick. In the spiritual marriage the union is like what we have when rain falls from the sky into a river or fount; all is water, for the rain that fell from heaven cannot be divided or separated from the water of the river. Or it is like what we have when a little stream enters the sea, there is no means of separating the two. Or, like the bright light entering a room through two different windows; although the streams of light are separate when entering the room, they become one.[18]

Teresa composed many other short tracts and testimonies, drawing on her wealth of self examination and insight. One of her lesser known works entitled *Meditations on the Song of Songs* is probably the pinnacle of her mystical eroticism, composed in roughly 1566. Only seven chapters long, she focuses on one particular translation of the verse, 'Your breasts are better than wine,' (*Song of Songs* 1:2) whereby the image of Christ, in the same manner as Julian of Norwich, is seen as the divine Mother, nourishing the individual soul with the milk of his breasts. Teresa writes:

> But when this most wealthy Spouse desires to enrich and comfort the Bride still more, He draws her so closely to him that she is like one who swoons from excess of pleasure and joy and seems to be suspended in those Divine breasts. Sustained by that divine milk with which her Spouse continually nourishes her and growing in grace so that she may be enabled to receive His comforts, she can do nothing but rejoice. Awakening from that sleep and heavenly inebriations, she is like one amazed and stupefied. It seems to me that she can say these words: 'Your breasts are better than wine.'[19]

It is no surprise, therefore, that when Teresa was on her deathbed on 4th October 1582 in Alba, she started reciting verses from the *Song of Songs*, ready to be received into the bosom of Christ. Indeed, her statue, *The Ecstasy of St Teresa*, sculpted by Gian Lorenzo Bernini and housed in the Cornaro Chapel in Rome, depicts a woman swathed in flowing robes, lost in the rapture of her love.

chapter eighteen

Grace Aguilar

Although the Spanish Inquisition perpetrated some of the most heinous crimes against humanity the modern world has ever seen in an attempt to crush unorthodox teachings, Spain itself was once a centre of a great mystical tradition. Conquered by Arabs in the eighth century, it was home to a handful of eminent Muslim sages who were learned in the esoteric message of Islam as well as the Platonist philosophy of the Greeks. Moreover, in the eleventh century, Spain also became refuge to a large Jewish population, who brought with them their own wisdom tradition of the *Apocrypha* and the Old Testament.

It is no surprise, therefore, that into this metaphysical melange was born Solomon Ibn Gabirol (1021–58) in Malaga in southern Spain, whose most famous prose work, *The Fountain of Life*, was an attempt to describe the nature of Reality and the creation of the universe. Nevertheless, it is in his poetry where Gabirol's mystical insight is the most beautifully crafted. And like so many enlightened sages before him, he employs the concept of the feminine soul as the manifested embodiment of the sacred:

> At Thy word, 'Be, O soul,' she took on existence,
> And from Thy Emptiness Thou didst draw her forth as light from the eye.
> It was Thee who didst breathe in her life; I shall proclaim and affirm
>   this with uplifted hands.

And therefore she shall pour out her thanks and give witness that she
was bidden to do by Thee.
While yet in the body, she serves Thee as a handmaid;
And on that day when she returns to the land from whence she came,
In Thee will she dwell, for in Thee is her being.
Whether she sits or rises, Thou art with her the same.
She was Thine before she was born and breathing;
She was nourished by Thee with wisdom and knowledge,
And it is to Thee she looks for her guidance and sustenance ...

Let her pour out her tears as the wine on the altar,
And let the breath of her sighs rise as fragrance to Thee.
At her gate and her doorway, she watches in prayer;
She is burning like flame with her passion for Thee.[1]

The idea of the sacred feminine would be developed further in a related but distinctly separate phenomenon known as the Kabbala, simply meaning 'the tradition', which flourished during the twelfth century in Spain and southern France. The Kabbalistic teaching was systematized by Moses de Leon (1240–1305) in his book, *Zohar* meaning 'Splendour', a mystical interpretation of the first five books of the Hebrew Bible, the *Torah*. Cunningly, in order to accelerate its popularity, he claimed that the text was an ancient tract written by Shimeon ben Yohai, a second-century CE Palestinian monk. It was only in the nineteenth century that scholars learnt of the fraud.

The *Zohar* starts by describing the birth of the created world out of the Infinite One (known as *En Sof*):

In the beginning, when the Will of the King began to take effect, He impressed His signs into the heavenly sphere within the Most Hidden, the Infinite [*En Sof*], a dark flame issued forth, like a fog forming in the Unformed.

Forming the concentric ring of [that] first sphere, [this flame was] neither white nor black, neither red nor green, of no colour whatever. Only after this flame began to assume size and dimension, did it produce radiant colours. From the innermost centre of the flame gushed forth a host of colours which spread on everything beneath. Concealed within all was the hidden mystery of the Infinite [*En Sof*].[2]

In the Kabbala, the Absolute or Yahweh is perceived as masculine and is hidden from normal comprehension. The soul, known as the Shekhinah, is feminine and is separated from Yahweh by ignorance. The purpose of each individual's life, therefore, is the removal of the veil of ignorance in order to find oneness with God – in other words, the union of the masculine and feminine.

Moreover, central to the teaching is the image of the Tree of Life; humankind is represented as a series of ten qualities, or *sefirot*, on the tree – humility (at the crown of the tree); understanding; wisdom; judgement; loving-kindness; splendour; endurance; foundation; the Shekhinah (at the base of the tree); and finally, *Tif'eret*, at the very heart of the tree, which is the beauty and compassion of God. Through meditation and various techniques, the Shekhinah rises up through each quality, eventually merging with the *Tif'eret* in divine union. It is no surprise, therefore, that the *Song of Songs* is one of the main mystical texts of Kabbala practice.

As well as being perceived as the individual soul, Shekhinah is also seen as an embodiment of the Holy Spirit, immanent in all creation and forming the ground of being in both men and women alike. Moreover, in the same manner in which Mary becomes the personification of Sophia as an object of worship, so too does *Matronit*, or the Matron, become the personification of Shekhinah, to whom affection and obeisance can be offered.

Unfortunately, however, as with so many other religious traditions, Jewish women were exiled from scholastic and mystical practice. Moreover, the Tree of Life itself took on a misogynistic interpretation, whereby the left-hand, feminine side of the tree became associated with darkness and evil, whereas the right-hand, masculine side represented goodness and light.

And yet, at the very heart of the Kabbala teaching is the egalitarian status of both men and women. Indeed, in the *Zohar* itself, Moses de Leon stresses the importance of both the male and female embodiments of the Divine. Commenting on the first two verses of Genesis 5, he emphasizes the simultaneous creation of both sexes, equal before God:

> *High mysteries are revealed in these two verses.*
> *'Male and female He created them.'*
> *To make known the Glory on high,*
> *the mystery of faith …*

> *'Male and female he created them.'*
> *From here we learn:*
> *Any image that does not embrace male and female*
> *is not a high and true image.*
> *We have established this in the mystery of our Mishnah [Bible commentary].*

> *Come and see:*
> *The Blessed Holy One does not place His abode*
> *in any place where male and female are not found together.*
> *Blessings are found only in a place where male and female are found,*
> *as it is written:*
> *'He blessed them and called their name Adam*
> *on the day they were created.'*
> *It is not written:*
> *'He blessed Him and called his name Adam.'*
> *A human being is only called Adam*
> *when male and female are as one.*[3]

Here we hear echoes of Jesus' words in *The Gospel of Thomas*: 'make the male and the female into a single one.'[4]

By the eighteenth century in Europe, the Kabbala was the province of male scholarship alone. It was during this time that women decided, therefore, to readdress the balance by creating a body of literature specifically for their own daily use, called *tkhines* –

Yiddish supplicatory prayers, written by women for women. Indeed, one specific *tkhine* redefines the symbolism of the candle-lighting ceremony on the Sabbath. Rather than accepting the traditional meaning that the lighting of the wick is an act of atonement for Eve's 'sinfulness' of bringing darkness in the world, it is reinterpreted as the celebration of the sacred Shekhinah.

It was around this time that the voice of an individual woman would emerge, championing further the cause of Jewish women. Grace Aguilar was born on 2nd June 1816 in Hackney, London, to Portuguese parents. As a child she contracted a mysterious illness that left her physically weak for the rest of her short life. She contracted measles at nineteen and later a spinal disease that almost paralyzed her. Being of a Sephardic family, her father was keen to teach Grace about her Portuguese Jewish inheritance. This culminated in her first attempt at writing – an historical romance set during the Spanish Inquisition, entitled *The Vale of Cedars*, completed before her twenties but which was published only posthumously in 1850.

After living in Devon for a number of years during her teens, the family settled in Brighton, where both parents became increasingly infirm. With two younger brothers to take care of, Grace took on the responsibility of providing financially for the family by earning an income through publishing her writing. Initially her output was predominantly mainstream – she produced a book of poems, *The Magic Wreath of Hidden Flowers* (1835), comprising riddles on particular flora, as well as regularly contributing short sketches on domestic life to magazines and journals. During this period, she also drafted a series of novels – *Home Influence: A Tale for Mothers and Daughters* (not published until 1847), *A Mother's Recompense* (1851) and *Women's Friendship* (1850), in which she offers portraits of female role models and the necessity for giving children a religious education.

Although Grace remained childless and never married, she was a keen advocate of the domestic life as a place for spiritual growth, which in turn provided a firm foundation for an enlightened society. In the manner of Plato and his analogy of children being like soft wax, Grace stressed the importance of shaping young minds with a moral hand. In *The Spirit of Judaism* (1842), a reworking of the Jewish teaching into a female-centred theology, she emphasizes the responsibility of Jewish mothers towards their offspring:

> There is a peculiar sweetness in the remembrance of a mother. When a young man has raised himself by his own virtues and talents in the world, when he feels himself esteemed and beloved by his fellow men: he will still think of his mother, if it have been from her lips, the first lesson of virtue were imbibed; and if religion were as zealously and carefully implanted, would not her memory have equal influence in guarding him from temptation, strengthening him to walk on the paths she loved? It may be that continued occupation, perhaps arduous labour, or severe thought and study have withdrawn his attention awhile from God; or that the paths of pleasure, encircling him with their delusive rays, conceal from his eyes the light of eternity.
>
> Some sudden recollection recalls his mother to his mind ... He hears again the sweet and gentle voice which first spoke to him of God; he sees again those happy hours when, seated at her feet, he rested his little hands upon her lap, and repeated with her the words of prayer or listened with tearful eyes, and swelling heart, to the tales of sacred love ...[5]

Essentially, Grace was honouring the oral tradition of the past. Moreover, she abhorred the way in which men and women were separated in the synagogue and made it quite clear that she believed that women should receive the same religious education as men.

In 1845, Grace published what is believed to be her masterpiece, the three-volumed *Women of Israel*, in which she further expounded the female cause by chronicling the biographical accounts of Jewish women from Eve right up to her current age. In it, she reaffirms women's religious experience and offers her own theological commentary; with passion and vigour, she takes the root of misogyny to task:

How or whence originated the charge that the law of Moses sank the Hebrew female to the lowest state of degradation, placed her on a level with slaves or heathens, and denied her all mental and spiritual enjoyment, we know not; yet certain it is that this most extraordinary and unfounded idea obtains credence even in this enlightened age. The word of God at once proves its falsity; for it is impossible to read the Mosaic law without the true and touching conviction that the female Hebrew was even more an object of the tender and soothing care of the Eternal than the male ...

The Eternal's provision for her temporal and spiritual happiness is proved in His unalterable word; and therefore no Hebrew can believe that He would issue another law for her degradation and abasement ...

The women of the Bible are but mirrors of ourselves. And if the Eternal, in His infinite mercy, extended love, compassion, forbearance, and forgiveness unto them, we may believe He extends them equally unto us ...[6]

In her reassessment of her Hebrew heritage, she also wrote a beautiful prose short story, 'Spirit of Night'. Composed in 1852, it is a Hebrew apologue or fable founded upon Morris Raphall's 'The Sun and the Moon', itself a creation tale based on Genesis 1:16. In Raphall's version, the female Moon only receives the reflected light of the male Sun; in Grace's text, however, the Moon's jealousy of the Sun prompts the Eternal to take pity on her and honour her with equal status:

Queen of the lovely night will thine orb be hailed; the tears of thy repentance shall be a reviving balm to all that languish; imparting consolation to the mourner, rest to the weary, soothing to the care-worn, strength to the exhausted. Peace shall be thy whisper, and in thy kingdom of stillness and repose, breathe thrillingly the promise of Heaven and its rest. Go forth, then, on thy mild and vivifying career. The Orb of Day will do his work, and be hailed with rejoicing mirth; but many a one shall turn to thee from him, and in the radiance of thy tears find consolation.[7]

Once again, the voice of the sacred feminine shines forth and the immanent lunar light radiates throughout the universe.

Grace also wrote poetry and was in fact one of the first Anglo-Jewish women to publish verse. Romantic in theme, she infuses her poems with the mystical presence of the Divine. In the opening stanzas of 'An Hour of Peace', Grace speaks of her wish to die and find union with God:

Oh, wake me not from this sweet dream
Now o'er my spirit stealing,
Of heaven's deep calm, a shadowy gleam,
This care-worn heart is feeling.

This is not suff'ring, though my frame,
Be weak and pain-struck lying;
While life's sad cares no thought can claim,
There is no need for sighing.

This – this is peace! Disturb it not,
To heav'n that dream has won me,
Oh let me lie, the world forgot –
God's eye alone upon me! …[8]

And in one of her most beautiful poems, 'The Address to the Ocean', which obliquely refers to Lord Byron's 'Childe Harold's Pilgrimage', Grace loses her soul in the crash and hiss of the heaving sea:

Sound on, thou mighty Deep, sound on, thou Sea,
Lash thy blue waves to snowy crested foam,
Wake into music, glorious and free,
Proclaim thee bulwark of our island home.

Sound on! Thou hast a voice of freedom, Sound!
My soul hath thrilling echoes to thy voice,
And throbs and bounds, as if on thee were found,
A home where life all chainless, might rejoice! ...

Let thy rich voice sound on! Roll on thy waves
'Mid storm and sunshine, still the blue, the free!
Life is upspringing from my soul's deep caves,
To hail, o bless thee, oh, thou glorious sea![9]

Once again, the sea – vast, immense, unfathomable – becomes the metaphor for the universal Source. Indeed, Grace was in no doubt of the immeasurable and indescribable oneness of God. In *The Spirit of Judaism*, she writes:

> The Hebrew word rendered *Lord* in the English of this sentence is in the original that awful and ineffable NAME, which no true Israelite will utter. It is the name peculiar to the Divine Essence, signifying He who WAS, IS and ever WILL BE – *Yahweh* ... We are told, first, that this Divine Essence – this ever-existing Being is our God, and then, that this Divine Essence is one.
>
> ... It is enough for us to know that not alone did our Father so reveal Himself in the impressive words with which He answered Moses – *ehyeh asher ehyeh* – I AM THAT I AM ...[10]

In 1847, Grace travelled to Frankfurt to visit her brother in order to improve her failing health. Diary entries from this period of her life reveal a woman in great physical pain and emotional turmoil. As she deteriorated further, her doctor advised her to stop writing and thus her journal ends abruptly mid-sentence on 29th July 1847. She was only thirty-one years old. Although she only had modest success during her lifetime, after her death Grace's vast body of work started to become well known through the efforts of her mother, Sarah Aguilar, who helped edit and posthumously publish her work.

Grace would never have dreamed that within a few decades, the emancipation of women in the home would spill over into the public arena, with the rise of feminism and the women's suffrage movement. And yet, as with all the women before her, she was instrumental in providing yet another stepping stone for the empowerment and liberation of women from all faiths and walks of life.

chapter nineteen

Emily Dickinson

By the time we reach the seventeenth and eighteenth centuries in Europe, a radical shift in human thinking was once again taking place. But whereas in the past, dogma and tradition were breaking down to allow for more enlightened attitudes towards universal consciousness, philosophers and scientists were now sidelining the spiritual realm in favour of a better understanding of the material world. With its emphasis on reason and empirical evidence, the somewhat ironically titled 'Age of Enlightenment' had dawned. Although God was still given credence for being the Creator of the world, it was man who was responsible for understanding him, unaided by any act of divine grace. Indeed, almost all of Christian theology was rejected and, in particular, the concept of original sin.

Out of the array of great thinkers of the period, it would be René Descartes (1596–1650) who would be responsible for inexorably changing the way in which man looked at the world. Using his 'method of doubt', he was able to deconstruct both the physical and mental world around him right up to the point of his very existence. It was only this fact – his own existence – of which he was in absolutely no doubt. This in turn led to his famous axiom, 'I think therefore I am'.

Immanuel Kant (1724–1804) would also develop Descartes' ideas by labelling the universe into its component parts – the physical world, which he called phenomenon; and the spiritual world, which he called noumenon. But despite Descartes' and Kant's belief in the existence of a divine power, it was now reduced to a philosophical abstraction.

Mankind's attention had subsequently shifted from the metaphysical to the physical, from the immanent Self to the limited form. Reason had triumphed over faith. However, the pendulum was about to swing back the other way; the following century saw one of the greatest philosophers ever to live who would synthesize Western philosophy with Eastern mysticism – the German scholar, Arthur Schopenhauer (1788–1860). In his most famous tract, *The World as Will and Representation*, first published in 1818, he outlines his unique vision of the cosmos:

> Past and future (apart from the consequences of their content) are as empty and unreal as any dream; but present is only the boundary between the two, having neither extension nor duration. In just the same way, we shall also recognize the same emptiness in all the other forms of the principle of sufficient reason, and shall see that, like time, space also, and like this, everything exists simultaneously in space and time, and hence everything that proceeds from causes or motives, has only a relative existence, is only through and for another like itself, i.e., only just as enduring. In essence this view is old; in it Heraclitus lamented the eternal flux of things; Plato spoke with contempt of its object as that which for ever becomes, but never is; Spinoza called it mere accidents of the sole substance that alone and endures; Kant opposed to the thing-in-itself that which is known as mere phenomenon; finally, the ancient wisdom of the Indians declares that 'it is maya, the veil of deception, which covers the eyes of mortals and causes them to see a world of which one cannot say either that it is or that it is not; for it is like a dream, like the sunshine on the sand which the traveller from a distance takes to be water or like the piece of rope on the ground which he regards as a snake.'[1]

Interestingly, Schopenhauer came to his nondualist vision *before* reading the ancient texts of the East, which merely confirmed his understanding.

Schopenhauer advocated that the appreciation of the arts could lead people to a momentary release of the individual will. Painting, sculpture, poetry and above all, music, lifted the soul above normal concerns, liberating and nourishing it on a wave of aesthetic ecstasy. Artists influenced by his ideas included the writers Leo Tolstoy (1828–1910), Thomas Mann (1875–1955) and Thomas Hardy (1840–1924) as well as the great composers, Richard Wagner (1813–83) and Gustav Mahler (1860–1911).

Another artistic movement that was influenced by the works of Schopenhauer was Romanticism. Propelled by the belief in the power of the subjective imagination, freedom of individual expression and the inherent sacredness of nature, the Romantic Age started in Europe in approximately 1750, lasting until roughly 1870. In contradistinction to Descartes, the French philosopher Jean-Jacques Rousseau (1712–78) famously said, 'I felt before I thought'. Thus the movement was an artistic backlash against the Age of Enlightenment, where the imagination triumphed over reason, emotion over logic and intuition over science. Above all, Romantic artists founded their interpretation of the world within the context of an immanent, all-pervading consciousness.

Many English poets would emerge during this period as accomplished exponents of Romantic literature – Samuel Taylor Coleridge (1772–1834), Lord Byron (1788–1824), Percy Bysshe Shelley (1792–1822), John Keats (1795–1821) and William Wordsworth (1770–1850). Indeed, Wordsworth's 'Intimations of Immortality from Recollections of Early Childhood' not only encapsulates the Romantic imagination but is also an exquisite example of the plight of the human soul, searching for its home:

Our birth is but a sleep and a forgetting:
The Soul that rises with us, our life's Star,
Hath had elsewhere its setting,
And cometh from afar:
Not in entire forgetfulness,
And not in utter nakedness,
But trailing clouds of glory do we come

From God, who is our home:
Heaven lies about us in our infancy!
Shades of the prison-house begin to close
Upon the growing Boy
But he
Beholds the light, and whence it flows,
He sees it in his joy;
The Youth, who daily farther from the east
Must travel, still is Nature's Priest,
And by the vision splendid
Is on his way attended;
At length the Man perceives it done away,
And fade into the light of common day.[2]

Freedom of individual expression meant that society was seeing the emergence more and more of women writers. Moreover, the realm of emotional sensitivity and the appreciation of nature were aptly suited for the female pen. Christina Rossetti (1830–94), sister of the Pre-Raphaelite painter Dante Gabriel Rossetti (1828–82), wrote many poems focusing on romantic and sacred love. Living as a recluse in the last fifteen years of her life, she was still popular and accomplished enough to be considered for the position of Poet Laureate. In the opening stanzas of 'Confluents', it is easy to see why:

As rivers seek the sea,
Much more deep than they,
So my soul seeks thee
Far away:
As running rivers moan
On their course alone,
So I moan
Left alone.

As the delicate rose
To the sun's sweet strength

Doth herself unclose,
Breadth and length;
So spreads my heart to thee
Unveiled utterly,
I to thee
Utterly ...[3]

Another eminent female writer who lived during this period was Elizabeth Barrett Browning (1806–61). Married to the poet Robert Browning, she too was considered by Wordsworth to be a contender for the illustrious position of Poet Laureate. A lover of classical poetry and aesthetic theory, she lived with her husband in Italy where she wrote her magnum opus, *Aurora Leigh* (1857), a 'novel in verse'. The 11,000-line story of a woman writer, it deals with issues of social responsibility and the position of women. Like her contemporary Romantic poets, Elizabeth is enchanted by the world around her and yet she is consciously aware of the way in which it is also the manifestation of something greater:

Truth, so far, in my book – the truth which draws
Through all things upwards – that a twofold world
Must go to a perfect cosmos. Natural things
And spiritual – who separates those two
In art, in morals or the social drift
Tears up the bond of nature and brings death,
Paints futile pictures, writes unreal verse,
Leads vulgar days, deals ignorantly with men,
Is wrong, in short, at all points. We divide
This apple of life, and cut it through the pips –
The perfect round which fitted Venus' hand
Has perished as utterly as if we ate
Both halves. Without the spiritual, observe,
The natural's impossible – no form,
No motion: without sensuous, spiritual
Is inappreciable – no beauty or power:

And in this twofold sphere the twofold man
(For still the artist is intensely a man)
Holds firmly by the natural, to reach
The spiritual beyond it – [4]

Not all women, however, believed that an emotional sensibility was the best means through which a woman could express herself. Indeed, the rising voice of feminism was growing in Europe fostered by the enormous political, economic and sociological changes of the time. The most notable feminist voice was Mary Wollstonecraft (1759–97), whose *A Vindication of the Rights of Women* was essentially the first great feminist treatise. For her, the intellect was the means to individual freedom and in a stunning piece of integrity and wit, she states her cause:

My own sex, I hope, will excuse me, if I treat them like rational creatures, instead of flattering their *fascinating* graces, and viewing them as if they were in a state of perpetual childhood, unable to stand alone. I earnestly wish to point out in what true dignity and human happiness consists – I wish to persuade women to endeavour to acquire strength, both of mind and body, and to convince them that the soft phrases, susceptibility of heart, delicacy of sentiment, and refinement of taste, are almost synonymous with epithets of weakness, and that those beings who are only the objects of pity and that kind of love, which has been termed its sister, will soon become objects of contempt. Dismissing then those pretty feminine phrases, which the men condescendingly use to soften our slavish dependence, and despising that weak elegancy of mind, exquisite sensibility, and sweet docility of manners, supposed to be the sexual characteristics of the weaker vessel, I wish to show that elegance is inferior to virtue, that the first object of laudable ambition is to obtain a character as a human being, regardless of the distinction of sex; and that secondary views should be brought to this simple touchstone.[5]

Interestingly, her daughter, Mary, would become the wife of Percy Bysshe Shelley and a writer in her own right.

The spirit of both feminism and Romanticism also spread across to America. A group of writers and thinkers emerged, predominantly male, who also placed emphasis on transcendental knowledge and the belief that the soul was immanent in all creation. Collectively known as the American Transcendentalists, the movement was a reaction to the intellectual rationalism of the eighteenth century and the strict Puritan attitudes arising out of New England, brought to America by Protestant Pilgrim Fathers in the seventeenth century. The Transcendentalists' chief exponent, Ralph Waldo Emerson (1803–82), speaking of the Eternal Spirit or 'Over Soul' commented that it constituted the 'unity within which every man's particular being is contained and made one with all other'.[6] Emerson also actively campaigned alongside female suffrage movements, championing the equal rights of women.

Born into this extraordinary transitional period of American history was the female poet, Emily Dickinson, on 10th December 1830. Raised in a New England village, Amherst, with an older brother and younger sister, her parents were respectable middle-class folk with strong Calvinist roots. However, this was the time of the Second Great Awakening, the Puritan revival that was sweeping through New England. Unable to participate in this wave of religious fervour, she suffered an acute religious breakdown in her early childhood, which affected her for the rest of her life. Indeed, she refused to associate herself with any religious denomination, simply calling herself a 'pagan'.

Emily started writing poetry in her late twenties. It was only then do we get a feeling of the full extent of her unhappiness and sense of isolation as a child. Brought up under strict parentage and religious discipline, she desperately searched for some form of happiness, beyond her mortal self:

A loss of something ever felt I –
The first that I could recollect
Bereft I was – of what I knew not
Too young that any should suspect

A Mourner walked among the children
I notwithstanding went about
As one bemoaning a Dominion
Itself the only Prince cast out –

Elder, Today, a session wiser
And fainter, too, as Wiseness is –
I find myself still softly searching
For my Delinquent Palaces –

And a Suspicion, like a Finger
Touches my Forehead now and then
That I looking oppositely
For the site of the Kingdom of Heaven –[7]

In 1862, she submitted four poems to the journal, *Atlantic Monthly*, whose editor, Colonel Thomas Wentworth Higginson, was less than enthusiastic about her verse. He found her poetry unruly and lacking any external structure. Moreover, he disliked Emily's use of metaphor and allusion and therefore advised her to delay publication. However, looking at her poetry through twenty-first-century eyes, we see a radical and revolutionary style, where the unconventional form mirrors subtle ideas and emotion. Indeed, her eccentric use of pauses, punctuation and irregular rhyming schemes reflect the unpredictability and transience of not only her own interior world but of the universe around all of us. Nevertheless, despite his ambivalence, Higginson and Emily went on to have a twenty-year correspondence.

Emily wrote about many themes – death, nature, romantic love. And yet despite the overt feeling of mutability and loss of the created world, there is always hope of eternal life beyond it. Like the Romanticists before her, her poetry is suffused with the mystical vision of a transcendental knowledge beyond all human comprehension.

I felt a Funeral, in my Brain,
And Mourners to and fro
Kept treading – treading – till it seemed
That Sense was breaking through –

And when they all were seated,
A Service, like a Drum –
Kept beating – beating – till I thought
My Mind was going numb –

And then I heard them lift a Box
And creak across my Soul
With those same Boots of Lead, again,
Then Space – began to toll,

As all the Heavens were a Bell,
And Being, but an Ear,
And I, and Silence, some strange Race
Wrecked, solitary, here –

And then a Plank in Reason, broke,
And I dropped down, and down –
And hit a World, at every plunge,
And finished knowing – then – [8]

And then? The poet is poignantly silent. Nonetheless, the death of self is a theme she returns to time and again:

Me and Myself – to banish –
Had I Art –
Impregnable my Fortress
Unto All Heart –

But since Myself – assault Me –
How have I peace

Except by subjugating
Consciousness?

And since We're mutual Monarch
How this be
Except by Abdication –
Me – of Me?[9]

The mistress of metaphor, Emily employs many images to represent her abstract ideas. Indeed she has often been compared to the Metaphysical Poets, owing to her brevity and wit of expression. Moreover, landscapes often assume the manifestation of the changing states of the soul's journey towards immortality:

I cross till I am weary
A Mountain – in my mind –
More Mountains – then a Sea –
More Seas – And then
A Desert – find –

And My Horizon blocks
With steady – drifting – Grains
Of unconjectured quantity –
As Asiatic Rains

Not this – defeat my Pace –
It hinder from the West
But as an Enemy's Salute
One hurrying to Rest –

What merit had the Goal –
Except there intervene
Faint Doubt – and far Competitor –
To jeopardise the Gain?

At last – the Grace in sight –
I shout unto my feet –
I offer them the Whole of Heaven
The instant that we meet –

They strive – and yet delay –
They perish – Do we die –
Or is this Death's Experiment –
Reversed – in Victory?[10]

Despite the literary freedom Emily enjoyed in her poems, she was, however, subjugated to the prevailing nineteenth-century ideology regarding women and, in particular, concepts regarding whether or not a female poet should be published. Emily was inconsistent on the issue, believing on the one hand equal rights should exist for both male and female artists, whereas on the other, she shied away from fame – in her own lifetime, she only published ten poems. It was only after she died of kidney disease in 1886 that her vast corpus of work – 1,775 short lyrics – was discovered, stitched into packets known as fascicles, accumulated in a bureau drawer. It was her publisher, Thomas Wentworth Higginson, who was left the main responsibility of editing and publishing her work.

One poet who had a profound effect on Emily was Elizabeth Barrett Browning – her verse novel *Aurora Leigh* had been given to her by Emily's brother's wife, Susan Dickinson. Emily outlines her debt of inspiration in one of her poems to her female muse:

I think I was enchanted
When first a sombre Girl –
I read that Foreign Lady –
The Dark – felt beautiful –

And whether it was noon at night –
Or only Heaven – at Noon –
For very Lunacy of Light
I had not power to tell – …

I could not have defined the change –
Conversion of the Mind
Like Sanctifying in the Soul –
Is witnessed – not explained –

'Twas a Divine Insanity
The danger to be Sane
Should I again experience –
'Tis an Antidote to turn –

To Tomes of solid Witchcraft –
Magicians be asleep –
But Magic – hath an Element
Like Deity – to keep –[11]

As Emily grew older, she shunned the outside world more and more. Indeed her reclusive behaviour even saw her closest friends refused entry into the family home. Various myths have arisen to describe such a stance – agoraphobia, a literary 'pose' enabling her to write, an unrequited love. Indeed, the only known black-and-white photograph of Emily shows a thin, gaunt-faced young woman, with serious dark eyes, betraying no hint of emotion – a façade, perhaps, to the swathe of feeling beneath.

Interestingly, although Emily was perceived as being ambivalent to marriage and resenting the restraint it placed on a woman's freedom, three draft letters were discovered after her death. Collectively known as the Master Letters, they are directed to an unidentified lover and are the intimate confessions of her love. Some commentators have suggested suitable candidates, both single and married, male and female, the most notable being Susan Dickinson (some feminist critics have identified a thread of homoeroticism in her verse).

Whomever the intended recipient, they reveal a side to Emily not prevalent in her poetry. In the three letters, the power of her emotion and heartfelt longing is breathtakingly moving. In the first letter, written in roughly 1858 and of the least intense, she wishes her

Master well after an illness. It is the second letter of the same year, however, which is unashamedly urgent and direct in its confession of her romantic feelings:

MASTER,

If you saw a bullet hit a Bird – and he told you he wasn't shot – you might weep at his courtesy but you would certainly doubt his word.

One drop more from the gash that stains your Daisy's bosom – then would you *believe*? … God made me – [Sir] Master – I didn't be – myself …

I am older – tonight, Master – but the love is the same – so are the moon and the crescent. If it had been God's will that I might breathe where you breathed – and find the place – myself – at night – if I [can] never forget that I am not with you – and that sorrow and frost are nearer than I – if I wish with a might I cannot repress – that mine were the Queen's place – the love of the Plantagenet is my only apology …

Have you a Heart in your breast – Sir – is it set like mine – a little to the left – has it the misgiving – if it wake in the night – perchance – itself to it – a timbrel is it – itself to it a tune?[12]

Emily fantasizes about a possible relationship with the Master but there is an undertone of doom, of hope fading into the unrequited reality of her love. The letter can also be read as a microcosm of Emily's life and her friendships with others. Not only did she remain single, she had not one sustaining relationship, platonic or otherwise. It is said that such was the intensity of her personality, both intellectually and emotionally, that any potential friends or suitors simply shied away.

The third letter, dated approximately 1862, is much more sombre and subdued in its acknowledgement of the utter hopelessness of her love:

You send the water over the Dam in my brown eyes – …

Oh how the sailor strains, when his boat is filling – Oh how the dying tug, till the angel comes. Master – open your life wide, and take me in forever, I will never be tired – I will never be noisy when you want to be still. I will be [glad] [as] your best little girl – nobody else will see me, but you – but that is enough – I shall not want any more – and all that Heaven only will disappoint me – will be because it's not so dear.[13]

The full realization of failure in the Master's eyes is apparent. The pain we feel for her is achingly palpable.

Interestingly, in 1876 Susan Dickinson also gave Emily a copy of *The Imitation of Christ* for Christmas, the mystical tract infused with the imagery of divine lovers. However, although it is highly unlikely that the Master of Emily's three letters was a reference to Christ, Thomas à Kempis' text had a subsequently profound effect on her. Not only does it advocate the solitary life but it speaks of the mystical union between lover and Beloved. Indeed, she imitates a number of her own poems in such a vein:

Given in Marriage unto Thee
Oh thou Celestial Host –
Bride of the Father and the Son
Bride of the Holy Ghost.

Other Betrothal shall dissolve –
Wedlock of Will, decay –
Only the Keeper of this Ring
Conquer Mortality – [14]

As with so many women who composed verse and prose with a radically unique style and meaning, she has only come to be appreciated after her death. And yet, like her male contemporary, Walt Whitman (1819–92), whose immortal lines in his poem, 'Song of Myself' – 'I celebrate myself, and sing myself'[15] – inspired generations of mystical poets, so too do the haunting lines of Emily Dickinson:

Behind Me – dips Eternity –
Before Me – Immortality –
Myself – the Term between –

Death but the Drift of Eastern Gray,
Dissolving into Dawn away,
Before the West begin –

'Tis Kingdom – afterward – they say –
In perfect – pauseless Monarchy –
Whose Prince – is Son of None –
Himself – His Dateless Dynasty –
Himself – Himself diversify –
In duplicate Divine –

'Tis Miracle before Me – then –
'Tis Miracle behind – between –
A Crescent in the Sea –
With midnight to the North of Her –
And Midnight to the South of Her –
And Maelstrom – in the Sky – 16

chapter twenty

Sharada Devi

Similar changes in human consciousness were taking place in the East but the effect was far less pronounced. Essentially, attitudes towards women in the Asian continents were still bound by their respective religious traditions as well as ongoing patriarchal structures. India would have to wait until the nineteenth century for another great teacher to emerge – one who would eclipse all those before him in terms of his wisdom and humility, and one who would venerate all women as the sacred feminine.

Born Gadadhar Chattopadyaya in Kamarpukur in Bengal, he is more commonly known to us as the sage Ramakrishna (1836–86). Interested in religion at a very young age, he would listen to the tales from the *Puranas* and would often sit with sannyasin passing through the village. It was at the tender age of six that Ramakrishna would have his first taste of the one Self. Walking through paddy fields on a hot summer's day carrying a basket of puffed rice, he looked up and saw a dark thundercloud. Suddenly, a flock of snow-white cranes flew by and the contrasting beauty of white on black was so overwhelming that he fell down in a swoon, immersed in a state of ecstasy.

At sixteen, his older brother, who lived in Calcutta, sent for Ramakrishna. He then took him to a local temple devoted to Mother Kali where he was the priest, just outside the city in Dakshineswar, on the east bank of the River Ganges. Ramakrishna was assigned to helping him in the running of the temple, a job which at first yielded little interest. However, over time, Ramakrishna began to love the temple and its paradisal surroundings – so much so that he would spend the rest of his life there in service and meditation.

The most interesting aspect of Ramakrishna's practice was his overwhelming desire to have an inner experience of the Divine Mother. For many nights sitting alone in the forest, he would implore her to reveal herself to him. Eventually, his dreams would come true:

> I felt as if my heart were being squeezed like a wet towel. I was overpowered with a great restlessness and a fear that it might not be my lot to realize Her in this life. I could not bear the separation from Her any longer. Life seemed to be not worth living. Suddenly my glance fell on the sword that was kept in the Mother's temple. I determined to put an end to my life. When I jumped up like a madman and seized it, suddenly the blessed Mother revealed Herself. The buildings with their different parts, the temple, and everything else vanished from my sight, leaving no trace whatsoever, and in their stead I saw a limitless, infinite, effulgent Ocean of Consciousness. As far as the eye could see, the shining billows were madly rushing at me from all sides with a terrific noise, to swallow me up! I was panting for breath. I was caught in the rush and collapsed, unconscious. What was happening in the outside world I did not know; but within me there was a steady flow of undiluted bliss, altogether new, and I felt the presence of the Divine Mother.[1]

Ramakrishna's behaviour became more and more eccentric as his perception of the sacred feminine grew, seeing everything as an embodiment of the Divine Mother. Indeed, one story recounts how during one of these states of divine madness, instead of offering rice to Kali in holy ritual, he fed it to the temple cat. A complaint was made but it had little effect:

> The Divine Mother revealed to me in the Kali temple that it was She who had become everything. She showed me that everything was full of Consciousness. The image was Consciousness, the altar

was Consciousness, the water-vessels were Consciousness, the door-sill was Consciousness, the marble floor was Consciousness – all was Consciousness. I found everything inside the room soaked, as it were, in Bliss, the Bliss of God. I saw a wicked man in front of the Kali temple; but in him also I saw the power of the Divine Mother vibrating. That was why I fed the cat with the food that was to be offered to the Divine Mother. I clearly perceived that all this was the Divine Mother – even the cat. The manager of the temple garden wrote to Mathur Babu saying that I was feeding the cat with the offering intended for the Divine Mother. But Mathur Babu had insight into the stage of my mind. He wrote back to the manager: 'Let him do whatever he likes. You must not say anything to him.'[2]

But this was only the beginning. Ramakrishna came under the wing of a wandering sannyasini, or female renunciate, known as Brahmani, who initiated him into Tantra. Moreover, she explained to Ramakrishna the nature of his ecstatic experiences in terms of the kundalini energy within his body. After he had become a Tantric adept, he then encountered another teacher, Topapuri, who was a strict *advaitin*, in the manner of Shankara, whose approach to reality was completely different to Brahmani's. Instead of dwelling on mystical visions, such as the Divine Mother, Topapuri urged Ramakrishna to go beyond all created phenomena:

In spite of all my attempts, I could not altogether cross the realm of name and form and bring my mind to the unconditioned state. I had no difficulty in taking my mind from all the objects of the world. But the radiant and too familiar figure of the Blissful Mother, the Embodiment of the essence of Pure Consciousness, appeared before me as a living reality. Her bewitching smile prevented me from passing into the Great Beyond. Again and again I tried, but She stood in my way every time. In despair I said to Nangta [Topapuri]: 'It is hopeless. I cannot raise my mind to the unconditioned state and come face to face with Atman.' He grew excited and sharply said, 'What? You can't do it? But you have to!'

He cast his eyes around. Finding a piece of glass, he took it up and stuck it between my eyebrows. 'Concentrate the mind on this point!' he thundered. Then with stern determination I again sat to meditate. As soon as the gracious form of the Divine Mother appeared before me, I used my discrimination as a sword and with it clove Her in two. The last barrier fell. My spirit at once soared beyond the relative plane and I lost myself in samadhi.'[3]

Ramakrishna remained in total samadhi for the following three days, whereupon he declared that he had now seen the Self in both its phenomenal and noumenal states, both as expressions of the One:

Kali is none other than He whom you call Brahman. Kali is the primal Shakti. When It is inactive, we call It Brahman. But when It has the function of creating, preserving or destroying, we call that Shakti or Kali. He whom you call Brahman, She whom I call Kali, are no more different from each other than fire and its power of burning …

When I think of the Supreme Being as inactive – neither creating nor preserving nor destroying – I call Him Brahman or Purusha, the Impersonal God. When I think of Him as active – creating, preserving destroying – I call Him Shakti or Maya or Prakriti, the Personal God. But the distinction between them does not mean a difference. The Personal and the Impersonal are the same thing, like milk and its whiteness, the diamond and its lustre, the snake and its wriggling motion. It is impossible to conceive of the one without the other. The Divine Mother and Brahman are one.[4]

This is the highest teaching – everything is One, whether existent or non-existent, created or uncreated, personal or impersonal. Expounding further, Ramakrishna said:

After the creation, the Primal Power dwells in the universe itself. She brings forth this phenomenal world and then pervades it. In the Vedas, creation is likened to the spider and its web. The spider brings the web out of itself and then remains in it. God is the container of the universe and also what is contained within it.[5]

Ramakrishna then embarked on a spiritual journey through all the world's faiths in an attempt to validate further his experience of unity. He studied Islam and Christianity, Buddhism, Jainism and Sikhism, acknowledging yet again that all faiths are paths to the One.

The more absorbed in the Self Ramakrishna became, the more devotees he attracted, eager to benefit from his wisdom and luminous presence. Over the years, a handful of devout followers collected around him, including Swami Vivekananda (1863–1905), who would go on to take his Master's message to the West, and most notably the World Parliament of Religions in Chicago in 1893. His most honoured disciple, however, was Sharada Devi, the Holy Mother, who was also his wife. Only six years old at the time of their marriage, which was not uncommon for Hindu women, she acted both as Ramakrishna's devotee and spiritual companion until his death in August 1886 of throat cancer.

Sharada Devi was born of Brahmin parents on 22nd December 1853, in the small village of Jayrambati, in Bengal. It is said that before her birth, both her mother, Syamasundari Devi, and her father, Ramachandra Mukherjee, had a dream in which they were holding a little girl in their arms.

Growing up, Sharada was considered a serious girl who took little interest in playing with her childhood friends or study and instead, found pleasure in making clay models of Kali and Laksmi, whom she decorated with flowers. In 1859, Sharada was betrothed to Ramakrishna, who at the time was living in Dakshineswar practising severe austerities. Indeed, it was his mother who initiated the arrangements for his marriage, greatly alarmed by her son's increasingly erratic behaviour, in the hope that married life would bring him back down to earth. Ramakrishna happily consented to the idea, even suggesting a suitable bride, apparently instructing his mother to go to the home of Ramachandra Mukherjee's house to find her.

Sharada and Ramakrishna only met for a few days during this

time. She would not meet him again until she was fourteen and even then it was only for a few months. However, Sharada quickly realized the unique godliness of his being. Referring to this period of her life, she would tell her devotees:

> At that time I always felt as if a jar of bliss was set in my heart. It is impossible to describe that divine joy, which was full to the brim.'[6]

Sharada didn't see Ramakrishna again until she was eighteen. Many rumours abounded about the mental state of her husband, which caused her great distress, so she resolved to be with him permanently. Setting out on the long journey with her father, Sharada was taken ill on the third day of their travels and had to stay at an inn to recuperate. During the night, she had a miraculous vision:

> I was lying unconscious owing to fever, without even any sense of decorum. Just then I saw a woman, pitch dark in complexion, sitting by my side. Though she was dark, I have never seen another as beautiful as she. She stroked my aching head with her soft cool hands and I felt the heat of my body subsiding. 'Where are you from?' I asked her. And she replied, 'From Dakshineswar.' At this I was speechless with wonder and exclaimed, 'From Dakshineswar! I too am going to Dakshineswar to see my husband. But this fever has unfortunately detained me on the way.' To this she replied, 'Don't worry. You will soon be all right to see your husband in Dakshineswar. It is for your sake that I have kept him there.' I said to her, 'Indeed! Is it so? But who are you to me?' 'I am your sister,' she replied. I was much astonished to hear this. After this conversation I feel asleep.[7]

Her sister was none other than the goddess, Kali, bidding her home to her Beloved. And indeed, Sharada arrived at Dakshineswar a few days later. Ramakrishna immediately set about helping her recover from her illness, installing her in the music room, or *nahabat* – a two-storey, octagonal building, situated on the banks of the Ganges.

As a married couple, they would spend the night together, sleeping side by side in Ramakrishna's bedchamber. And in a test of her spiritual purity, he asked her: 'Tell me if you have come here to drag me down the road leading to the worldly life.' 'Certainly not,' she replied, without a moment's hesitation. 'Why should I drag you to the world? I am here to help you realize your spiritual ideal.'[8] Sharada then asked Ramakrishna what he thought of her, to which he said:

> The Mother who is worshipped in the temple, and the mother who gave birth to this [pointing to his body] and is now living in the *nahabat* – the same mother is now stroking my feet. Really and truly, I always regard you as the embodiment of the blissful Mother of the Universe.[9]

Indeed, as part of Ramakrishna's ascetic practice, he would perform Shodasi Puja – the worship of the Divine Mother in one of her ten aspects, namely Shodasi, a sixteen-year-old virgin. Ramakrishna would then direct his attention onto Sharada so that she too would assume the status of Shodasi. Offering garlands of flowers and fruits at her feet, he would cry:

> O Divine Mother, Thou Eternal Woman, possessor of all Power! Please open the gate of perfection. Purify her body and mind, and manifest Thyself through her for the welfare of all ... O most auspicious of all auspicious beings, O Consort of Siva, Fulfiller of all desires, O Refuge of all, O three-eyed Goddess of golden complexion, O Power of Narayana, I salute Thee again and again.[10]

As the divine couple, both would support and honour the other. Speaking of this time together, Sharada observed:

> During my days at Dakshineswar, I used to get up at three o'clock in the morning and sit in meditation. Often I used to be totally absorbed in it. Once, on a moonlit night, doing *japa*, I was sitting on the steps of the *nahabat*. Everything was quiet. I did

not even know when the Master passed that way. On other days
I would hear the sound of his slippers but on this, I did not. I was
totally absorbed in meditation ... On this day the cloth had
slipped off from my back owing to the breeze but I was uncon-
scious of it ...

Ah! The ecstasy of those days. On moonlit nights I would look
at the moon and pray with folded hands, 'May my heart be as pure
as the rays of yonder moon!' If one is steady in meditation, one can
clearly see the Lord in one's heart and hear His voice. The
moment an idea flashes in the mind of such a one, it will be
fulfilled then and there. One will be bathed in peace. Ah! What a
mind I had at that time ...

In the fullness of one's spiritual realization, one will find that He
who resides in one's heart resides in the hearts of others as well –
the oppressed, the persecuted, the Untouchable and the outcast.
This realization makes one truly humble.[11]

Ramakrishna knew that Sharada would carry on his work of helping
humanity to understand the immanence of the sacred feminine. During
their time together, he taught her many spiritual practices and austerities; all the while, she cooked and cleaned for him, tending to his every
need, and always remaining discreetly out of the limelight. Indeed, one
day, Ramakrishna told a woman disciple:

She is Saraswati. She has assumed a human body to impart wisdom
to men; but she has hidden her celestial beauty lest people, by
looking at her, should befoul their minds with sinful thoughts.[12]

Throughout his illness and the last months of his life, Sharada
remained by Ramakrishna's side, only travelling back to Jayrambati
occasionally. It was around this time that she had a dream in which
she saw the image of Kali, with her neck bent over to one side. Asking
what was wrong with her, Kali replied, 'It is because of this [pointing
to the cancer in the throat of Sri Ramakrishna], that I also have it in
My throat.'[13] Ramakrishna died on 15th August 1886; just before he

closed his eyes for the final time, he lifted himself up and cried out, 'Kali! Kali! Kali!'

The next day, Ramakrishna's body was cremated. In the evening, distraught with grief, Sharada began to discard her jewellery, following the custom of Hindu widows. As she was about to remove her bracelets, a vision of Ramakrishna allegedly appeared before her and said, 'Am I dead that you are acting like a widow? I have just moved from one room to another.'[14] From that day forth, she never took off her bracelets for as long as she lived.

The handful of disciples that Ramakrishna had collected around him decided to renounce their worldly activities and form a monastery in a small dilapidated house in Barangore, a northern suburb of Calcutta. Known as the Belur Math, it became the permanent headquarters of the Monks of the Ramakrishna Order and housed Ramakrishna's ashes. Sharada herself embarked on a pilgrimage, visiting Vrindavan, the birthplace of Krishna, where she identified with Radha's grief at the loss of her beloved Lord and Master. Nevertheless, she once again was visited by an image of Ramakrishna on three consecutive nights, instructing her to initiate her devotees with a mantra that he revealed to her in the dream. From that moment, she resolved to carry on her Master's work for the rest of her life.

Sharada thus became the perfected embodiment of the Holy Mother, the living manifestation of the sacred feminine. She spent the rest of her days between her home in Calcutta, near Belur Math, and Jayrambati, where she shared her home with many relatives, one of whom was Radhu, her niece. Mentally unstable, Radhu tried the patience of Sharada to the very limit, constantly making selfish demands on her attention. But when asked about her relationship with Radhu, Sharada replied:

> People think that I worry about Radhu and I am strongly attached to her. But they do not know that without this attachment, my body would not have been preserved after the Master's death. He himself kept the body alive, through Radhu, for the sake of his work. When my mind withdraws from her I shall give up the body.[15]

Indeed, her soul yearned to free itself from the shackles of the physical body. And in one rare moment of sublime samadhi, she tasted the entirety of the universe:

> I found in that state that I had travelled into a distant country. Everybody there was very affectionate to me. My beauty was beyond description. Sri Ramakrishna was also there. With great tenderness they made me sit by his side. I cannot describe to you the nature of that ecstatic joy. When my mind came down from that exalted mood, I found my body lying there. I thought, 'How can I possibly enter into this ugly body?' I could not at all persuade my mind to do so. After a long while, it did and the body became conscious again.[16]

Throughout the last years of her life, in a white sari and still wearing her marriage bangles, Sharada was surrounded by many devotees, eager for her compassion and maternal love – indeed, Ramakrishna would often tell his disciples to be like unto children before the Holy Mother. Moreover, as her Master's consort, the presence of Ramakrishna could still live on – as she said herself: 'The Master told me that he would dwell in my body in a subtle form.'[17] Through her nondual teaching, with particular emphasis on meditation and detachment, she helped hundreds of men and women come to the understanding that all that matters in life is the realization of the Self:

> The aim of life is to realize God and remain immersed in contemplation of Him. God alone is real and everything else is false. God is one's very own, and this is the eternal relationship between God and creatures. One realizes God in proportion to the intensity of one's feelings for Him. He who is really eager to cross the ocean of the world will somehow break the bonds.[18]

And in a beautiful analogy, she expounds the veil of the mind:

> The moon is in the sky but it is hidden by a cloud. The cloud must be slowly blown away by the wind and then you will see the moon.

Can anything happen abruptly? The vision of God is also like that. Slowly one gets rid of one's past karma ... That is nature's law. Haven't you noticed the new moon and full moon? The mind, likewise, sometimes feels pure and sometimes impure.[19]

It is said that the guru takes on the suffering of his or her devotees and Sharada was no exception. Throughout her life, she was afflicted with acute physical pain. By early 1920, she was seriously ill with black fever, and was confined to bed in her Calcutta home. Asked about the care of Radhu, Sharada said: 'I have withdrawn my mind. I don't want her here any more.' A woman devotee, also distressed by Sharada's dying body, pressed her further about what would happen to all her followers without her:

'Why should you be afraid? You have seen the Master. What should frighten you? Let me tell you something. My child, if you want peace, then do not look into anybody's faults. Look into your own faults. Learn to make the world your own, no one is a stranger, my child; the whole world is your own.'[20]

On 21st July, 1920, Sharada's last moments were at hand. Devotees started to chant the Lord's name. At about one o'clock in the morning, she breathed deeply several times and entered into samadhi and then passed away. The following morning, Sharada's body was taken across the Ganges to the Belur Math, where it was bathed and dressed in a new cloth. A funeral pyre of sandalwood was constructed and at about three in the afternoon, Sharada was cremated. Her ashes were placed in the Ramakrishna temple.

Throughout her life, Sharada was accompanied by a handful of devoted female disciples, amongst whom was the English woman, Sister Nivedita. Speaking of Sharada, she said:

In her one sees realized that wisdom and sweetness to which the simplest of women may attain. And yet to myself the stateliness of her courtesy and her great open mind are almost as wonderful as her saintliness. I have never known her hesitate in giving utterance to large and generous judgement, however new and complex might be the question put before her. Her life is one long stillness of prayer.[21]

What Sharada Devi showed the world, through her modesty and piety, was that even the humblest of women is in fact an embodiment of the sacred feminine. And what Ramakrishna taught was the way in which she should be honoured as such. His treatment of his wife as a manifestation of the Divine Mother not only gave Sharada the status she deserved but also raised the position of Hindu women in general, at a time when Western materialism, perpetuated by British imperial rule, was devaluing traditional roles within society.

Thus, despite the fact that feminism was unleashing women from the ties that bound them to domesticity and patriarchal dominance, it came at a price. The softness and grace normally associated with women was becoming undermined through their weary struggle for independence. Indeed, Swami Vivekananda remarked after his trip to the United States:

> In the West the women did not very often seem to be women at all, they appeared to be replicas of men ... In India alone the sight of feminine modesty and reserve soothes the eye ... Still on this sacred soil of India, this land of Sita and Savitri, among women may be found such character, such spirit of service, such affection, such compassion, contentment and reverence, as I could not find anywhere else in the world.[22]

And in a letter written in America sent to one of his fellow monks at Belur Math, he observed:

> You have not understood the wonderful significance of the Mother's life. But gradually you will know. Without Shakti there is no regeneration for the world ... Mother has been born to revive that wonderful Shakti in India; and making her the nucleus, once more will Gargis and Maitreyas be born into the world.[23]

Photographs of the Holy Mother, Sri Sharada Devi, show a beautifully serene woman, with large dark eyes, soothing the eye with her
grace and bestowing upon us the maternal love of the Divine Mother
– the living embodiment of the sacred feminine.

Mirra Alfassa

Vivekananda's observations about women in the West were refreshingly blunt, however, they were made through the eyes of an Indian male, accustomed to clearly defined female roles and a religion that honoured the sacred feminine principle. Women in America and Europe had had to live through political, economic and sociological changes not witnessed in the East, significantly altering their societal and psychological status in both the eyes of men and themselves.

Indeed, the Women's Movement in Europe at the turn of the twentieth century was rigorously campaigning for control of personal property, equality of opportunity in education and employment, women's suffrage and sexual freedom. In Britain, the feminist Emmeline Pankhurst (1858–1928) founded the Women's Social and Political Union and was one of the first women to be instrumental in pushing through political reform and women's right to vote. In France, the existential writer Simone de Beauvoir (1908–1986), companion and lover of Jean-Paul Sartre, was outlining her feminist theories in her classic text, *The Second Sex*. Speaking about the feminine sensibility, she makes an examination of the female mystic:

> Love has been assigned to woman as her supreme vocation, and when she directs it towards a man, she is seeking God in him: but if human love is denied her by circumstances, if she is disappointed

or over-particular, she may choose to adore divinity in the person
of God Himself. To be sure, there have been men who burned with
that flame, but they are rare, and their fervour is of a highly refined
intellectual cast; whereas the women who abandon themselves to
the joys of the heavenly nuptials are legion, and their experience is
of a peculiarly emotional nature.[1]

For Simone the absoluteness of female love is akin to her most natural
state:

> There is no other way out for her than to lose herself, body and
> soul, in him who is represented to her as the absolute, as the
> essential.[2]

Interestingly, rather than find fault with men, as was the custom with
many feminists of her day, she speaks of the woman's dependency on
him for her spiritual salvation.

Interest in feminine, rather than feminist, spirituality was on
the increase, with a particular leaning towards spiritualism,
occultism and theosophy. Another powerful French woman who
would establish her own esoteric organization in the pursuit of
universal Truth was the charismatic Mirra Alfassa. Always associated with her life companion, the Indian sage and political activist,
Aurobindo Ghose, together they were responsible for one of the
most important metaphysical renaissances the modern world has
ever known, attracting a significant following of disciples from
around the world.

Born in Paris in 1878 of an Egyptian mother and Turkish father,
even at a very young age, Mirra was already aware of her life's
mission:

> I started doing or contemplating my Yoga from the age of four.
> There was a small chair for me on which I used to sit, engrossed in
> my meditation. A very brilliant light would then descend over my
> head and produce some turmoil inside my brain. Of course, I under-

stood nothing, it was not the age for understanding. But gradually I began to feel, 'I shall have to do some tremendously great work that nobody yet knows.'[3]

Through her teens, she continued to indulge herself in profound mystical phenomena, all as an expression within herself:

> When I was a child of about thirteen, for nearly a year every night as soon as I had gone to bed it seemed to me that I went out of my body and rose straight up above the house, then above the city, very high above. Then I used to see myself clad in a magnificent robe, much longer than myself; as I rose higher, the robe would stretch, spreading out in a circle around me to form a kind of immense roof over the city. Then I would see men, women, children, old men, the sick, the unfortunate coming out from every side; they would gather under the outspread robe, begging for help, telling their miseries, their suffering, their hardships. In reply, the robe, supple and alive, would extend towards each one of them individually, and as soon as they had touched it, they were comforted or healed, and went back into their bodies happier and stronger than they had come out of them.[4]

Moreover, whilst in these ecstatic states, Mirra would encounter teachers and holy beings, one of whom she called Krishna. She said she always knew that one day she would meet him here on earth.

Growing up with the avant-garde in Paris during the great Impressionistic Age, Mirra studied painting at the École des Beaux Arts and was even exhibited at the Parisian *salons*. Indeed, a black-and-white photographic portrait of her shows a woman with smiling kohl eyes wearing an elaborate brocaded headscarf – the quintessential embodiment of Parisian chic. At nineteen, she married Henri Morisset, a student of the painter, Gustave Moreau, and together they had a son, André. And yet despite her family life and love of the fine arts, it wasn't enough – personal fulfilment for her lay far beyond the material world:

> Between the age of eighteen and twenty I had attained a conscious
> and constant union with the divine Presence and ... I had done it
> *all alone*, with *absolutely nobody* to help me, not even books, you
> understand![5]

Around this time, Mirra read Vivekananda's *Raja Yoga* as well as a
French translation of the *Bhagavad Gita*, in which she realized that not
only was Krishna the immanent Godhead but he was also the Divine
within each and every one of us. Equipped with this understanding,
she claimed, 'In one month, the whole work was done.'[6]

In 1905, Mirra met an occultist by the name of Max Theon in
Paris, a Polish Jew who had been the Grand Master of a group in
Egypt known as the Hermetic Brotherhood of Luxor. Theon had a
house in Tlecmen, South Algeria, and invited Mirra to stay with him
and his wife. She thus spent the following three years learning about
the occult and the Kabbala, practising her new-found mystical
powers.

Returning to Paris, with her marriage to Henri Morisset now
over, she took a new husband, Paul Richard, a man deeply interested
in philosophy and Vedantic yoga. She started a study group called
'Cosmique', in which she taught the perennial wisdom of the
Upanishads, the *Bhagavad Gita* and the *Yoga Sutras*. Richard also had
political aspirations and, in connection with an election campaign,
journeyed to Pondicherry in order to further his ambitions. Whilst
staying there, he determined to seek the advice of a holy man, and in
1910 he had his first encounter with Aurobindo.

Born in Calcutta in 1872, Aurobindo Ghose was taken with his two
elder brothers to Manchester, England, for his education where he
lived with an English family. At twelve, he attended St Paul's public
school in London and then King's College, University of Cambridge.
Returning to India in 1893, he became vigorously interested in Indian
nationalism and campaigned for total independence from British rule,
editing a Nationalist newspaper, the *Bande Mataram*. He also became
deeply passionate about *raja* yoga and in 1907, he experienced a
moment of transcendental awareness:

An absolute stillness and blotting out, as it were, of all mental, emotional and other inner activities – the body continued indeed to see, walk, speak, and do its other business but as an empty automatic machine and nothing more. I did not become aware of any pure 'I' nor even of any self, impersonal or other – there was only an awareness of That as the sole reality, all else being quite insubstantial, void, non-real. As to what realized that Reality, it was a nameless consciousness which was other than That … Neither was I aware of any lower soul or outer self called by such and such a personal name that was performing this feat of arriving at the consciousness of Nirvana …[7]

A year later, Aurobindo was remanded in custody, suspected of terrorist acts against the British. In prison, he experienced the taste of nirvana again, whereupon he resolved to devote his life to the spiritual path. After his release, he moved to Pondicherry, then under French rule, where he developed his theories of 'Integral Yoga'. For Aurobindo, enlightenment came about through realizing the Supermind, the Truth-Consciousness of the Divine within oneself, which ultimately lead to man's transfiguration into the 'Superman'. Through a series of three distinct steps, the somewhat complex *sadhana* of Integral Yoga proceeds through psychic, spiritual and supramental transformation, leading to identification with the Absolute. Moreover, this process is helped by universal Shakti, the Divine Mother, who acts as an intermediary between mankind and the Supermind:

> The supramental change is a thing decreed and inevitable in the evolution of the earth-consciousness, for its upward ascent is not ended and mind is not its last summit. But that the change may arise, take form, and endure, there is needed the call from below with a will to recognize and not deny the light when it comes. There is needed the sanction of the Supreme from above. The power that mediates between the sanction and the call is the presence and power of the Divine Mother.[8]

Thus, after four years of practising silently on his own, Aurobindo began publication of his ideas in a monthly philosophical journal, *Arya*. Most of his important works, including *The Divine Life*, *The Synthesis of Yoga*, *Essays on the Gita* and *The Isha Upanishad* were initially serialised in the *Arya*. The journal ceased publication after six and a half years, however, by this time a handful of devotees had started to surround Aurobindo and a community of *sadhaks* (devotees) formed into what is now known as the Sri Aurobindo Ashram.

Paul was so impressed by his presence, he could not wait to tell Mirra about Aurobindo when he returned to Paris. Inspired by all she heard, Mirra immediately started a correspondence with him. Four years later, in 1914, Paul and Mirra set sail for India to meet Aurobindo in person. In a diary note describing the sea journey and the boat they were travelling in, she says:

> ... [it is] a marvellous abode of peace, a temple sailing in Thy honour over the waves of the subconscious passivity which we have to conquer and awaken to the consciousness of Thy divine Presence.[9]

The very next day after their arrival in Pondicherry, Mirra Alfassa met Aurobindo Ghose and immediately Mirra recognized in him the special being she had called Krishna. Moreover, she believed that her whole life had merely been a preparation for this moment: 'I seem to have at last arrived at the threshold which I have long sought.'[10] The Richards subsequently spent each afternoon conversing with Aurobindo and during their year-long stay, helped collaborate on the journal, *Arya*, contributing philosophical pieces and poems.

The Richards returned to Paris in the midst of the First World War, and Mirra and Aurobindo resumed their correspondence. In 1917 the Richards set sail again, this time for Japan, where they remained until 1920. However, the yearning to be with Aurobindo was so intense that Mirra decided to return to Pondicherry to be by his side forever – her marriage to Paul was now at an end.

For the first six years, Mirra blended in with the other disciples within the ashram, content just to receive his darshan and help with all the domestic chores. But soon her powerful personality was conducting meditation groups, rather in the manner of her Cosmique days in Paris. More importantly, Aurobindo was withdrawing more and more from public view, appearing only on special occasions, leaving Mirra to orchestrate activities within the ashram.

Then, on 24th November 1926, a remarkable event took place. Aurobindo declared that Krishna had descended into the physical realm enabling humanity to work towards realizing its full divine potential in order to become one with the Supermind. Various 'miracles' allegedly took place but most significantly, Aurobindo started calling Mirra, 'Sweet Mother'. For Aurobindo, the Mother's grace was the nourishing and life-sustaining force of the created universe. Indeed, out of all his prolific philosophical writings is a small book entitled *The Mother*, in which he extols the quadruple aspects of the sacred feminine:

Four great Aspects of the Mother, four of her leading Powers and Personalities have stood in front in her guidance of this Universe and in her dealings with the terrestrial play. One is her personality of calm wideness and comprehending wisdom and tranquil benignity and inexhaustible compassion and sovereign and unsurpassing majesty and all-ruling greatness. Another embodies her power of splendid strength and irresistible passion, her warrior mood, her overwhelming will, her impetuous swiftness and world-shaking force. A third is vivid and sweet and wonderful with her deep secret of beauty and harmony and fine rhythm, her intricate and subtle opulence, her compelling attracting and captivating grace. The fourth equipped with her close and profound capacity of intimate knowledge and careful flawless work and quiet and exact perfection in all things. Wisdom, Strength, Harmony, Perfection are their several attributes and it is these powers that they bring with them into the world ... To the four we give the four great names, Maheshwari, Mahakali, Mahalakshmi, Mahasaraswati ...[11]

When asked whether Mirra and the Mother were synonymous, Aurobindo was in no doubt that they were one and the same. And yet the Divine Mother is also for him so much more than the four physical manifestations of phenomenal existence:

> There are three ways of being of the Mother of which you can become aware when you enter into touch of oneness with the Conscious Force that upholds us and the universe. *Transcendent*, the original supreme Shakti, she stands above the worlds and links the creation to the ever-unmanifest mystery of the Supreme. *Universal*, the cosmic Mahashakti, she creates all these beings and contains and enters, supports and conducts all these million processes and forces. *Individual*, she embodies the power of these two vast arrays of her existence, makes them living and near to us and mediates between the human personality and the divine Nature.[12]

Moreover, for Aurobindo, one's whole life should be dedicated in service to the divine feminine, a surrendering to her ineffable beauty and infinite grace:

> There must be a total and sincere surrender; there must be an exclusive self-opening to the divine Power; there must be a constant and integral choice of the Truth that is descending, a constant and integral rejection of the falsehood of the mental, vital and physical Powers and Appearances that still rule the earth-Nature ...
>
> The surrender must be total and seize all the parts of the being. It is not enough that the physic should respond and the higher mental accept or even the inner vital submit and the inner physical consciousness feel the influence. There must be in no part of the being, even the most external, anything that makes a reserve, anything that hides behind doubts, confusions, and subterfuges, anything that revolts or refuses ...
>
> All your life must be an offering and a sacrifice to the Supreme; your only object in action shall be to serve, to receive, to fulfil, to

become a manifestating instrument of the Divine Shakti in her works. You must grow in the divine consciousness till there is no difference between your will and hers, no motive except her impulsion in you, no action that is not her conscious action in you and through you.[13]

Aurobindo is not saying, however, that the path is easy or instantaneous – three gradual and distant stages can be recognized in one's journey to the Divine:

Until you are capable of this complete dynamic identification, you have to regard yourself as a soul and body created for her service, one who does all for her sake ...

There must be no demand for fruit and no seeking for reward; the only fruit for you is the pleasure of the Divine Mother and the fulfilment of her work, your only reward a constant progression in divine consciousness and calm and strength and bliss ...

And afterwards you will realize that the divine Shakti not only inspires and guides, but initiates and carries out your works; all your movements are originated by her, all your powers are hers, mind, life and body are conscious and joyful instruments of her action, means for her play, moulds for manifestation in the physical universe ...

The last stage of this perfection will come when you are completely identified with the Divine Mother and feel yourself to be no longer another and separate being, instrument, servant or worker, but truly a child and eternal portion of her consciousness and force. Always she will be in you and you in her; it will be your constant, simple and natural experience that all your thought and seeing and action, your very breathing or moving come from her and are hers. You will know and see and feel that you are a person and power formed by her out of herself, put out from her for the play and yet always safe in her, being of her being, consciousness of her consciousness, force of her force, Ananda of her Ananda.[14]

By the time Aurobindo died in 1950, he felt his mission had come to its rightful end, leaving Sweet Mother to take over responsibility for the work of enlightening humanity. Indeed, another important date was looming ahead – the year 1967 when the supramental consciousness would enter into a higher stage of realizing power. Perhaps the countercultural revolution in the West, albeit precipitated by LSD, and the infamous Summer of Love were products of that power. Who can tell? Nonetheless, Mirra forged ahead during this period, establishing an International Centre of Education as well as her *cause célèbre*, the town of Auroville, meaning 'City of Dawn', where the principles of Integral Yoga could be put into practice within the context of a community.

Mirra lived out her remaining life under strict self discipline, following the same regime every day – rising early at four in the morning, giving darshan on the balcony of the ashram at around six, meditation, interviews with *sadhaks*, and supervision of the distribution of food; then sports and children's games in the afternoon, followed by evening meditation and darshan.

One night in 1969 she had an experience in which she announced that there had been a descent of the Superman-consciousness, an intermediary between mankind and the Supermind:

> It was something very material, I mean it was very external – very external – and it was luminous, with a golden light. It was very strong, very powerful; but even so, its character was a smiling benevolence, a peaceful delight ... very, very gently, very smiling, *very benevolent* ... My own impression was that of a immense personality ... for it the earth was small, small ... like a little ball ... It gave the impression of a personal divinity ... who comes to help, and so strong, so strong and at the same time so gentle, so all-embracing ...[15]

It is a vision reminiscent of Julian of Norwich's apperception of the world as a tiny hazelnut in the palm of her hand. And yet, despite celestial inspiration, Mirra's own bodily health was fading and on

17th November 1973, she passed away at the age of ninety-five. For the next three days, her body was laid in state in the meditation room of the ashram, whereupon thousands of devotees paid their respects.

Mirra's legacy is of equal merit and profundity to Aurobindo's. But unlike her spiritual companion's zest for writing philosophical poems and prose, Mirra's work comprises in the main transcripts of her speeches, given in French and English, which were recorded on tape. Her only written work is *Prayers and Meditations*, which were selected from her diary notes.

Like Aurobindo, she was very thorough in her exposition of Integral Yoga and her understanding of the teaching. And yet her words are suffused with an elegance and sophistication, a *joie de vivre*, uniquely her own. Speaking on the nature of love, she says:

> Love is a supreme force which the Eternal Consciousness sent down from itself into an obscure and darkened world that it might bring back that world and its beings to the Divine. The material world in its darkness and ignorance had forgotten the Divine. Love came into the darkness; it awakened all that lay there asleep; it whispered, opening the ears that were sealed, 'There is something that is worth waking to, worth living for, and it is love!' And with the awakening to love there entered into the world the possibility of coming back to the Divine ...[16]

Aurobindo and Mirra were not lovers in the physical sense; however, between them there existed a passionate relationship founded in respect and a mutual love of Truth. 'The Mother and I are one and equal,' wrote Aurobindo one day in his diary. Mirra confirmed this, writing 'Without him, I exist not; without me, he is unmanifest.'[17]

The twentieth century saw the arising of many celebrated embodiments of the Divine Mother, and yet, unlike Mirra, they are predominantly Indian: Anandamayi Ma (1896–1982), Anasuya Devi (1923–1985), Karunamayi (1958–), Gurumayi (1955–) and Ammachi (1953–). But whatever their nationality, the history of the world has returned to its veneration of the sacred feminine and the knowledge that everything in the universe is an expression of the Divine Mother.

chapter twenty-two

Irina Tweedie

In the west the sun was setting in a sea of shimmering golden clouds. The whole world seemed to be illumined by this vivid gold, was transformed by it. I had to cross the *chowraha* [circus] to get to the baker's shop. Before entering, I stopped and turned and saw that right across the *chowraha* was a magnificent rainbow. So clear, so vivid and bright, against the golden sky; and I must have walked right under it. I stood for a while, enchanted. There is a Russian saying that when one walks under a rainbow it means that if one has a wish or a desire it will be fulfilled. What an omen! My Master told me that my troubles are passing away. I don't think that I ever was so happy in my life ... with this special happiness never experienced before ...[1]

Reading Irina Tweedie's spiritual autobiography is to be transported to India and experience directly the beauty and overwhelming magnificence of existing in a subcontinental wonderland. Aryanagar, the district where Irina lived for two years regularly visiting a Sufi Master, enters into our consciousness as a place where the magic and the mystery of the Unknown are revealed. Her diary entries, written between October 1961 and December 1966 and encompassing her time spent in Aryanagar, London and then finally the Himalayas, take the reader on their own spiritual odyssey. Indeed, the overall effect is to taste the very living presence of her Master and his enduring wisdom for ourselves.

With unashamed honesty, Irina Tweedie records her thoughts and emotions as she embarks on her path of self discovery. Her Naqshbandi Sufi Master, Bhai Sahib (which in Hindi means Elder Brother) is an enigmatic character – cryptic, compassionate, aloof. Not given to long and verbose discourses on the nature of Reality, Irina is, nevertheless, moved by his presence. In her first formal meeting with him, Bhai Sahib asks her, 'Why did you come to me?' Irina's words come spilling out:

> 'I want God,' I heard myself saying, 'But not the Christian idea of an anthropomorphic deity. I want the Rootless Root, the Causeless Cause of the Upanishads.'
> 'Nothing less than that?' He lifted an eyebrow …[2]

By the twentieth century in the West, the belief in an immanent Reality for most people was on shaky ground. Indeed, unlike the revival in the East of the universal Mother immanent in all creation, the Post Modernist world had deconstructed all philosophical and religious belief into meaningless abstractions: 'God is dead,' Friedrich Nietzsche (1844–1900) famously declared. Nevertheless, in a climate where dogma and ideological ignorance were crumbling, it gave rise to new possibilities. The pioneering spirit of women like Mirra Alfassa enabled more and more women to search independently for their own salvation, to find the Truth for themselves beyond domestic restraints. Irina Tweedie's own search for spiritual fulfilment is yet another example of an independent Western woman taking a stand against what society expected of her.

Irina speaks very little of her past prior to visiting India. Born in 1907 in Russia, she was educated in Vienna and Paris. She then moved to England where she was happily married to a naval officer. His death in 1954 caused a grief of such profundity that she sought solace in religion and philosophy, turning eventually to the Theosophical Society. But it failed to inspire. An intense longing for freedom still prevailed and nothing she did would suffice. She then felt compelled to travel to India.

Continuing to explain her reasons for coming to Bhai Sahib, she tells him of the theosophical belief that not even a guru is necessary for liberation, salvation being achievable through our own independent efforts:

'Not even in a hundred years!' he laughed outright. 'It cannot be done without a Teacher!'

I told him that I did not know what Sufism was.

'Sufism is a way of life. It is neither a religion nor a philosophy. There are Hindu Sufis, Muslim Sufis, Christian Sufis. My Revered Guru Maharaj was a Muslim.' He said it very softly, with a tender expression, his eyes dreamy and veiled. And then I noticed something which in my excitement and eagerness I had not noticed before; there was a feeling of great peace in the room. He himself was full of peace. He radiated it; it was all around us and it seemed eternal. As if this special peace always was and always would be, forever ...[3]

Immediately, Bhai Sahib instructs her to keep a diary of her experiences. *The Daughter of Fire: A Woman's Experience of Liberation through the Teachings of a Sufi Master* meticulously records Irina's day-to-day existence (which was later abridged to a much shorter version, *The Chasm of Fire* and published first). It charts her meetings and conversations with Bhai Sahib, as well as her attitudes and frustrations, her insights and dreams.

At first, her entries tell of the sheer physical endurance of Indian life, which becomes an almost insurmountable obstacle: the smells and the noise and the chaos in temperatures well over a hundred degrees. Nevertheless, provoked by her feisty and often quarrelsome character, Bhai Sahib is forced to break her attachment to the senses and her overriding sense of 'poor me'. Irina is regularly made to sit outside his house, often in the blinding dust or pouring rain, whilst welcoming other devotees into his presence. He also demands that she hand over to him all of her income as a test of her dependence on money. Her protestations are loud but the Master knows it is for her own good:

'The world is for us as we create it: if you say there is a *bhut* [ghost] in the tree, then there will be a *bhut* for you. This is all *manas* [mind]. But what is *manas*? Nothing. *Manas* is maya [illusion]. You want everything but are not prepared to make sacrifices, to pay the price …

'People are not prepared to give anything up. If you want to go anywhere you will have to take the train or the plane, you are expected to pay the fare, is it not so? Be always a friend of the Almighty and you *will never die*. Prayer should be done always, even in ordinary prayer; but of course the only *real* prayer is merging, *oneness* with God.[4]

Her heart responds to the essence of his words but her mind is still sloshing with anxiety and confusion. Her desire for permanent release provokes a tireless demand for her Master's assistance:

'Oh please help me! I am so confused!'

'Why should I?' He looked straight at me. 'If I begin to help, you will ask again and again for help: how will you cross the stream? You must do it yourself, I will not help. If I do, you will get used to it and will never be able to do without my help. We all have to cross the stream alone. Don't you realize that this is the way? I am telling you, showing you the way. THE ONLY WAY. Why don't you realize that you are nothing? It means complete surrender. It takes time. It is not done in one day. It takes time to surrender.'[5]

Bhai Sahib goes on to tell her that his method is the Way of the Silent Sufi. Always in silence and dependent on the maturity of the devotee, practice [*dzikr*] can either be the path of contemplative meditation [*dhyana*] in the mind (self-enquiry) or the path of complete renunciation [*tyaga*] in the heart (surrender). Although both paths ultimately lead to the same goal, the Teacher places greater emphasis on surrender:

'It is like love; it cannot be hidden. If I don't speak to you for days, you just sit. If I speak, you speak and never, never must you complain ... This is the door, the *only door* to the *King of the Heart*. What is surrender of the heart? You people do not even imagine. Not only Western people, I mean Indians too ... Learn to be *nothing*, this is the only way.'[6]

And it is only through the heart chakra where true surrender can take place and the individual can fall in love with God. Nevertheless, he continues to taunt her:

> To say 'I love you' is easy but to realize it is difficult. Here is hidden the mystery of the Realization of God or Truth. Because you have to realize one fact: 'You are in my heart, you are everything, I am nothing.' If you begin to realize that, then you really love, and your own self diminishes, the external things begin to lose all importance. The self, and everything else, remains with the Beloved from then on, and the Beloved remains with you permanently when there is no self anymore.'[7]

Despite these wise words, her diary entries reveal the personal torment she repeatedly endures. Her antagonisms and resentments are seething inside her, with little outlet for release. At night, she sleeps badly. In the darkness she can find no peace. Her body starts to shake violently, her skin is weeping sweat. Her mind is wrestling with visions of creatures and demons:

> Without the slightest indication that it may be coming, I was flooded with a powerful sexual desire. It was just the desire, for no object in particular, just the desire, per se, uncontrollable, a kind of wild cosmic force ... I sat there helpless, shaking with fear ... Good heavens, what was happening? Tried to listen, to *feel* from where this vibration came, where it was exactly. Then I knew; it was at the base of the spine, just above the anus. I could feel it there distinctly. It must be the *muladhara chakra* [psychic centre at the base of the spine]. I went ice-cold with terror ... This was the *coup de grace*! I thought; he has activated the chakra

at the base of the spine and left the kundalini energy there to ...
to what?

The most terrifying night of my life began. Never, not even in
its young days had this body known anything even faintly compa-
rable, or similar to this! This was not just desire; it was madness in
its lowest, animal form; a paroxysm of sex-craving. A wild howling
of everything female in me, for a male. The whole body was SEX
ONLY; every cell, every particle, was shouting for it; even the skin,
the hands, the nails, every atom ...

Waves of wild goose-flesh ran over my whole body making all the
hair stand stiff, as if filled with electricity. The sensation was painful,
but the inexplicable thing was that the idea of intercourse did not
even occur to me ... The body was shaking, I was biting the pillow
so as not to howl like a wild animal. I was beside myself; the craziest,
the maddest thing one could imagine, so sudden, so violent.[8]

And she continues:

The body seemed to break under this force; all I could do was to
hold it stiff, still and completely stretched out. I felt the over-
stretched muscles full of pain as in a kind of cramp. I was rigid, I
could not move. The mind was absolutely void, emptied of its
content. There was no imagery; only an uncontrollable fear, primitive, animal fear and it went on for hours. I was shaking like a leaf
... a mute, trembling jelly carried away by forces completely
beyond any human control. A fire was burning inside my bowels
and the sensation of heat increased and decreased in waves. I could
do nothing. I was in complete psychological turmoil.

I don't know how long it lasted, don't know if I had slept out of
sheer exhaustion or if I fainted ...

The whole body was shaking and trembling in the morning. The
cup of tea tasted bitter. Felt like vomiting.[9]

But Bhai Sahib reassures her that this is all perfectly natural – it is the
awakening of the kundalini energy in the base of her spine, it is the

initiation of the soul's longing for union with God. And unlike men, the Teacher continues, women are already well attuned to this mystical relationship:

> Women, because they are nearer to Prakriti, are fertilized by the Divine Energy which they retain in their chakras and, because of this, very few practices are needed. Women are taken up through the Path of Love, for love is feminine mystery. Woman is the cup waiting to be filled, offering herself up in her longing which is her very being.[10]

Through the ensuing days and months, Irina is tossed upon the tidal waves of ecstasy and pain; for every drop of understanding, there is a backwash of unmitigated ignorance. But gradually, the path of love begins to arise within her, the feminine mystery starts to overflow. India, in all her kaleidoscopic splendour, blossoms in front of her eyes; astonishing beauty is everywhere. And now Bhai Sahib also stands before her – Beloved Teacher and guide. Her gratitude is over-whelming; she offers herself up completely and drowns in a sea of unfathomable bliss:

> Deepest peace. And I nearly fall down when I salute him lately. And the feeling of nothingness before him represents such happiness. He will be resting, his eyes closed or open, I sit, bent in two (a comfort-able position for me in his presence) under the blow from the two fans; he and I alone somewhere, where nothing is but peace.
>
> Lately it becomes increasingly lovely. Deep happiness welling from within. From the deepest depth ... Also at home, when I think of him, it comes over me ... Soft, gentle. A bliss of non-being; not existing at all. It is difficult to believe, unless one has experienced it, that it is so glorious 'not to be'.[11]

The feeling of nothingness is taking over. All the humiliations and agonies of the past are leading to an unshakeable experience of the Self:

> Walking to his place amongst the busy morning traffic, the noise of
> children going to school, cows wandering aimlessly, rickshaws
> driving at greatest speed, dogs fighting and the sky covered with
> white clouds, I reflected that the feeling of nothingness is not only
> now in his presence. It stays with me ... I feel like that before God,
> before life; it seems slowly to have become my very being.[12]

Irina treasured this experience for the rest of her life. Indeed,
returning to London years later and embarking on giving lectures
at the Theosophical Society on Sufism, she often became carried
away with the memory of her beloved teacher. Having taken a vow
never to speak of anything other than her experience, her talks
essentially became the records of a living tradition, imparted to all
those eager to hear.

One day in the reading room of the British Library, Irina chanced
upon a book elucidating the metaphysics of Rumi, by Khalifa Abdul
Hakim, a Pakistani scholar. Reading it, she realized that what Bhai
Sahib and Rumi were saying were identical. She immediately went
home and made two copies – one by hand and the other typed:

> ... there is only one way of rising from the lower to the higher stage
> and that is by assimilation of the lower into the higher ... [Rumi]
> believed that necessity is not only the mother of invention, it is the
> mother of creation as well. Even God would not have created the
> heaven and earth if He had not been urged by an irresistible inner
> necessity ... For Rumi ... life is nothing but a product of the will to
> live, and ever dissatisfied with the present equipment, life creates
> new desires, to fulfil which new organs come into existence.[13]

Irina retired from teaching publicly in 1992 but continued giving
talks in her home in London until her death in 1999. A photographic portrait of her taken around this time shows a
striking-looking woman, with vivid blue eyes gazing peacefully into
the distance. Speaking about the way of surrender to a student one
day, she said:

Here again, the terrible paradox. Complete surrender, complete nothingness, 'yes' to everything. This is the greatest power. I find this path is especially difficult for men, especially for the Western man because of the education, you know, the competition: 'I am better than thou' in sport, in everything. For women, somehow it is easier. Guruji explains one place in the book, how a woman can reach Reality just by being a woman. So I'm very glad, and I said, 'Oh, really, wonderful!'

It's not [always] like that. It is just as difficult for everybody. To men, I give many practices, women need only one practice: the detachment from worldly things. Because we by our very nature are attached to comfort, to children; because a woman has to bear children, she needs security. Women are attached to security. If a woman is prepared to give up security ... because spiritual life is utmost insecurity, no-man's land, it's like walking on water, walking on air, you have nothing under your feet. It's a chasm of fire. Actually, the title, *Chasm of Fire* is from Gregory of Nisa, the Christian mystic, a contemporary of St Augustine. He said, 'The path of love is like a bridge of hair across the chasm of fire.' Of hair, you know. You walk on it; it falls, you fall into the fire ... very insecure indeed.[14]

Irina's final diary entries are made on solitary retreat in 1966 in the Himalayas, where she is at the end of her journey. Three months have passed since Bhai Sahib left his physical body after a series of heart attacks, and she now reflects on their relationship and the wisdom he has transferred. Who would have thought that a widow in her fifties could have endured so much suffering in the search for the ultimate Truth? But through surrendering to the Path of Love, everything has been revealed; through the grace of her Master Bai Sahib's compassion, lover and Beloved have merged into One:

The sunrise, the sunset, the garden, the people, the whole daily life seems outwardly the same. But the values have changed. The meaning underlying it all is not the same as before. Something which seemed intangible, unattainable, slowly, very slowly becomes a permanent reality. There is nothing but Him. At the beginning it was sporadic; later of shorter or longer duration, when I was acutely conscious of it. But now … The infinite, endless Him … Nothing else is there. And all the beauty of nature which surrounds me is as if only on the edge of my consciousness. Deep within I am resting in the peace of His Heart. The body feels so light at times. As if it were made of the pure, thin air of the snow peaks. This constant vision of the One is deepening and increasing in the mind, giving eternal peace …[15]

Epilogue

Now, in the twenty-first century, the sacred feminine, the immanent life-sustaining power of all creation, is being honoured once again in all aspects of life – goddess mythology and comparative religion, feminist studies, ecology and quantum science. Indeed, veneration of the feminine principle has finally come full circle since the early days of Mesopotamia and Egypt, India and ancient Greece.

But more importantly, however, the sacred feminine is also being rediscovered from within as a means to spiritual salvation and individual freedom. Through the example of both women and men alike, reconnecting with the female force of nature in all her myriad forms puts individuals back in touch with the expansive totality of the universe. As one of the greatest Indian sages of the twentieth century, Bhagavan Sri Ramana Maharshi (1879–1950), makes clear:

> It is impossible for anyone to get established in the experience of reality, being-consciousness, except through the power of grace, the Mother.
>
> Other than through grace, the Mother, no one can attain reality ... which is truth.
>
> Except through that exalted light, which is grace of consciousness, the supreme power, it is impossible to transcend the conceptualizing power of the mind.
>
> The ego can only be destroyed by the power of grace, not by the dark perverted knowledge ...[1]

In order for any of us to go beyond the mind, to return to the indisputable fact 'I AM' and the ordinary individual's unshakeable belief in his or her own existence, there has to be a form of surrender. And through the act of surrendering, reconciliation and harmony between the masculine and feminine principles can finally be gained, leading all of us to the mysterious and ineffable glory of the One:

> If you naturally remain in submission to her authority, she will unite you with the realization of the state of Siva.
>
> Harmoniously and with delight live forever in your Heart, embracing that tender Lady.
>
> Let your life, in which you live in the state of blissful oneness, beguiled by her charms, stand as a delightful example to others.
>
> With you yourself as she, and she herself as you, becoming one, merge together within the Heart.[2]

Notes & References

Prologue

1 *Mysticism*, Evelyn Underhill, p5

Chapter One – Enheduanna

1 *Sumerian and Babylonian Psalms*, Stephen Langdon, quoted in *The Myth of the Goddess*, Anne Baring & Jules Cashford, p193
2 'Hymn to Ishtar', *Myths of Babylonia and Assyria*, D A Mackenzie, quoted in *Ibid*, p193
3 'Hymn to Inanna', *The Exaltation of Inanna*, William W Hallo & J J A van Dijk, quoted in *Women in Praise of the Sacred*, Jane Hirshfield, p4
4 *Inanna, Lady of Largest Heart: Enheduanna*, Betty De Shong Meador, p92
5 *Ibid*, p133, p175
6 *Ibid*, p96
7 *Ibid*, p94
8 *Ibid*, p125
9 *Ibid*, p122
10 *Ibid*, p128
11 *Ibid*, p175
12 *Ibid*, p179
13 *Ibid*, p174

Chapter Two – Hatchepsut

1 *Egyptian Mysteries: New Light on Ancient Knowledge*, Lucie Lamy, quoted in *The Myth of the Goddess*, Anne Baring & Jules Cashford, p255
2 'Hymn VII', *Hymns to Isis in Her Temple at Philae*, L Zabkar, quoted in *The Divine Feminine*, Andrew Harvey & Anne Baring, p50
3 'Spell 834', *Pyramidentexte*, quoted in *The Origins and History of Consciousness*, Erich Neumann, p222

4 *Egyptian Mysteries: New Light on Ancient Knowledge*, Lucie Lamy, quoted in *The Myth of the Goddess*, Anne Baring & Jules Cashford, pp261–2

5 *Ancient Egyptian Literature*, Miriam Lichtheim, quoted in *An Anthology of Sacred Texts by and about Women*, Serinity Young, p132

6 *Ancient Egyptian Literature*, Miriam Lichtheim, quoted in *Ibid*, p133

7 'Bulletin of the Metropolitan Museum of Art, New York', 23.2:47, quoted in *Hatchepsut: The Female Pharaoh*, Joyce Tyldesley, p129

8 *Ancient Egyptian Literature*, Miriam Lichtheim, quoted in *An Anthology of Sacred Texts by and about Women*, Serinity Young, pp132–3

9 *Royal Sarcophagi of the XVIII Dynasty*, W C Hayes, quoted in *Hatchepsut: The Female Pharaoh*, Joyce Tyldesley, p86

Chapter Three – Vach

1 'Hymn of Creation', *Rig Veda*, X, cxxix, quoted in *History of Mysticism*, S Abhayananda, pp 24–6

2 *The Hymns of the Rig Veda*, VIII, xxv, trans Ralph T H Griffith, p416

3 *Selections from Vedic Hymns*, trans Daniel Smith, quoted in *An Anthology of Sacred Texts by and About Women*, Serinity Young, p271

4 *Hymns of the Atharva Veda*, Maurice Bloomfield, quoted in *Ibid*, p272

5 *Rig Veda*, X, cxxv, quoted in *Great Women of India*, ed Swami Madhavananda, p131

6 *Rig Veda*, X, cxxv, quoted in *Ibid*, p132

7 'Isa Upanishad', *The Principal Upanishads*, trans Alan Jacobs, p3

8 'Devi Upanishad', quoted in *The Divine Feminine*, Andrew Harvey & Anne Baring, p158

9 'Brihadaranyaka Upanishad', *The Thirteen Principal Upanishads*, trans Robert Ernest Hume, quoted in *An Anthology of Sacred Texts by and about Women*, Serinity Young, pp274–5

10 *The Laws of Manu*, trans G Bühler, quoted in *Ibid*, p277

Chapter Four – Makeda, Queen of Sheba

1 Genesis, 2:7

2 Genesis, 2:21–3

3 *Sirach*, 1:2–10

4 *Sirach*, 15:2–3

5 *Sirach*, 25:24

6 *Wisdom of Solomon*, 6:12–20

7 *Wisdom of Solomon*, 8:2–5

8 Proverbs, 8:22–31

9 *Jewish Antiquities*, Josphus Flavius, quoted in *Makeda, Queen of Sheba*, Torrey Philemon on www.windweaver.com/sheba

10 *Women in Praise of the Sacred*, ed Jane Hirshfield, p13
11 *Kebra Nagast*, 24
12 *Kebra Nagast*, 24
13 *Kebra Nagast*, 26
14 *Poetry for the Spirit*, ed Alan Jacobs, pp4–5
15 *Ibid*, p5
16 *Ibid*, p6
17 *Ibid*, p14
18 *Women in Praise of the Sacred*, ed Jane Hirshfield, p14

Chapter Five – Sappho

1 *Symposium*, Plato, trans Christopher John Gill, pp47–9
2 'Hymn to the Earth: Mother of All', trans P B Shelley, quoted in *Poetry for the Spirit*, ed Alan Jacobs, p17
3 Homeric 'Hymn to Athena', trans Jules Cashford, quoted in *The Myth of the Goddess*, Anne Baring & Jules Cashford, p343
4 Homeric 'Hymn to Artemis', trans Jules Cashford, quoted in *Harvest*, Vol 33, quoted in *Ibid*, pp320–1
5 Homeric 'Hymn to Aphrodite', trans. Jules Cashford, quoted in *Harvest*, Vol 33, quoted in *Ibid*, p349
6 Poem 1, *Sappho: Poems and Fragments*, trans Stanley Lombardo, p1
7 Poem 6, *Ibid*, p6
8 Poem 54, *Ibid*, p54
9 Poem 62, *Sappho: Poems and Fragments*, trans Josephine Balmer, p56
10 Poem 106, *Ibid*, p80

Chapter Six – Therigatha Nuns

1 *Dhammapada*, XI, Babbitt, quoted in *History of Mysticism*, S Abhayananda, pp73–4
2 Adaptation of *Cullavagga*, Max Müller, quoted in *The First Buddhist Women*, Susan Murcott, pp 15–6
3 *Ibid*, p17
4 *Ibid*, pp18–9
5 *Ibid*, pp33–4
6 *Ibid*, pp65–6
7 *Ibid*, pp87–8
8 *Ibid*, p196

Chapter Seven – Mary Magdalene

1 *An Anthology of Sacred Texts by and about Women*, Serinity Young, p63
2 Ephesians, 5: 22–24

3 I Corinthians, 14:34–35
4 I Timothy, 2:8–15
5 St Luke, 17:21
6 St John, 14:6, 10, 18–20
7 St John, 13:19; cf Exodus, 3:14
8 St John, 1:1–4
9 *Apophasis Megale*, Simon Magus, quoted in *The Ante-Nicene Christian Library*, ed Roberts, Donaldson & Clarke, quoted in *History of Mysticism*, S Abhayananda, p132
10 'The Great Announcement', *Refutations*, VI.18, Hippolytus, quoted in *Jung and the Lost Gospels*, Stephan Hoeller, p68
11 *The Gospel According to Thomas*, Log 1
12 *Ibid*, Log 77
13 *Ibid*, Log 67
14 *Ibid*, Log 22
15 St Luke, 8:2
16 *The Gospel of Mary Magdalene*, trans Jean-Yves Leloup, p25,
17 *Ibid*, p27
18 *Ibid*, p27
19 *Ibid*, p31
20 *Ibid*, p31
21 *Ibid*, p25
22 *Ibid*, p25
23 *Ibid*, p37
24 *Ibid*, p39
25 *The Gospel of Philip*, 59:9
26 *Gospel According to Thomas*, Log 108
27 *Dialogue of the Saviour*, 139:12–3
28 *Gospel of Thomas*, Log 114, quoted in *The Gospel of Mary Magdalene*, trans Jean-Yves Leloup, p102
29 *Ibid*, p39
30 *Ibid*, p37
31 *The Thunder, Perfect Mind*, quoted in *The Nag Hammadi Library*, ed James M Robinson, pp297–8
32 *Trimorphic Protennoia*, quoted in *Ibid*, p513
33 *The Sophia of Jesus Christ*, quoted in *Ibid*, pp239–40, pp232–3
34 *Pistis Sophia*, I, Log 17, 19
35 *On the Origin of the World*, quoted in *The Nag Hammadi Library*, p182
36 *The Reality of the Rulers*, (or *The Hypostasis of the Archons*), quoted in *Ibid*, pp164–5

Chapter Eight – Chinese Nuns

1 *Visuddhi-Magga*, XIII, quoted in *Buddhism in Translation*, trans Henry Clarke Warren, quoted in *An Anthology of Sacred Texts by and about Women*, Serinity Young, p308
2 *The Holy Teaching of Vimalakirti*, trans Robert Thurman, quoted in *Ibid*, p319
3 *The Holy Teaching of Vimalakirti*, trans Robert Thurman, quoted in *Ibid*, p319
4 *Women in Buddhism*, Diana Paul, quoted in *Ibid*, p322
5 *The Journey to the West*, trans Athony C Yu, quoted in *The Goddesses' Mirror*, David Kinsley, pp25–6
5 *The Position of Women in Early China*, Alber Richard O'Hara quoted in *An Anthology of Sacred Texts by and about Women*, Serinity Young, p361
7 *Lives of the Nuns*, trans Kathryn Ann Tsai, p15
8 *Ibid*, p15
9 *Ibid*, p18
10 *Ibid*, p24
11 *Ibid*, p39
12 *Ibid*, pp52–3
13 *Ibid*, p57
14 *Ibid*, p83
15 *Original Teachings of Ch'an Buddhism*, Chang Chung-yuan, quoted in *History of Mysticism*, S Abhayananda, p219
16 *Studies in Shinto Thought*, trans Delmer M Brown & James T Araki, quoted in *The Goddesses' Mirror*, David Kinsley, p71
17 *Sources of Chinese Tradition*, ed W Theodore de Bary, quoted in *An Anthology of Sacred Texts by and about Women*, Serinity Young, pp340–1
18 *The I Ching*, trans Cary F Baynes, quoted in *Ibid*, p343
19 *The Analects of Confucius*, trans Arthur Waley, quoted in *Ibid*, p353

Chapter Nine – Rabi'a al-'Adawiyya

1 Surah 37:4–5
2 Surah 24:35
3 Surah 4:1
4 *Kitab al-Ta'arruf*, Kalabadhi, quoted in *Muslim Women Mystics*, Margaret Smith, pp161–2
5 Surah 28:88
6 *Bezels of Wisdom*, trans R W J Austin, quoted in *An Anthology of Sacred Texts by and about Women*, Serinity Young, p119
7 *Memoir of the Saints*, Attar, quoted in *Muslim Women Mystics*, Margaret Smith, p21
8 *Ibid*, p23
9 *Ibid*, pp23–4
10 *Ibid*, p24

11 *Doorkeeper of the Heart*, Charles Upton, p58
12 *Ibid*, p31
13 *Ibid*, p2
14 *Ibid*, p9
15 *Ibid*, p11
16 *Ibid*, p6
17 *Ibid*, p48
18 *Muslim Women Mystics*, Margaret Smith, pp32–3
19 *Doorkeeper of the Heart*, Charles Upton, p66
20 'Love in Absence', *Rumi: Poet and Mystic*, ed Reynold A Nicholson, quoted in *An Anthology of Sacred Texts by and about Women*, Serinity Young, p120
21 'The Love of Woman', *Rumi: Poet and Mystic*, quoted in *Ibid*, p120
22 *Doorkeeper of the Heart*, Charles Upton, p61

Chapter Ten – Yeshe Tsogyal

1 *History of Mysticism*, S Abhayananda, p177
2 *Buddhist Texts through the Ages*, ed Edward Conze, quoted in *An Anthology of Sacred Texts by and about Women*, Serinity Young, p327
3 *Buddhist Texts through the Ages*, ed Edward Conze, quoted in *Ibid*, p327
4 *The Origin of the Tara Tantra*, trans David Templeman, quoted in *Ibid*, p331
5 'Hymn to Tara', Vagisvarakirti, quoted in *The Divine Feminine*, Andrew Harvey & Anne Baring, p145
6 'Padma-Shambhava', *The World of the Buddha*, ed Lucien Stryck, quoted in *History of Mysticism*, S Abhayananda, p85
7 *Lady of the Lotus Born*, trans Padmakara Translation Group, p9
8 *Ibid*, pp94–5
9 *Ibid*, pp21–2
10 *Ibid*, pp23–4
11 *Ibid*, pp139–40
12 *Ibid*, p91
13 *Ibid*, p141
14 *Ibid*, pp145–6
15 *Ibid*, pp176–7
16 *Ibid*, p164
17 *Tibetan Yoga and Secret Doctrines*, ed W Y Evans-Wentz, quoted in *An Anthology of Sacred Texts by and about Women*, Serinity Young, p337
18 *Ibid*, p337

Chapter Eleven – Andal

1 *Devi Mahatmya*, Thomas B Coburn, quoted in *An Anthology of Scared Texts by and about Women*, Serinity Young, p303

2 *Devi Mahatmya*, Thomas B Coburn, quoted in *Ibid*, p300
3 www.sanskrit.safire.com
4 *Classical Hindu Mythology*, trans Cornelia Dimmitt & J A B van Buitenen, quoted in *An Anthology of Sacred Texts by and about Women*, Serinity Young, p302
5 *Devi Mahatmya*, Thomas B Coburn, quoted in *Ibid*, p301
6 *Ramayana*, Valmiki, trans Hari Prasad Shastri, quoted in *Ibid*, p293
7 *Mahabharata*, trans J A B van Buitenen, quoted in *Ibid*, p286
8 *The Geeta*, trans Shri Purohit Swami, IV: 9–11
9 *Ibid*, VI: 26–28
10 *Ibid*, IX: 13–19
11 *Srimad Bhagavatam*, trans Kamala Subramaniam, p375
12 *Bhakti Sutras*, 1–6, trans Prem Prakash
13 *Ibid*, 51–55
14 *Ibid*, 28–30
15 *Ibid*, 82
16 *Tiruppavai*, Andal, trans P S Sundaram, p3
17 *Ibid*, 29, p31
18 *Ibid*, 30, p32
19 *Nachiyar Tirumozhi*, I:8, Andal, trans P S Sundaram, p42
20 *Ibid*, V:7, p83
21 *Ibid*, VI:4, p90
22 *Ibid*, XI: 2–3, pp124–5
23 *Ibid*, VIII:10, p149

Chapter Twelve – Hildegard of Bingen

1 *The Consolation of Philosophy*, Boethius, trans V W Cooper, I:2, quoted on www.etext.lib.virginia.edu/
2 *Ibid*, II:37
3 *Ibid*, III:95
4 *La Vita Nuova*, Dante Alighieri, trans Dante Gabriel Rossetti, p1
5 *Selected Writings*, Hildegard of Bingen, trans Mark Atherton, p3
6 *Women Writers of the Middle Ages*, Peter Dronke, p145
7 *Ibid*, p168
8 *Selected Writings*, Hildegard of Bingen, trans Mark Atherton, p91
9 *Scivias*, Hildegard of Bingen, trans Mother Columba Hart and Jane Bishop, p109
10 *Ibid*, p133
11 *Ibid*, p124
12 *Selected Writings*, Hildegard of Bingen, trans Mark Atherton, p171
13 *Ibid*, pp172–3
14 *Women Writers of the Middle Ages*, Peter Dronke, p175

15 *Ibid*, p176
16 *Selected Writings*, Hildegard of Bingen, trans Mark Atherton, pxv
17 *Ibid*, p122

Chapter Thirteen – Sun Bu-er

1 *Ways to Paradise*, Michael Loewe, quoted in *An Anthology of Sacred Texts by and about Women*, Serinity Young, p392
2 *The Eight Immortals of Taoism*, trans Kwok Man Ho & Joanne O'Brien, quoted in *Ibid*, p395
3 *Tao Te Ching*, Lao Tsu, trans Gia-Fu Feng & Jane English, p3
4 *Ibid*, VI, p8
5 *Ibid*, XX, p22
6 *Chuang Tzu*, quoted in *History of Mysticism*, S Abhayananda, p 67
7 *Ibid*, p68
8 'The Jade Woman of Greatest Mystery', *History of Religion*, Edward H Schafer, quoted in *An Anthology of Sacred Texts by and about Women*, Serinity Young, p383
9 *Seven Taoist Masters*, trans Eva Wang, quoted in *Ibid*, p387
10 *Seven Taoist Masters*, trans Eva Wang, quoted in *Ibid*, p389
11 'Gathering the Mind', *Immortal Sisters*, trans Thomas Cleary, p7
12 'The Womb Breath', *Ibid*, p22
13 'Facing a Wall', *Ibid*, p38
14 *Ibid*, pp46–7
15 *Ibid*, p48
16 *Ibid*, pp49–50
17 *Ibid*, pp51–2
18 *Ibid*, pp53–4

Chapter Fourteen – The Beguines

1 *Summa Theologica of St Thomas Aquinas*, trans Fathers of the English Dominican Province, quoted in *An Anthology of Sacred Texts by and about Women*, Serinity Young, p69
2 *The Oxford Companion to Philosophy*, ed Ted Honderich, p43
3 *Selected Writings: Meister Eckhart*, trans Oliver Davies, p258
4 *Ibid*, p108
5 Sermon 27, *Meister Eckhart*, trans Raymond B Blackney, quoted in *History of Mysticism*, S Abhayananda, p281
6 Sermon 52, *The Essential Sermons, Commentaries, Treatises and Defence*, trans Edmund Colledge, quoted on www.franic.net/mistica/
7 *The Mirror of Simple Souls*, trans Ellen L Babinsky, p79
8 *Ibid*, pp192–3

9   *Ibid*, p193
10 Psalms, 46:10
11 *The Mirror of Simple Souls*, trans Ellen L Babinsky, p129
12 *Ibid*, p129
13 *Ibid*, p195
14 *Ibid*, p200
15 *Ibid*, p201
16 *Mechthild of Magdeburg: The Flowing Light of the Godhead*, trans Frank Tobin, p40
17 *Ibid*, p39
18 *Ibid*, p62
19 *Ibid*, p111
20 *Ibid*, pp53–4
21 *Ibid*, p49
22 *Ibid*, pp96–7
23 *Hadewijch: The Complete Works*, trans Mother Columba Hart, p280
24 *Ibid*, p66
25 *Visions and Longing: Medieval Women Mystics*, Monica Furlong, pp107–8
26 *The Malleus Maleficarum*, Heinrich Kramer & James Sprenger, trans Montague Summers, quoted in *An Anthology of Sacred Texts by and about Women*, Serinity Young, p79
27 *The Malleus Maleficarum*, Heinrich Kramer & James Sprenger, trans Montague Summers, quoted in *Ibid*, pp79–80

Chapter Fifteen – Julian of Norwich

1   *Of the Marvellous Effect of the Love of God*, Thomas à Kempis, quoted in *On the Love of God*, trans S Abhayananda, quoted in *History of Mysticism*, S Abhayananda, p294
2   *The Cloud of Unknowing*, ed Evelyn Underhill, p16
3   *The Form of Living*, Richard Rolle, quoted in *Women and Mystical Experience in the Middle Ages*, Frances Beer, p129
4   *Anchoritic Spirituality: Ancrene Wisse and Associated Works*, trans Anne Savage & Nicholas Watson, pp189–190
5   *Revelations of Divine Love*, Julian of Norwich, trans Elizabeth Spearing, 'The Short Text', p5
6   *Ibid*, 'The Short Text', p6
7   *Ibid*, 'The Short Text', pp10–11
8   *Ibid*, 'The Long Text', p137
9   *Ibid*, 'The Long Text', p138
10 *Ibid*, 'The Short Text, p7
11 *Ibid*, 'The Short Text', p12
12 *Ibid*, 'The Long Text', p80
13 *Ibid*, The Long Text', p139

14 *Ibid*, 'The Long Text', p160
15 *Ibid*, 'The Short Text', p8
16 *Ibid*, 'The Short Text', p10
17 *Ibid*, 'The Long Text', p179

Chapter Sixteen – Mirabai

1 *Jnaneshvar: The Life and Works*, trans S Abhayananda, quoted in *History of Mysticism*, S Abhayananda, pp270–3
2 *The Song of the Goddess: The Devi Gita*, trans C Mackenzie Brown, pp45,47
3 *Ibid*, pp53–4
4 *Ibid*, p63
5 *Naked Song: Lalla*, trans Coleman Barks, p19
6 *Ibid*, p42
7 *Ibid*, p54
8 *Ibid*, p21
9 *Love Song of the Dark Lord: Jayadeva's Gitagovinda*, trans Barbara Stoler Miller, p112
10 *Ibid*, pp123–4
11 *Mirabai: Ecstatic Poems*, trans Robert Bly & Jane Hirshfield, p6
12 *For Love of the Dark One: Songs of Mirabai*, trans Andrew Schelling, p23
13 *Mirabai: Ecstatic Poems*, trans Robert Bly & Jane Hirshfield, p57
14 *For Love of the Dark One: Songs of Mirabai*, trans Andrew Schelling, p30
15 www.sacred-texts.com

Chapter Seventeen – Teresa of Avila

1 *Corpus Hermeticum*, XI & XII, trans Scott, quoted in *The Fall of Sophia*, Violet Macdermot, p54
2 *The Faerie Queene*, Book I: 28–34, quoted in *The Norton Anthology of English Literature*, M H Abrams, p153 (my modern spelling)
3 *The Tempest*, William Shakespeare, IV, I, 148–158
4 'The Garden', v–vi, *Andrew Marvell: The Complete Poems*, ed Elizabeth Story Donno, p101
5 *De Sapientia*, Nicholas of Cusa, ed John P Dolan, quoted in *History of Mysticism*, S Abhayanda, p309
6 *Luther's Works*, ed Jaroslav Pelikan, quoted in *An Anthology of Sacred Texts by and about Women*, Serinity Young, p85
7 *Luther's Works*, ed Jaroslav Pelikan, quoted in *Ibid*, p85
8 *Dark Night of the Soul*, www.ccel.org/j/john_of _the_cross/dark_night
9 'The Ascent of Mount Carmel', *The Collected Works of John of the Cross*, trans Kieran Kavanagh & Otilio Rodriguez, quoted in *History of Mysticism*, S Abhayananda, p321
10 *The Life of Saint Teresa of Avila by Herself*, trans J M Cohen, p74

11   *Ibid*, p125
12   *Ibid*, p127
13   *The Way of Perfection*, trans E Allison Peers, pp65–6
14   *Ibid*, p199
15   *The Interior Castle*, trans Kieran Kavanaugh & Otilio Rodriguez, p35
16   *Ibid*, p37
17   *Ibid*, p93
18   *Ibid*, p179
19   *Meditations on the Song of Songs*, quoted in *Medieval Women Mystics and the Song of Songs*, E Ann Matter, quoted on www.pendlehill.org

Chapter Eighteen – Grace Aguilar

1   'The Royal Crown', *Selected Religious Poems of Solomon Ibn Gabirol*, trans Israel Zangwill, quoted in *History of Mysticism*, S Abhayananda, p247
2   *Zohar*, Sholem, quoted in *Ibid*, p250
3   *Zohar*, trans Daniel C Matt, quoted in *An Anthology of Sacred Texts by and about Women*, Serinity, Young, p31
4   *The Gospel of Thomas*, Log 22
5   *Grace Aguilar: Selected Writings*, ed Michael Galchinsky, pp225–6
6   *Ibid*, pp248–9, p255
7   *Ibid*, p183
8   *Ibid*, p191
9   *Ibid*, pp198, 200
10 *The Spirit of Judaism*, Grace Aguilar, quoted in *Four Centuries of Jewish Women's Spirituality*, ed Ellen M Umansky & Dianne Ashton, pp79–80

Chapter Nineteen – Emily Dickinson

1   *The World as Will and Representation*, Arthur Schopenhauer, trans E F J Payne, pp7–8
2   *The Norton Anthology of Poetry*, ed Margaret Ferguson, Mary Jo Salter & Jon Stallworthy, p729
3   'Confluents', Christina Rossetti, quoted in *Poetry for the Spirit*, Alan Jacobs, p337
4   *Aurora Leigh*, Elizabeth Barrett Browning, quoted in *Ibid*, pp280–1
5   *A Vindication of the Rights of Women*, Mary Wollstonecraft, quoted on www.bartleby.com
6   *A Glossary of Literary Terms*, M H Abrams, p194
7   #959, quoted in *The Life of Emily Dickinson*, Richard B Sewall, p328
8   #280, *Emily Dickinson*, ed Helen McNeil, p15
9   #642 *Ibid*, p64
10 #550, quoted in *The Life of Emily Dickinson*, Richard B Sewall, pp458–9
11 #593, *Emily Dickinson*, ed Helen McNeil, pp56–7

12 *The Life of Emily Dickinson*, Richard B Sewall, pp514–5
13 *Ibid*, pp518–9
14 #817, *Ibid*, p693
15 'Song of Myself', Walt Whitman, quoted in *The Norton Anthology of Poetry*, ed Margaret Ferguson, Mary Jo Salter & Jon Stallworthy, p961
16 #721, *Emily Dickinson*, ed Helen McNeil, p70

Chapter Twenty – Sharada Devi

1 *The Gospel of Ramakrishna*, Swami Nikhilananda, quoted in *History of Mysticism*, S Abhayananda, p362
2 *The Gospel of Ramakrishna*, Swami Nikhilananda, quoted in *Ibid*, p363
3 *The Gospel of Ramakrishna*, Swami Nikhilananda, quoted in *Ibid*, p367
4 *The Gospel of Ramakrishna*, Swami Nikhilananda, quoted in *Ibid*, p368
5 *The Gospel of Ramakrishna*, Swami Nikhilananda, quoted in *The Return of the Mother*, Andrew Harvey, p61
6 *Holy Mother*, Swami Nikhilananda, p30
7 *Women Saints East and West*, ed Swami Ghanananda & Sir John Stewart-Wallace, p99
8 *Holy Mother*, Swami Nikhilananda, p40
9 *Ibid*, p40
10 *Ibid*, pp42–3
11 *Women Saints East and West*, ed Swami Ghanananda & Sir John Stewart-Wallace, pp102–3
12 *Holy Mother*, Swami Nikhilananda, p79
13 *Women Saints East and West*, ed Swami Ghanananda & Sir John Stewart-Wallace, p105
14 *Holy Mother*, Swami Nikhilananda, pp93–4
15 *Ibid*, p139
16 *Women Saints East and West*, ed Swami Ghanananda & Sir John Stewart-Wallace, p109
17 *Holy Mother*, Swami Nikhilananda, p191
18 *Ibid*, p214
19 *Ibid*, p235
20 *Ibid*, p319
21 *Ibid*, p237
22 *Great Women of India*, ed Swami Madhavananda & Ramesh Chandra Majumdar, p537
23 *Ibid*, p538

Chapter Twenty-one – Mirra Alfassa

1 *The Second Sex*, Simone de Beauvoir, trans H M Parshley, p679
2 *Ibid*, p653

3   *The Mother: A Short Biography*, Wilfred, p3
4   *Ibid*, pp5–6
5   *Ibid*, p10
6   *Ibid*, p10
7   Quoted in *The Spiritual Tourist*, Mick Brown, pp151–2
8   *The Mother*, Aurobindo, quoted in *The Return of the Mother*, Andrew Harvey, p127
9   *The Mother: A Short Biography*, Wilfred, p18
10 *Ibid*, p20
11 *Ibid*, p54
12 *The Mother*, Aurobindo, quoted in *The Return of the Mother*, Andrew Harvey, p135
13 *The Mother*, Aurobindo, quoted in *Great Women of India*, ed Swami Madhavananda & Ramesh Chandra Majumdar, p84
14 *The Mother*, Aurobindo, quoted in *Ibid*, pp84–5
15 *The Mother: A Short Biography*, Wilfred, p93
16 *The Mother's Vision*, pp188–9
17 *The Mother: A Short Biography*, Wilfred, p58

Chapter Twenty-two – Irina Tweedie

1   25 June, *The Chasm of Fire*, Irina Tweedie, p191
2   3 October, *Ibid*, p12
3   3 October, *Ibid*, p13
4   8 June, *Ibid*, p42
5   8 June, *Ibid*, p104
6   8 June, *Ibid*, p105
7   9 March, *Ibid*, pp77–8
8   20 January, *Ibid*, pp57–8
9   20 January, *Ibid*, p58
10 7 January, *Ibid*, p150
11 30 June, *Ibid*, p191
12 24 July, *Ibid*, p194
13 *Metaphysics of Rumi*, Abdul Hakim, quoted in *The Taste of Hidden Things*, Sara Sviri, p193
14 Interview courtesy Golden Sufi Center, California, quoted in *Women of Sufism*, Camille Adams Helminski, p274
15 8 November, *The Chasm of Fire*, p201

Epilogue

1   *Padamalai: The Teachings of Sri Ramana Maharshi recorded by Muruganar*, ed David Godman p250
2   *Ibid*, p196

Bibliography

Primary Sources & Critical Texts

Abhayananda, S, *History of Mysticism: The Unchanging Testament* (Watkins Publishing, London, 2002)

Armstrong, Karen, *A History of God*, (Vintage, London, 1993)

Atherton, Mark (trans), *Hildegard of Bingen: Selected Writings* (Penguin, London, 2001)

Babinsky, Ellen (trans), *Marguerite Porete: The Mirror of Simple Souls* (Paulist Press, New York, 1993)

Balmer, Josephine (trans), *Sappho: Poems and Fragments* (Bloodaxe Books, Newcastle upon Tyne, 1992)

Baring, Anne & Cashford, Jules, *The Myth of the Goddess: Evolution of an Image* (Penguin, London, 1993)

Cahill, Susan (ed), *Wise Women: Over 2000 Years of Spiritual Writing by Women* (W W Norton & Co, New York, 1996)

Barks, Coleman (trans), *Naked Song: Lalla* (Maypop Books, Athens, 1992)

Barnstone, Aliki & Barnstone, Willis (eds), *Women Poets from Antiquity to Now* (Schocken Books, New York, 1992)

Beauvoir, Simone de, *The Second Sex* (Vintage, London, 1997)

Beer, Frances, *Women and Mystical Experience in the Middle Ages* (The Boydell Press, Woodbridge, 1992)

Bly, Robert & Hirshfield, Jane (eds), *Mirabai: Ecstatic Poems* (Beacon Press, Boston, 2004)

Brooks, Miguel F (trans), *Kebra Nagast* (The Red Sea Press, New Jersey, 2002)

Brown, Mackenzie (trans), *The Song of the Goddess: The Devi Gita* (State University of New York Press, 2002)

Brown, Mick, *The Spiritual Tourist* (Bloomsbury, London, 1998)

Busby, Margaret (ed), *Daughters of Africa: An International Anthology of Works and Writings by Women of African Descent from the Ancient Eqyptian to the Present* (Ballantine Books, New York, 1992)

Campbell, Joseph, *The Hero with a Thousand Faces* (Fontana Press, London, 1993)

Carpenter, Jennifer, *Worshipping Women, 'Women, Religion and Society: The Experience of the Medieval Women Mystics'* (Sydney, 1997)

Chittick, William, *Sufism: A Short Introduction* (Oneworld, Oxford, 2001)

Cleary, Thomas (trans), *Immortal Sisters: Secret Teachings of Taoist Women* (North Atlantic Books, Berkeley, 1996)

Cohen, J M (trans), *The Life of Saint Teresa of Avila by Herself* (Penguin, London, 1957)

Davies, Oliver (trans), *Meister Eckhart: Selected Writings* (Penguin, London, 1994)

Dronke, Peter, *Women Writers of the Middle Ages* (Cambridge University Press, Cambridge, 1996)

Eliot, T S, *Collected Poems: 1909–1962* (Faber & Faber, London, 1963)

Ellis, Ralph, *Solomon: Falcon of Sheba* (Edfu Boks, Cheshire, 2002)

Feng, Gia-Fu & English, Jane (trans), *Tao Te Ching* (Vintage Books, New York, 1989)

Ferguson, Margaret, & Salter, Mary Jo & Stallworthy, Jon (eds), *The Norton Anthology of Poetry* (Norton, New York, 1996)

Ford-Grabowsky, Mary (ed), *Sacred Voices: Essential Women's Wisdom through the Ages* (HarperSanFrancisco, New York, 2002)

Godman, David (ed), *Padamalai: Teachings of Sri Ramana Maharshi Recorded by Muruganar* (David Godman, Boulder, 2004)

Guillaumont, A, *The Gospel According to Thomas* (Leiden, 1976)

Flinders, Carol Lee, *Enduring Grace: Living Portraits of Seven Women Mystics* (HarperSanFrancisco, 1993)

Furlong, Monica *Visions and Longings: Medieval Women Mystics* (Mowbray, New York, 1996)

Galchinsky, Michael (ed), *Grace Aguilar: Selected Writings* (Broadview Literary Texts, Ontario, 1993)

Ghananda & Stewart-Wallace, Sir John (ed), *Women Saints: East and West* (Vedanta Press, Hollywood, 1979)

Gilbert R A, *The Elements of Mysticism* (Element, Shaftsbury, 1991)

Giles, Mary, *The Feminist Mystic and other Essays on Women and Spirituality* (Crossroad, New York, 1985)

Gill, Christopher John (trans), *Symposium*, Plato (Penguin, London, 1999)

Griffith, Ralph (trans), *The Hymns of the Rig Veda* (Motilal Banarsidass Publishers, Delhi, 1995)

Hart, Mother Columba (trans), *Hadewijch: The Complete Works* (Paulist Press, New York, 1980)

Hart, Mother Columba & Bishop, Jane (trans), *Hildegard of Bingen: Scivias* (Paulist Press, 1990)

Harvey, Andrew & Baring, Anne, *The Divine Feminine: Exploring the Feminine Face of God around the World* (Conari Press, Berkeley, 1996)

Harvey, Andrew, *The Return of the Mother* (Frog, Berkeley, 1995)

Helminski, Camille Adams, *Women of Sufism: A Hidden Treasure* (Shambhala, Boston, 2003)

Hinnells, John R, *Who's Who of Religion*, (Penguin Reference, London, 1991)

Hirshfield, Jane, *Women in Praise of the Sacred: 43 Centuries of Spiritual Poetry by Women* (Harper Perennial, New York, 1994)

Hoeller, Stephan, *Jung and the Lost Gospels* (Quest Books, Illinois, 1989)

Jacobs, Alan (ed), *Poetry for the Spirit: An Original and Insightful Anthology of Mystical Poems*, (Watkins, London, 2002)

Jacobs, Alan (trans), *The Principal Upanishads* (O Books, London, 2003)

James, William, *The Varieties of Religious Experience* (Touchstone, New York, 1997)

Jantzen, Grace, *Julian of Norwich: Mystic and Theologian* (SPCK, London, 2000)

Jung, Carl Gustav, *Aspects of the Feminine* (Routledge, London, 2003)

Kavanaugh, Kieran & Rodriguez, Otilio, *Teresa of Avila: The Interior Castle* (Paulist Press, New York, 1979)

King, Karen L, *The Gospel of Mary of Magdala: Jesus and the First Woman Apostle* (Polebridge Press, Santa Rosa, 2003)

Kinsley, David, *The Goddesses' Mirror: Visions of the Divine from East and West* (State University of New York Press, 1989)

Leloup, Jean-Yves (trans), *The Gospel of Mary Magdalene* (Inner Traditions, Vermont, 2002)

Lombardo, Stanley (trans), *Sappho Poems and Fragments* (Hackett Publishing, Indianapolis, 2002)

MacDermot, Violet (trans), *The Fall of Sophia: A Gnostic Text on the Redemption of Universal Consciousness* (Lindisfarne Books, 2001)

Madhavananda & Majumdar, *Great Women of India: The Holy Mother Birth Centenary Memorial* (Advaita Ashrama, Kolkata, 2001)

Madigan, Shawn (ed), *Mystics, Visionaries & Prophets: A Historical Anthology of Women's Spiritual Writings* (Fortress Press, Minneapolis, 1998)

McGill, Bernard (ed), *Meister Eckhart and the Beguine Mystics* (Continuum, New York, 1994)

McNeil, Helen (ed), *Emily Dickinson* (Everyman, London, 2004)

Miller, Barbara Stoler (trans), *Love Songs of the Dark Lord: Jayadeva's Gitagovinda* (Columbia University Press, New York, 1997)

Meyer, Marvin (ed), *The Gospels of Mary Magdalene* (HarperSanFrancisco, 2004)

Murcott, Susan, *The First Buddhist Women: Translations and Commentary on the Therigatha* (Parallax Press, Berkeley, 1991)

Neumann, *The Origins and History of Consciousness* (Princeton University Press, 1973)

Nicholson, D H S, & Lee, A H E, *The Oxford Book of Mystical Verse* (Clarendon Press, Oxford, 1932)

Nikhilananda, Swami, *Holy Mother* (Ramakrishna Vivekananda Centre Press, 1962)

Noffke, Suzanne (trans), *Catherine of Siena: The Dialogue* (Paulist Press, New York, 1980)

Padmakara Translation Group (trans), *Lady of the Lotus Born: The Life and Enlightenment of Yeshe Tsogyl* (Shambhala, Boston, 2002)

Pagels, Elaine, *Adam, Eve and the Serpent* (Vintage Books, New York, 1989)

Pagels, Elaine, *The Gnostic Gospels* (Penguin, London, 1990)

Payne, E F (trans), *Arthur Schopenhauer: The World as Will and Representation* (Dover Publications, New York, 1969)

Peers, Alison (trans), *The Way of Perfection: Teresa of Avila* (Image, 2004)

Picknett, Lynn, *Mary Magdalene* (Robinson, London, 2003)

Prakash, Prem (trans), *The Yoga of Spiritual Devotion: A Modern Translation of the Narada Bhakti Sutras* (Inner Traditions International, Vermont, 1998)

Ricks, Christopher (ed), *Andrew Marvell: The Complete Poems* (Penguin, London, 1985)

Robinson (ed), *The Nag Hammadi Library* (HarperSanFrancisco, 1990)

Rossetti, Dante Gabriel (trans), *La Vita Nuova: Dante Alighieri* (Dover Publications, New York, 2001)

Savage, Anne & Watson, Nicholas (trans), *Anchoritic Spirituality: Ancrene Wisse and Associated Works* (Paulist Press, New York, 1991)

Schelling, Andrew (trans), *For the Love of the Dark One: Songs of Mirabai* (Hohm Press, Arizona, 1998)

Sewall, Richard, *The Life of Emily Dickinson* (Harvard University Press, Cambridge, 1980)

Shong Meador, Betty de, *Inanna: Lady of Largest Heart, Poems of the Sumerian High Priestess, Enheduanna* (University of Texas Press, Austin, 2000)

Smith, Margaret, *Muslim Women Mystics: The Life and Work of Rabi'a and other Women Mystics in Islam* (Oneworld, Oxford, 1994)

Smith, Margaret, *Studies in Early Mysticism in the Inner and Middle East* (Oneworld Publications, Oxford, 1995)

Spearing, Elizabeth (trans), *Julian of Norwich: Revelations of Divine Love* (Penguin, London, 1998)

Subramaniam, Kamala, *Srimad Bhagavatam* (Bharatiya Vidya Bhavan, Mumbai, 1993)

Sundaram, P S (trans), *Andal: Tiruppavai & Nachiyar Tirumozhi* (Ananthacharya Indological Research Institute, Mumbia, 1987)

Sviri, Sara, *The Taste of Hidden Things* (Golden Sufi Centre, Inverness, 1997)

Teasdale, Wayne, *The Mystic Heart: Discovering a Universal Spirituality in the World's Religions* (New World Library, Novato, 2001)

Tharu, Susie & Lalita, K (eds), *Women Writing in India: 600 BC to the Present*, Vol I (The Feminist Press, New York, 1991)

Tobin, Frank (trans), *Mechthild of Magdeburg: The Flowing Light of the Godhead* (Paulist Press, New York, 1998)

Tsai, Kathryn Ann, *Lives of the Nuns: Biographies of Chinese Buddhist Nuns from the Fourth to Sixth Centuries* (University of Hawaii Press, Honolulu, 1994)

Tweedie, Irina, *The Chasm of Fire: A Woman's Experience of Liberation through the Teachings of a Sufi Master* (Element, Tisbury, 1979)

Tyldesey, Joyce, *Daughters of Isis: Women of Ancient Egypt* (Penguin, London, 1995)

Tyldesley, Joyce, *Hatchepsut: The Female Pharaoh* (Penguin, London, 1998)

Umansky, Ellen, & Ashton, Dianne (eds), *Four Centuries of Jewish Women's Spirituality: A Sourcebook* (Beacon Press, Boston, 1992)

Underhill, Evelyn, *Mysticism: The Nature and Development of Spiritual Consciousness* (Oneworld, Oxford, 1993)

Underhill, Evelyn (ed), *The Cloud of Unknowing: The Classic of Medieval Mysticism* (Dover, New York, 2003)

Upton, Charles, *Doorkeeper of the Heart: Versions of Rabi'a* (Pir Press, New York, 2003)

Wilfred, *The Mother: A Short Biography* (Sri Aurobindo Ashram, Pondicherry, 2002)

The Mother's Vision: Selections from Questions and Answers (Sri Aurobindo Ashram, Pondicherry, 2002)

Young, Serinity, *An Anthology of Sacred Texts by and about Women* (Rivers Oram Press/Pandora, 1993)

Texts Cited in Secondary Sources

Abhayananda, S, *Thomas à Kempis: On the Love of God* (Atma Books, Washington, 1992)

Abhayananda, S, *Jnaneshvar: The Life and Works of the Celebrated Indian Mystic Poet* (Atma Books, Washington, 1989)

Aurobindo, Ghose, *The Mother* (Sri Aurobindo Ashram, Pondicherry, 1928)

Austin, R W J (trans), *The Bezels of Wisdom* (Paulist Press, New York, 1980)

Babbitt, Irving (trans), *Dhammapada* (New Directions, New York, 1965)

Bary, W Theodore de, et al, *Sources of Chinese Tradition* (Columbia University Press, New York, 1964)

Baynes, Cary F (trans), *The I Ching or Book of Changes* (Princeton University Press, Princeton, 1967)

Blackney, Raymond B, *Meister Eckhart, A Modern Translation* (Harper Torchbook, New York, 1941)

Bloomfield, Maurice, *Hymns of the Atharva Veda* (Motilal Banarsidass, Delhi, 1964)

Bowie, Fiona & Davies, Oliver, *Beguine Spirituality* (SPCK, London, 1989)

Brown, Delmer M & Araki, James T, *Studies in Shinto Thought* (Ministry of Education, Japan, 1964)

Bühler, G (trans), *The Laws of Manu* (Motilal Banarsidass, Delhi, 1964)

Buitenen, J A B van (trans), *Mahabharata*, 2 Vols (University of Chicago Press, Chicago, 1975)

Chung-yuan, Chang, *Original Teachings of Ch'an Buddhism* (Pantheon Book, New York, 1975)

Coburn, Thomas, B, *Devi Mahatmya: The Crystallization of the Goddess Tradition* (Motilal Banarsidass, Delhi, 1984)

Colledge, Edmund & McGinn, Bernard, *Meister Eckhart: The Essential Sermons, Commentaries, Treatises & Defence* (Paulist Press, New York, 1981)

Conze, Edward (ed), *Buddhist Texts through the Ages* (Harper & Row, New York, 1964)

Dimmitt, Cornelia & Buitenen, J A B van, *Classical Hindu Mythology: A Reader in the Sanskrit Puranas* (Temple University Press, Philadelphia, 1978)

Dolan, John P (ed), *Unity and Reform: Selected Writing of Nicholas de Cusa* (University of Notre Dame Press, Notre Dame, 1962)

Evans-Wentz, W Y, *Tibetan Yoga and Secret Doctrines* (Oxford University Press, London, 1967)

Fathers of the Dominican Province (trans), *Summa Theologica of St Thomas Aquinas* (Burns Oats & Washbourne, 1912)

Hallo, William W & Van Dijk, J J A, *The Exaltation of Inanna* (Yale University Press, New Haven, 1968)

Hakim, Khalifa Abdul, *The Metaphysics of Rumi* (Shaikh Muhammad Ashraf, 1945)

Hayes, W C, *Royal Sarcophagi of the XVIII Dynasty* (Princeton University Press, Princeton, 1935)

Ho, Kwok Man, & O'Brien, Joanne, *The Eight Immortals of Taoism* (Penguin, New York, 1990)

Hume, Robert Ernest (trans), *The Thirteen Principal Upanishads* (Oxford University Press, Oxford, 1931)

O'Hara, Alber Richard, *The Position of Women in Early China according to Lieh Nu Chuan: 'The Biographies of Chinese Women'*, (Mei Ya Publications, Taiwan, 1971)

Kalabadhi, M b I b I al-, *Kitab al-Ta'arruf* (Ms Collection Prof Nicholson)

Kavanaugh, K & Rodriguez, O (trans), *The Collected Works of John of the Cross* (ICS Publications, Washington, 1973)

Lamy, Lucie, *Egyptian Mysteries: New Light on Ancient Knowledge* (Thames & Hudson, London, 1981)

Langdon, Stephen, *Sumerian and Babylonia Psalms* (Libraire Paul Geuthner, Paris, 1909)

Lichtheim, Miriam, *Ancient Egyptian Literature: A Book of Readings, Vol 2, The New Kingdom* (University of California, Berkeley, 1976)

Loewe, Michael, *Ways to Paradise: The Chinese Quest for Immortality* (George Allen & Unwin, London, 1979)

Mackenzie, D A, *Myths of Babylonia and Assyria* (Gresham Publishing, London, 1915)

Matt, Daniel C (trans), *Zohar: The Book of Enlightenment* (Paulist Press, New York, 1982)

Nicholson, Reynold A (ed), *Rumi: Poet and Mystic* (Allen & Unwin, London, 1950)

Nikhilananda, Swami (trans), *The Gospel of Ramakrishna* (Ramakrishna-Vivekananda Center, Madras, 1985)

Paul, Diana, *Women in Buddhism: Images of the Feminine in the Mahayana Tradition* (University of California Press, Berkeley, 1985)

Pelikan, Jaroslav (ed), *Luther's Works: Lectures on Genesis* (Concordia, Saint Louis, 1958)

Roberts, Rev A, Donaldson J, & Clarke T, *The Ante-Nicene Christian Library* (Continuum International Publishing, Edinburgh, 1892)

Schafer, Edward H, *History of Religion* (1978)

Scholem, Gershom (ed), *Zohar: The Book of Splendour* (Schocken Books, 1949)

Scott, Walter (ed), *Hermetica: The Ancient Greek and Latin Writings which contain*

Religious or Philosophic Teachings Ascribed to Hermes Trismegistus, 4 Vols (Shambhala, Boston, 1985)

Shastri, Hari Prasad (trans), *Ramayana of Valmiki* (Shanti Sadan, London, 1959)

Smith, Daniel (trans), *Selections from the Vedic Hymns* (University of California Press, Berkeley, 1968)

Stryck, Lucien (ed), *The World of the Buddha* (Doubleday, New York, 1968)

Summers, Montague, *The Malleus Maleficarum of Heinrich Kramer & James Sprenger* (Dover Publications, New York, 1971)

Templeman, David (trans), *The Origin of Tara Tantra* (Library of Tibetan Works and Archives, Dharamsala, 1981)

Thurman, Robert (trans), *The Holy Teaching of Vimalakirti: A Mahayana Scripture* (Pen State University Press, 1976)

Waley, Arthur, *The Analects of Confucius* (Vintage Books, New York, 1989)

Wang, Eva, *Seven Taoist Sisters: A Folk Novel of China* (Shambhala, Boston, 1990)

Warren, Henry Clarke, *Buddhism in Translation* (Atheneum, New York, 1962)

Yu, Athony C, *The Journey to the West* (University of Chicago Press, Chicago, 1983)

Zabkar, L, *Hymns to Isis in Her Temple at Philae* (University Press of New England, Hanover, 1988)

Zangwill, Israel (trans), *Selected Religious Poems of Solomon Ibn Gabirol* (Jewish Publication Society, Philadelphia, 1974)

Journals

Harvest: Journal for Jungian Studies (Karnac Books, London)

Internet sites

www.gnosis.org
(Gnostic Gospels Library)

www.sacred-texts.com
(Sacred Texts Library)

home.infionline.net/~ddisse/
(Translations of women's writing before 1700, compiled by Dorothy Disse)

www.windweaver.com/sheba
(Research on Makeda, Queen of Sheba, compiled by Torrey Philemon)

Acknowledgements & Permissions

The author would like to thank the following for permission to reproduce their material. Every care has been taken to trace copyright holders. However, if I have omitted anyone I apologize and will, if informed, make corrections to any future edition.

Advaita Ashrama: *Great Women of India: The Holy Mother Birth Centenary Memorial*, Madhavananda & Majumdar (2001)

Alderman Electronic Library: *The Consolation of Philosophy*, Boethius (2005)

Ananthacharya Indological Research Institute: *Andal: Tiruppavai & Nachiyar Tirumozhi*, Sundaram, P S (1987)

Asian Humanities Press: *Women in Buddhism: Images of the Feminine in the Mahayana Tradition*, Paul, Diana (1985)

Atma Books: *Jnaneshvar: The Life and Works of the Celebrated Indian Mystic Poet*, Abhayananda, S (1989), *Thomas à Kempis: On the Love of God*, Abhayananda, S (1992)

Sri Aurobindo Ashram: *The Mother*, Aurobindo (1928), *The Mother: A Short Biography*, Wilfred (2002), *The Mother's Vision: Selections from Questions and Answers* (2002)

Avadhuta Foundation: *Padamalai: Teachings of Sri Ramana Maharshi Recorded by Muruganar*, Godman, David (2004)

Beacon Press: *Mirabai: Ecstatic Poems*, Bly, Robert & Hirshfield, Jane (2004)

Bharatiya Vidya Bhavan: *Srimad Bhagavatam*, Subramaniam, Kamala (1993)

Bloodaxe Books: *Sappho: Poems and Fragments*, Balmer, Josephine (1992)

Boydell & Brewer: *Women and Mystical Experience in the Middle Ages*, Beer, Frances (1992)

Brill Academic Publishers: *The Gospel According to Thomas*, Guillaumont, A (1976)

Broadview Press: *Grace Aguilar: Selected Writings*, Galchinsky, Michael (1993)

Bruno Cassirer: *Buddhist Texts through the Ages*, Conze, Edward (1964)

Cambridge University Press: *Women Writers of the Middle Ages*, Dronke, Peter (1996)

Columbia University Press: *Sources of Chinese Tradition*, Bary, W Theodore de (1964), *Love Songs of the Dark Lord: Jayadeva's Gitagovinda*, Miller, Barbara Stoler (1997)

Conari Press: *The Divine Feminine: Exploring the Feminine Face of God around the World*, Harvey, Andrew & Baring, Anne (1996)

Concordia Publishing House: *Luther's Works: Lectures on Genesis*, Pelikan, Jaroslav (1958)

Continuum Books: *Summa Theologica of St Thomas Aquinas*, Fathers of the Dominican Province (1912), *The Ante-Nicene Christian Library*, Roberts, Rev A, Donaldson J & Clarke T (1892)

Dover Publications: *Arthur Schopenhauer: The World as Will and Representation*, Payne, E F (1969), *The Malleus Maleficarum of Heinrich Kramer & James Sprenger*, Summers, Montague (1971)

Faber & Faber: *The Geeta*, Shri Purohit Swami (1965)

Gresham Publishing: *Myths of Babylonia and Assyria*, Mackenzie, D A (1915)

Golden Sufi Center: Irina Tweedie interview

Greenwood Publishing: *Studies in Shinto Thought*, Brown, Delmer M & Araki, James T (1964)

Hackett Publishing: *Sappho Poems and Fragments*, Lombardo, Stanley (2002)

HarperCollins Publishers: *Buddhist Texts through the Ages*, Conze, Edward (1964), *Women in Praise of the Sacred: 43 Centuries of Spiritual Poetry by Women*, Hirshfield, Jane (1994), *Ways to Paradise: The Chinese Quest for Immortality*, Loewe, Michael (1979), *Rumi: Poet and Mystic*, Nicholson, Reynold A (1950), *The Nag Hammadi Library*, Robinson, James (1990), *The Chasm of Fire*, Tweedie, Irina (1979)

Harvard University Press: *The Life of Emily Dickinson*, Sewall, Richard (1980), *Buddhism in Translation*, Warren, Henry Clarke (1962)

Holm Press: *For the Love of the Dark One: Songs of Mirabai*, Schelling, Andrew (1998)

ICS Publications: *The Collected Works of St. John of the Cross*, translated by Kieran Kavanaugh and Otilio Rodriguez Copyright © 1964, 1979, 1991 by Washington Province of Discalced Carmelites ICS Publications 2131 Lincoln Road, N.E. Washington, DC 20002-1199 U.S.A. www.icspublications.org

Inner Traditions: *The Gospel of Mary Magdalene*, Leloup, Jean-Yves (2002), *The Yoga of Spiritual Devotion: A Modern Translation of the Narada Bhakti Sutras*, Prakash, Prem (1998)

Jewish Publication Society: *Selected Religious Poems of Solomon Ibn Gabirol*, Zangwill, Israel (1974)

Karnac Books: *Harvest: Journal for Jungian Studies*

Libraire Paul Geuthner: *Sumerian and Babylonia Psalms*, Langdon, Stephen (1909)

Library of Tibetan Works & Archives: *The Origin of Tara Tantra*, Templeman, David (1981)

Lindisfarne Books: *The Fall of Sophia: A Gnostic Text on the Redemption of Universal Consciousness*, MacDermot, Violet (2001)

Maypop Books: *Naked Song: Lalla*, Barks, Coleman (1992)

Mei Ya Publications: *The Position of Women in Early China according to Lieh Nu Chuan: 'The Biographies of Chinese Women'*, O'Hara, Alber Richard (1971)

Metropolitan Museum of Art: *Bulletin of the Metropolitan Museum of Art*

Motilal Banarsidass Publishers: *Devi Mahatmya: The Crystallization of the Goddess Tradition*, Coburn, Thomas, B (1984)

New Directions Publishing: *Dhammapada*, Babbitt, Irving (1965)

North Atlantic Books: *Immortal Sisters: Secret Teachings of Taoist Women*, Cleary, Thomas (1996)

O Books: *The Principal Upanishads*, Jacobs, Alan (2003)

Oneworld Publications: *Muslim Women Mystics: The Life and Work of Rabi'a and other Women Mystics in Islam*, Smith, Margaret (1994), *Mysticism: The Nature and Development of Spiritual Consciousness*, Underhill, Evelyn (1993)

Oxford University Press: *The Laws of Manu*, Bühler, G (1886), *Tibetan Yoga and Secret Doctrines*, Evans-Wentz, W Y, (1967), *The Thirteen Principal Upanishads*, Hume, Robert Ernest (1931)

Paulist Press: *The Bezels of Wisdom*, Austin, R W J (1980), *Marguerite Porete: The Mirror of Simple Souls*, Babinsky, Ellen (1993), *Meister Eckhart: The Essential Sermons, Commentaries, Treatises and Defence*, Colledge, Edmund & McGinn, Bernard (1981), *Hadewijch: The Complete Works*, Hart, Mother Columba (1980), *Hildegard of Bingen: Scivias*, Hart, Mother Columba & Bishop, Jane (1990), *Teresa of Avila: The Interior Castle*, Kavanaugh, Kieran & Rodriguez, Otilio (1979), *Zohar: The Book of Enlightenment*, Matt, Daniel C (1982), *Anchoritic Spirituality: Ancrene Wisse and Associated Works*, Savage, Anne & Watson, Nicholas (1991), *Mechthild of Magdeburg: The Flowing Light of the Godhead*, Tobin, Frank (1998)

Penguin: *Hildegard of Bingen: Selected Writings*, Atherton, Mark (2001), *The Myth of the Goddess: Evolution of an Image*, Baring, Anne & Cashford, Jules (1993), *The Life of Saint Teresa of Avila by Herself*, Cohen, J M (1957), *Meister Eckhart: Selected Writings*, Davies, Oliver (1994), *Plato: Symposium*, Gill, Christopher John (1999), *The Eight Immortals of Taoism* Ho, Kwok Man, & O'Brien, Joanne (1990), *Julian of Norwich: Revelations of Divine Love*, Spearing, Elizabeth (1998)

Parallax Press: Reprinted from *The First Buddhist Women: Translations and Commentary on the Therigatha* (1991) by Susan Murcott with permission of Parallax Press, Berkeley, California. www.parallax.org

Penn State University Press: *The Holy Teaching of Vimalakirti: A Mahayana Scripture*, Thurman, Robert (1976)

Pir Press: *Doorkeeper of the Heart: Versions of Rabi'a*, Upton, Charles (2003)

Princeton University Press: *The I Ching or Book of Changes*, Baynes, Cary F (1967)

Ramakrishna-Vivekananda Center of New York: *The Gospel of Ramakrishna*, Nikhilananda, Swami (1985), *Holy Mother*, Nikhilananda, Swami (1962)

Random House: *The World of the Buddha*, Stryck, Lucien (Doubleday, 1968), *Original Teachings of Ch'an Buddhism*, Chung-yuan, Chang (Pantheon, 1975), *The Way of Perfection: Teresa of Avila*, Peers, Alison (Image, 2004), *Zohar: The Book of Splendour*, Scholem, Gershom (Schockem, 1949)

Shambhala Publications: *Lady of the Lotus Born: The Life and Enlightenment of Yeshe Tsogyl*, Padmakara Translation Group (2002), *Seven Taoist Sisters: A Folk Novel of China*, Wang, Eva (1990)

Shanti Sadan: *Ramayana of Valmiki*, Shastri, Hari Prasad (1959)

Simon & Schuster: *The Analects of Confucius*, Waley, Arthur (1989)

SPCK: *Beguine Spirituality*, Bowie, Fiona & Davies, Oliver (1989)

State University of New York Press: *The Song of the Goddess: The Devi Gita*, Brown, Mackenzie (2002)

Thames & Hudson: *Egyptian Mysteries: New Light on Ancient Knowledge*, Lamy, Lucie (1981)

Theosophical Publishing House: *Jung and the Lost Gospels*, Hoeller, Stephan (1989)

Temple University Press: *Classical Hindu Mythology: A Reader in the Sanskrit Puranas*, Dimmitt, Cornelia & Buitenen, J A B van (1978)

University of California: *Ancient Egyptian Literature: A Book of Readings, Vol 2, The New Kingdom* Lichtheim, Miriam (1976), *Selections from the Vedic Hymns*, Smith, Daniel (1968)

University of Chicago Press: *History of Religion*, Schafer, Edward H (1978), *The Journey to the West*, Yu, Athony C (1983)

University of Hawaii Press: *Lives of the Nuns: Biographies of Chinese Buddhist Nuns from the Fourth to Sixth Centuries*, Tsai, Kathryn Ann (1994)

University of Notre Dame: *Unity and Reform: Selected Writing of Nicholas de Cusa*, Dolan, John P (1962)

University of Texas Press: *Inanna: Lady of Largest Heart, Poems of the Sumerian High Priestess, Enheduanna*, Shong Meador, Betty de (2000)

University Press of New England: *Hymns to Isis in Her Temple at Philae*, Zabkar, L (1988)

Van Pelt-Dietrich Electronic Library: 'Dark Night of the Soul', St John of the Cross (2005)

Vintage Books: *The Second Sex*, Beauvoir, Simone de (1997), *Tao Te Ching*, Feng, Gia-Fu & English, Jane (1989), *The Analects of Confucius*, Waley, Arthur (1989)

Yale University Press: *The Exaltation of Inanna*, Hallo, William W & Van Dijk, J J A (1968)

Index